The Lectionary 2025

First published in Great Britain in 2024

Society for Promoting Christian Knowledge
SPCK Group
Studio 101
The Record Hall
16–16A Baldwin's Gardens
London EC1N 7RJ
www.spckpublishing.co.uk

British Library Cataloguing-in-Publication Data
A catalogue record for this book is available from the British Library

ISBN 978-0-281-09056-3
ISBN 978-0-281-09057-0 (spiral-bound)

1 3 5 7 9 10 8 6 4 2

Designed by Colin Hall, Refined Practice
Typeset by Fakenham Prepress Solutions, Fakenham, Norfolk NR21 8NL
Printed in Great Britain by Ashford Colour Press

Produced on paper from sustainable sources

CONTENTS

UNDERSTANDING THE LECTIONARY

Common Worship on left-hand page

		Sunday Principal Service Weekday Eucharist	Third Service Morning Prayer	Second Service Evening Prayer
13 Sunday	**THE FOURTH SUNDAY AFTER TRINITY (Proper 10)**			
G	*Track 1* Amos 7. 7–end Ps. 82 Col. 1. 1–14 Luke 10. 25–37	*Track 2* Deut. 30. 9–14 Ps. 25. 1–10 Col. 1. 1–14 Luke 10. 25–37	Ps. 76 Deut. 28. 1–14 Acts 28. 17–end	Ps. 77 (*or* 77. 1–12) Gen. 32. 9–30 Mark 7. 1–23
14 Monday	**John Keble, Priest, Tractarian, Poet, 1866**			
Gw **DEL 15**	Com. Pastor *or* *also* Lam. 3. 19–26 Matt. 5. 1–8	Exod. 1. 8–14, 22 Ps. 124 Matt. 10.34 - 11.1	Ps. ***80***; 82 Job ch. 33 Rom. 14. 13–end	Ps. ***85***; 86 Judg. 13. 1–24 Luke 17. 20–end
15 Tuesday	**Swithun, Bishop of Winchester, c. 862** *Bonaventure, Friar, Bishop, Teacher, 1274*			
Gw	Com. Bishop *or* *also* James 5. 7–11, 13–18	Exod. 2. 1–15 Ps. 69. 1–2, 31–end Matt. 11. 20–24	Ps. 87; ***89. 1–18*** Job ch. 39 Rom. 15. 14–21	Ps. 89. 19–end Judg. 15.1 - 16.3 Luke 18. 15–30

Column 1

- **Date**
- **Colour:** An upper-case letter indicates the liturgical colour of the day. A lower-case second colour indicates the colour for a Lesser Festival while the upper-case letter indicates the continuing seasonal colour.
- **DEL:** Week number of Daily Eucharistic Lectionary.

Column 2

- Name of the Principal Holy Day, Sunday, Festival or Lesser Festival;
- a note of other Commemorations for mention in prayers;
- any general note that applies to the whole *Common Worship* provision for the day;
- one of the options where there are two options for readings at the Eucharist or Principal Service.

Readings: Readings occur in this column only in two circumstances.

1. **On Sundays after Trinity** where there are two 'tracks' for the Principal Service readings (where there is a choice of first reading and psalm, but the second reading and Gospel are the same in both tracks), Track I appears in this column.
2. **On Lesser Festivals throughout the year** where there are readings for that festival that are alternative to the semi-continuous Daily Eucharistic Lectionary, these also appear in this column.

Column 3

On Principal Feasts, Principal Holy Days, Sundays and Festivals this gives the Principal Service Lectionary, intended for use at the main service of the day (in most churches the mid-morning service), whether or not it is a Eucharist.

On other weekdays this gives the Daily Eucharistic Lectionary for those wanting a semi-continuous pattern of readings and a psalm for Holy Communion. It is most useful in a church where there is a daily celebration and a core community that worships together day by day, though its use is not restricted to that.

On Sundays after Trinity where there are two 'tracks' for the Principal Service readings (where there is a choice of first reading and psalm, but the second reading and Gospel are the same in both tracks), Track 2 appears in this column.

Column 4

On Principal Feasts, Principal Holy Days, Sundays and Festivals this gives the Third Service Lectionary. Many churches will have no need of it, for it comes into use only if the Principal and Second Service Lectionaries have been used. Its most likely use is at Morning Prayer (when this is not the Principal Service). Where psalms are recommended for use in the morning, these also appear in this column.

On other weekdays this provides the psalmody and readings for Morning Prayer. Where two or more psalms are appointed, the psalm in bold italic may be used as the only psalm. Psalms printed in round brackets ( ) may be omitted if they are used as an opening canticle at Morning Prayer. Where † is printed after the psalm number, the psalm may be shortened if desired. For those wishing to follow the Ordinary Time psalm cycle throughout the year (except for the period between 19 December and the Epiphany and from the Monday of Holy Week to the Saturday of Easter Week), this is printed as an alternative to the seasonal provision.

Column 5

On Principal Feasts, Principal Holy Days, Sundays and Festivals this gives the Second Service Lectionary, intended for use when a second set of readings is required. Its most likely use is in the evening, when the Principal Service Lectionary has been used in the morning. Sometimes it might be used at an evening Eucharist. Where the second reading is not a Gospel reading, an alternative to meet this need is provided. Where psalms are recommended for use in the evening, these also appear in this column.

On other weekdays this provides the psalmody and readings for Evening Prayer. Where two or more psalms are provided, the psalm in bold italic may be used as the only psalm. Psalms printed in round brackets ( ) may be omitted if they are used as an opening canticle at Evening Prayer. Where † is printed after the psalm number, the psalm may be shortened if desired. For those wishing to follow the Ordinary Time psalm cycle throughout the year (except for the period between 19 December and the Epiphany and from the Monday of Holy Week to the Saturday of Easter Week), this is printed as an alternative to the seasonal provision.

Book of Common Prayer and space for notes on right-hand page

	Calendar and Holy Communion	Morning Prayer	Evening Prayer	**NOTES**
	THE FOURTH SUNDAY AFTER TRINITY			
G	Gen. 3. 17–19 Ps. 79. 8–10 Rom. 8. 18–23 Luke 6. 36–42	Ps. 76 Deut. 28. 1–14 Acts 28. 17–end	Ps. 77 (*or* 77. 1–12) Gen. 32. 9–30 Mark 7. 1–23	
G		Job ch. 33 Rom. 14. 13–end	Judg. 13. 1–24 Luke 17. 20–end	
	Swithun, Bishop of Winchester, c. 862			
Gw	Com. Bishop	Job ch. 39 Rom. 15. 14–21	Judg. 15.1 – 16.3 Luke 18. 15–30	

Column 6

- Liturgical colour (***see column 1***).

Column 7

- The name of the Principal Holy Day, Sunday, Festival or Lesser Festival;
- any general note that applies to the whole Prayer Book provision for the day and an indication of points at which users may wish to draw on *Common Worship* material on the opposite page where the BCP has no provision;
- the Lectionary for the Eucharist on any day for which provision is made.

Column 8

This provides the readings for Morning Prayer, together with psalm provision where it varies from the BCP monthly cycle.

Column 9

This provides the readings for Evening Prayer, together with psalm provision where it varies from the BCP monthly cycle.

A letter to indicate liturgical colour in this column indicates a change of colour for Evening Prayer. The symbol in bold lower case, **ct**, indicates that the Collect at Evening Prayer should be that of the following day. This also applies to column 5.

Column 10

Space for notes.

ABBREVIATIONS OF BOOKS OF THE BIBLE

Old Testament

Gen. (Genesis)
Exod. (Exodus)
Lev. (Leviticus)
Num. (Numbers)
Deut. (Deuteronomy)
Josh. (Joshua)
Judg. (Judges)
Ruth
Sam. (Samuel)
Kings
Chron. (Chronicles)
Ezra
Neh. (Nehemiah)
Esther
Job
Ps. (Psalms)
Prov. (Proverbs)
Eccles. (Ecclesiastes)
Song of Sol. (Song of Solomon)
Isa. (Isaiah)
Jer. (Jeremiah)
Lam. (Lamentations)
Ezek. (Ezekiel)
Dan. (Daniel)
Hos. (Hosea)
Joel
Amos
Obadiah
Jonah
Mic. (Micah)
Nahum
Hab. (Habakkuk)
Zeph. (Zephaniah)
Hag. (Haggai)
Zech. (Zechariah)
Mal. (Malachi)

Apocrypha

Esdras
Tobit
Judith
Wisd. (Wisdom of Solomon)
Ecclus. (Ecclesiasticus)
Baruch
Song of the Three (Song of the Three Children)
Susanna (The History of Susanna)
Bel and the Dragon
Prayer of Manasseh
Macc. (Maccabees)

New Testament

Matt. (Matthew)
Mark
Luke
John
Acts (Acts of the Apostles)
Rom. (Romans)
Cor. (Corinthians)
Gal. (Galatians)
Eph. (Ephesians)
Phil. (Philippians)
Col. (Colossians)
Thess. (Thessalonians)
Tim. (Timothy)
Titus
Philemon
Heb. (Hebrews)
James
Pet. (Peter)
John (letters of John)
Jude
Rev. (Revelation)

MAKING CHOICES IN *COMMON WORSHIP*

Common Worship makes provision for a variety of pastoral and liturgical circumstances. It needs to, for it has to serve some church communities where Morning Prayer, Holy Communion and Evening Prayer are all celebrated every day, and yet be useful also in a church with only one service a week, and that service varying in form and time from week to week.

At the beginning of the year, some decisions in principle need to be taken.

In relation to the Calendar, whether to keep The Epiphany on Monday 6 January or on Sunday 5 January, and whether to keep the Feast of All Saints on Saturday 1 November or on Sunday 2 November.

In relation to the Lectionary, the initial choices every year to decide in relation to Sundays are:

- which of the services on a Principal Feast, Principal Holy Day, Sunday or Festival constitutes the 'Principal Service'; then use the Principal Service Lectionary (column 3) consistently for that service through the year;
- during the Sundays after Trinity, whether to use Track I of the Principal Service Lectionary (column 2), where the first reading stays over several weeks with one Old Testament book read semi-continuously, or Track 2 (column 3), where the first reading is chosen for its relationship to the Gospel reading of the day;
- which, if any, service on a Principal Feast, Principal Holy Day, Sunday or Festival constitutes the 'Second Service'; then use the Second Service Lectionary (column 5) consistently for that service through the year;
- which, if any, service on a Principal Feast, Principal Holy Day, Sunday or Festival constitutes the 'Third Service'; then use the Third Service Lectionary (column 4) consistently for that service through the year.

And in relation to weekdays:

- whether to use the Daily Eucharistic Lectionary (column 3) consistently for weekday celebrations of Holy Communion (with the exception of Principal Feasts, Principal Holy Days and Festivals) or to make some use of the Lesser Festival provision;
- whether to follow the first psalm provision in column 4 (morning) and column 5 (evening), where psalms during the seasons have a seasonal flavour but in ordinary time follow a sequential pattern; or to follow the alternative provision in the same columns, where psalms follow the sequential pattern throughout the year, except for the period between 19 December and The Epiphany and from the Monday of Holy Week to the Saturday of Easter Week; or to follow the psalm cycle in the Book of Common Prayer, where they are nearly always used 'in course';
- whether to use the Additional Weekday Lectionary (which begins on page 120) for weekday services (other than Holy Communion). It provides a one-year cycle of two readings for each day (except for Sundays, Principal Feasts, Principal Holy Days, Festivals and during Holy Week). Since each of the readings is designed to 'stand alone' (that is, it is complete in itself and will make sense to the worshipper who has not attended on the previous day and who will not be present on the next day), it is intended particularly for use in those churches and cathedrals that attract occasional rather than regular congregations.

The flexibility of *Common Worship* is intended to enable the church and the minister to find the most helpful provision for them. But once a decision is made, it is advisable to stay with that decision through the year or at the very least through a complete season.

Where optional additional verses or psalms are set, the references are placed in square parentheses [. . .]. A simple choice between two alternative readings is indicated by an italicized *or*, placed between references.

All Bible references (except to the psalms) are to the New Revised Standard Version, Anglicized edition (1995). Those who use other Bible translations should check the verse numbers against the NRSV. References to the psalms are to the *Common Worship* Psalter.

BOOK OF COMMON PRAYER

A separate Lectionary for the Book of Common Prayer is no longer issued. Provision is made on the right-hand pages of this Lectionary for BCP worship on all Sundays in the year, for the major festivals and for Morning and Evening Prayer. The Epistles and Gospels for Holy Communion are those of 1662, with the additions and variations of 1928, now authorized under the *Common Worship* overall provision. The Old Testament readings and psalms for these services, formerly appended to the Series One Holy Communion service, may be used but are not mandatory with the 1662 order.

Readings for Morning and Evening Prayer, which are the same as those for *Common Worship*, are set out in the BCP section for Sundays and weekdays. The special psalm provision of the BCP is given; however, where the *Common Worship* psalm provision is used, verse numbering may occasionally differ slightly from that in the BCP Psalter, and appropriate adjustment will have to be made (a table of variations in verse numbering can be found at www.churchofengland.org/prayer-and-worship/worship-texts-and-resources/common-worship/daily-prayer/psalter/psalter-verse). Otherwise the Psalter is read in course daily through each month.

The Calendar observes BCP dates when these differ from those of *Common Worship*; for example, St Thomas on 21 December. Additional commemorations in the *Common Worship* Calendar are not included, but those who wish to observe them may use the *Collects and Post Communions in Traditional Language: Lesser Festivals, Common of the Saints, Special Occasions* (Church House Publishing).

The Lectionaries of 1871 and 1922, to be found in many copies of the BCP, are still authorized and may be used, but – with the exception of the psalms and readings for Holy Communion mentioned above – the Additional Alternative Lectionary (1961) is no longer authorized for public worship.

Although those who use the BCP, for private or public worship or both, are free to follow any of the authorized lectionaries, there is much to be said for common usage across the Church of England, so that the same passages are being read by all. It is of course appropriate that BCP readings should be taken from the Authorized or King James Version for harmony of style, with the daily recitation of the BCP Psalter.

The integrity of the BCP as the traditional source of worship in the Church of England is not in any way affected by the use of a common lectionary for the daily offices.

CERTAIN DAYS AND OCCASIONS COMMONLY OBSERVED

Plough Sunday may be observed on 12 January 2025.

The Week of Prayer for Christian Unity may be observed from 18 to 25 January 2025.

Education Sunday may be observed on 14 September 2025.

Rogation Sunday may be observed on 25 May 2025.

The Feast of Dedication is observed on the anniversary of the dedication or consecration of a church, or, when the actual date is unknown, on 5 October 2025. In *Common Worship*, 26 October 2025 is an alternative date.

Ember Days. *Common Worship* encourages the bishop to set the Ember Days in each diocese in the week before the ordinations, whereas in BCP the dates are fixed.

Days of Discipline and Self-Denial in *Common Worship* are the weekdays of Lent and all Fridays in the year, except all Principal Feasts and festivals outside Lent and Fridays between Easter Day and Pentecost. The eves of Principal Feasts are also appropriately kept as days of discipline and self-denial in preparation for the feast.

Days of Fasting and Abstinence according to the BCP are the forty days of Lent, the Ember Days at the four seasons, the three Rogation Days, and all Fridays in the year except Christmas Day. The BCP also orders the observance of the Evens or Vigils before The Nativity of our Lord, The Purification of the Blessed Virgin Mary, The Annunciation of the Blessed Virgin Mary, Easter Day, Ascension Day, Pentecost, and before the following saints' days: Matthias, John the Baptist, Peter, James, Bartholomew, Matthew, Simon and Jude, Andrew, Thomas, and All Saints. (If any of these days falls on Monday, the Vigil is to be kept on the previous Saturday.)

KEY TO LITURGICAL COLOURS

Common Worship suggests appropriate liturgical colours. They are not mandatory, and traditional or local use may be followed.

For a detailed discussion of when colours may be used, see *Common Worship: Services and Prayers for the Church of England* (Church House Publishing), *New Handbook of Pastoral Liturgy* (SPCK) or *A Companion to Common Worship: Volume I* (SPCK).

When a lower-case letter accompanies an upper-case letter, the lower-case letter indicates the liturgical colour appropriate to the Lesser Festival of that day, while the upper-case letter indicates the continuing seasonal colour.

- **W** White
- **𝔚** Gold or white
- **R** Red
- **P** Purple (may vary from 'Roman purple' to violet, with blue as an alternative; a Lent array of sackcloth may be used in Lent, and rose pink on The Third Sunday of Advent and Fourth Sunday of Lent)
- **G** Green

PRINCIPAL FEASTS, HOLY DAYS AND FESTIVALS

Principal Feasts and other Principal Holy Days (Ash Wednesday, Maundy Thursday, Good Friday) are printed in **LARGE BOLD CAPITALS** in the Lectionary.

There are no longer proper readings relating to the Holy Spirit on the six days after Pentecost. Instead they have been located on the nine days before Pentecost.

When Patronal and Dedication Festivals are kept as Principal Feasts, they may be transferred to the nearest Sunday, unless that day is already either a Principal Feast or The First Sunday of Advent, The Baptism of Christ, The First Sunday of Lent or Palm Sunday.

Festivals are printed in the Lectionary in **SMALL BOLD CAPITALS**.

For each day there is a full liturgical provision for the Holy Communion and for Morning and Evening Prayer. Most holy days that are in the category 'Festival' are provided with an optional First Evening Prayer. Its use is entirely at the discretion of the minister. Where it is used, the liturgical colour for the next day should be used at that First Evening Prayer, and this has been indicated in the provision on the following pages.

LESSER FESTIVALS AND COMMEMORATIONS

Lesser Festivals (printed in **medium-bold roman** typeface) are observed at the level appropriate to a particular church. The readings and psalms for The Common of the Saints are listed on page 10. In addition, there are special readings appropriate to the Festival listed in the first column. The daily psalms and readings at Morning and Evening Prayer are not usually superseded by those for Lesser Festivals, but the readings and psalms for Holy Communion may on occasion be used at Morning or Evening Prayer.

Commemorations are printed in the Lectionary in *italic* typeface. They do not have Collect, psalm or readings, but may be observed by mention in prayers of intercession and thanksgiving. For local reasons, or where there is an established tradition in the wider Church, they may be kept as Lesser Festivals using the appropriate material from The Common of the Saints. Equally, it may be desirable to observe some Lesser Festivals as Commemorations.

If a Lesser Festival or a Commemoration falls on a Principal Feast, Principal Holy Day, Sunday or Festival, it is not normally observed that year, although it may be celebrated, where there is sufficient reason, on the nearest available day. Lesser Festivals and Commemorations which, for this reason, would not be celebrated in 2024–25 are listed on pages 9–10, so that, if desired, they may be mentioned in prayers of intercession and thanksgiving.

LESSER FESTIVALS AND COMMEMORATIONS NOT OBSERVED IN 2024–25

The Lesser Festivals and Commemorations (shown in italics) listed below fall on a Sunday or during Holy Week or Easter Week this year, and are thus not observed in this lectionary.

COMMON WORSHIP

2024

December

1 *Charles de Foucauld, Hermit in the Sahara, 1916*
8 The Conception of the Blessed Virgin Mary
29 Thomas Becket, Archbishop of Canterbury, Martyr, 1170

2025

January

12 Aelred of Hexham, Abbot of Rievaulx, 1167
Benedict Biscop, Abbot of Wearmouth, Scholar, 689
19 Wulfstan, Bishop of Worcester, 1095
26 Timothy and Titus, Companions of Paul

February

23 Polycarp, Bishop of Smyrna, Martyr, c. 155

March

2 Chad, Bishop of Lichfield, Missionary, 672

April

16 *Isabella Gilmore, Deaconess, 1923*
19 Alphege, Archbishop of Canterbury, Martyr, 1012
21 Anselm, Abbot of Le Bec, Archbishop of Canterbury, Teacher, 1109
24 *Mellitus, Bishop of London, first Bishop of St Paul's, 624*
The Seven Martyrs of the Melanesian Brotherhood, Solomon Islands, 2003
27 *Christina Rossetti, Poet, 1894*
28 *Peter Chanel, Missionary in the South Pacific, Martyr, 1841*
29 Catherine of Siena, Teacher, 1380

May

4 English Saints and Martyrs of the Reformation Era
25 The Venerable Bede, Monk at Jarrow, Scholar, Historian, 735
Aldhelm, Bishop of Sherborne, 709

June

1 Justin, Martyr at Rome, c. 165
8 Thomas Ken, Bishop of Bath and Wells, Nonjuror, Hymn Writer, 1711
15 *Evelyn Underhill, Spiritual Writer, 1941*
22 Alban, first Martyr of Britain, c. 250

July

6 *Thomas More, Scholar, and John Fisher, Bishop of Rochester, Reformation Martyrs, 1535*
20 *Margaret of Antioch, Martyr, 4th century*
Bartolomé de las Casas, Apostle to the Indies, 1566
27 *Brooke Foss Westcott, Bishop of Durham, Teacher, 1901*

August

10 Laurence, Deacon at Rome, Martyr, 258
31 Aidan, Bishop of Lindisfarne, Missionary, 651

October

12 Wilfrid of Ripon, Bishop, Missionary, 709
Elizabeth Fry, Prison Reformer, 1845
Edith Cavell, Nurse, 1915
19 Henry Martyn, Translator of the Scriptures, Missionary in India and Persia, 1812
26 Alfred the Great, King of the West Saxons, Scholar, 899
Cedd, Abbot of Lastingham, Bishop of the East Saxons, 664

November

2 Commemoration of the Faithful Departed (All Souls' Day)
9 *Margery Kempe, Mystic, c. 1440*
16 Margaret, Queen of Scotland, Philanthropist, Reformer of the Church, 1093
Edmund Rich of Abingdon, Archbishop of Canterbury, 1240
23 Clement, Bishop of Rome, Martyr, c. 100

December

1 *Charles de Foucauld, Hermit in the Sahara, 1916*
7 Ambrose, Bishop of Milan, Teacher, 397
14 John of the Cross, Poet, Teacher, 1591

BOOK OF COMMON PRAYER

2024

December
8 The Conception of the Blessed Virgin Mary

2025

March
2 Chad, Bishop of Lichfield, Missionary, 672

April
19 Alphege, Archbishop of Canterbury, Martyr, 1012
21 Anselm, Abbot of Le Bec, Archbishop of Canterbury, Teacher, 1109
23 George, Martyr, Patron of England, *c.* 304

June
1 Nicomede, Priest and Martyr at Rome (date unknown)

July
20 Margaret of Antioch, Martyr, 4th century

August
10 Laurence, Deacon at Rome, Martyr, 258

September
7 Evurtius, Bishop of Orleans, 4th century

November
23 Clement, Bishop of Rome, Martyr, *c.* 100

THE COMMON OF THE SAINTS

The Blessed Virgin Mary
Genesis 3. 8–15, 20; Isaiah 7. 10–14; Micah 5. 1–4
Psalms 45. 10–17; 113; 131
Acts 1. 12–14; Romans 8. 18–30; Galatians 4. 4–7
Luke 1. 26–38; I. 39–47; John 19. 25–27

Martyrs
2 Chronicles 24. 17–21; Isaiah 43. 1–7; Jeremiah 11. 18–20; Wisdom 4. 10–15
Psalms 3; 11; 31. 1–5; 44. 18–24; 126
Romans 8. 35–end; 2 Corinthians 4. 7–15; 2 Timothy 2. 3–7 [8–13]; Hebrews 11. 32–end; 1 Peter 4. 12–end; Revelation 12. 10–12a
Matthew 10. 16–22; 10. 28–39; 16. 24–26; John 12. 24–26; 15. 18–21

Teachers of the Faith and Spiritual Writers
I Kings 3. [6–10] 11–14; Proverbs 4. 1–9; Wisdom 7. 7–10, 15–16; Ecclesiasticus 39. 1–10
Psalms 19. 7–10; 34. 11–17; 37. 31–35; 119. 89–96; 119. 97–104
I Corinthians 1. 18–25; 2. 1–10; 2. 9–end; Ephesians 3. 8–12; 2 Timothy 4. 1–8; Titus 2. 1–8
Matthew 5. 13–19; 13. 52–end; 23. 8–12; Mark 4. 1–9; John 16. 12–15

Bishops and Other Pastors
I Samuel 16. I, 6–13; Isaiah 6. 1–8; Jeremiah 1. 4–10; Ezekiel 3. 16–21; Malachi 2. 5–7
Psalms 1; 15; 16. 5–end; 96; 110
Acts 20. 28–35; I Corinthians 4. 1–5; 2 Corinthians 4. 1–10 (*or* 1–2, 5–7); 5. 14–20; 1 Peter 5. 1–4
Matthew 11. 25–end; 24. 42–46; John 10. 11–16; 15. 9–17; 21. 15–17

Members of Religious Communities
I Kings 19. 9–18; Proverbs 10. 27–end; Song of Solomon 8. 6–7; Isaiah 61.10 - 62.5; Hosea 2. 14–15, 19–20
Psalms 34. 1–8; 112. 1–9; 119. 57–64; 123; 131
Acts 4. 32–35; 2 Corinthians 10.17 - 11.2; Philippians 3. 7–14; 1 John 2. 15–17; Revelation 19. 1, 5–9
Matthew 11. 25–end; 19. 3–12; 19. 23–end; Luke 9. 57–end; 12. 32–37

Missionaries
Isaiah 52. 7–10; 61. 1–3a; Ezekiel 34. 11–16; Jonah 3. 1–5
Psalms 67; 87; 97; 100; 117
Acts 2. 14, 22–36; 13. 46–49; 16. 6–10; 26. 19–23; Romans 15. 17–21; 2 Corinthians 5.11 - 6.2
Matthew 9. 35–end; 28. 16–end; Mark 16. 15–20; Luke 5. 1–11; 10. 1–9

Any Saint
Genesis 12. 1–4; Proverbs 8. 1–11; Micah 6. 6–8; Ecclesiasticus 2. 7–13 [14–end]
Psalms 32; 33. 1–5; 119. 1–8; 139. 1–4 [5–12]; 145. 8–14
Ephesians 3. 14–19; 6. 11–18; Hebrews 13. 7–8, 15–16; James 2. 14–17; 1 John 4. 7–16; Revelation 21. [1–4] 5–7
Matthew 19. 16–21; 25. 1–13; 25. 14–30; John 15. 1–8; 17. 20–end

SPECIAL OCCASIONS

The Guidance of the Holy Spirit
Proverbs 24. 3–7; Isaiah 30. 15–21; Wisdom 9. 13–17
Psalms 25. 1–9; 104. 26–33; 143. 8–10
Acts 15. 23–29; Romans 8. 22–27;
1 Corinthians 12. 4–13
Luke 14. 27–33; John 14. 23–26; 16. 13–15

The Commemoration of the Faithful Departed
Lamentations 3. 17–26, 31–33 *or* Wisdom 3. 1–9
Psalm 23 *or* 27. 1–6, 16–end
Romans 5. 5–11 *or* I Peter 1. 3–9
John 5. 19–25 *or* 6. 37–40

Rogation Days
Deuteronomy 8. 1–10; 1 Kings 8. 35–40; Job 28. 1–11
Psalms 104. 21–30; 107. 1–9; 121
Philippians 4. 4–7; 2 Thessalonians 3. 6–13;
1 John 5. 12–15
Matthew 6. 1–15; Mark 11. 22–24; Luke 11. 5–13

Harvest Thanksgiving

Year A
Deuteronomy 8. 7–18 *or* 28. 1–14
Psalm 65
2 Corinthians 9. 6–end
Luke 12. 16–30 *or* 17. 11–19

Year B
Joel 2. 21–27
Psalm 126
1 Timothy 2. 1–7 *or* 6. 6–10
Matthew 6. 25–33

Year C
Deuteronomy 26. 1–11
Psalm 100
Philippians 4. 4–9 *or* Revelation 14. 14–18
John 6. 25–35

Mission and Evangelism
Isaiah 49. 1–6; 52. 7–10; Micah 4. 1–5
Psalms 2; 46; 67
Acts 17. 12–end; 2 Corinthians 5.14 - 6.2;
Ephesians 2. 13–end
Matthew 5. 13–16; 28. 16–end; John 17. 20–end

The Unity of the Church
Jeremiah 33. 6–9a; Ezekiel 36. 23–28;
Zephaniah 3. 16–end
Psalms 100; 122; 133
Ephesians 4. 1–6; Colossians 3. 9–17;
1 John 4. 9–15
Matthew 18. 19–22; John 11. 45–52; 17. 11b–23

The Peace of the World
Isaiah 9. 1–6; 57. 15–19; Micah 4. 1–5
Psalms 40. 14–17; 72. 1–7; 85. 8–13
Philippians 4. 6–9; 1 Timothy 2. 1–6;
James 3. 13–18
Matthew 5. 43–end; John 14. 23–29; 15. 9–17

Social Justice and Responsibility
Isaiah 32. 15–end; Amos 5. 21–24; 8. 4–7;
Acts 5. 1–11
Psalms 31. 21–24; 85. 1–7; 146. 5–10
Colossians 3. 12–15; James 2. 1–4
Matthew 5. 1–12; 25. 31–end;
Luke 16. 19–end

Ministry (including Ember Days)
Numbers 11. 16–17, 24–29; 27. 15–end;
1 Samuel 16. 1–13a; Isaiah 6. 1–8; 61. 1–3;
Jeremiah 1. 4–10
Psalms 40. 8–13; 84. 8–12; 89. 19–25;
101. 1–5, 7; 122
Acts 20. 28–35; 1 Corinthians 3. 3–11;
Ephesians 4. 4–16; Philippians 3. 7–14
Luke 4. 16–21; 12. 35–43; 22. 24–27;
John 4. 31–38; 15. 5–17

In Time of Trouble
Genesis 9. 8–17; Job 1. 13–end; Isaiah 38. 6–11
Psalms 86. 1–7; 107. 4–15; 142. 1–7
Romans 3. 21–26; 8. 18–25;
2 Corinthians 8. 1–5, 9
Mark 4. 35–end; Luke 12. 1–7; John 16. 31–end

For the Sovereign
Joshua 1. 1–9; Proverbs 8. 1–16
Psalms 20; 101; 121
Romans 13. 1–10; Revelation 21.22 - 22.4
Matthew 22. 16–22; Luke 22. 24–30

		Sunday Principal Service Weekday Eucharist	Third Service Morning Prayer	Second Service Evening Prayer
December 2024				
1 Sunday	**THE FIRST SUNDAY OF ADVENT** *Common Worship* Year C begins			
P		Jer. 33. 14–16 Ps. 25. 1–9 1 Thess. 3. 9–end Luke 21. 25–36	Ps. 44 Isa. 51. 4–11 Rom. 13. 11–end	Ps. 9 (*or* 9. 1–8) Joel 3. 9–end Rev. 14.13 – 15.4 *Gospel*: John 3. 1–17
2 Monday	Daily Eucharistic Lectionary Year 1 begins			
P		Isa. 2. 1–5 Ps. 122 Matt. 8. 5–11	Ps. ***50***; 54 *alt.* Ps. ***1***; 2; 3 Isa. 42. 18–end Rev. ch. 19	Ps. 70; ***71*** *alt.* Ps. ***4***; 7 Isa. 25. 1–9 Matt. 12. 1–21
3 Tuesday	*Francis Xavier, Missionary, Apostle of the Indies, 1552*			
P		Isa. 11. 1–10 Ps. 72. 1–4, 18–19 Luke 10. 21–24	Ps. ***80***; 82 *alt.* Ps. ***5***; 6; (8) Isa. 43. 1–13 Rev. ch. 20	Ps. ***74***; 75 *alt.* Ps. ***9***; 10† Isa. 26. 1–13 Matt. 12. 22–37
4 Wednesday	*John of Damascus, Monk, Teacher, c. 749; Nicholas Ferrar, Deacon, Founder of the Little Gidding Community, 1637*			
P		Isa. 25. 6–10a Ps. 23 Matt. 15. 29–37	Ps. 5; ***7*** *alt.* Ps. 119. 1–32 Isa. 43. 14–end Rev. 21. 1–8	Ps. 76; ***77*** *alt.* Ps. ***11***; 12; 13 Isa. 28. 1–13 Matt. 12. 38–end
5 Thursday				
P		Isa. 26. 1–6 Ps. 118. 18–27a Matt. 7. 21, 24–27	Ps. ***42***; 43 *alt.* Ps. 14; ***15***; 16 Isa. 44. 1–8 Rev. 21. 9–21	Ps. ***40***; 46 *alt.* Ps. 18† Isa. 28. 14–end Matt. 13. 1–23
6 Friday	**Nicholas, Bishop of Myra, c. 326**			
Pw	Com. Bishop *or* *also* Isa. 61. 1–3 1 Tim. 6. 6–11 Mark 10. 13–16	Isa. 29. 17–end Ps. 27. 1–4, 16–17 Matt. 9. 27–31	Ps. ***25***; 26 *alt.* Ps. 17; ***19*** Isa. 44. 9–23 Rev. 21.22 – 22.5	Ps. 16; ***17*** *alt.* Ps. 22 Isa. 29. 1–14 Matt. 13. 24–43
7 Saturday	**Ambrose, Bishop of Milan, Teacher, 397**			
Pw	Com. Teacher *or* *also* Isa. 41. 9b–13 Luke 22. 24–30	Isa. 30. 19–21, 23–26 Ps. 146. 4–9 Matt. 9.35 – 10.1, 6–8	Ps. ***9***; 10 *alt.* Ps. 20; 21; ***23*** Isa. 44.24 – 45.13 Rev. 22. 6–end	Ps. ***27***; 28 *alt.* Ps. ***24***; 25 Isa. 29. 15–end Matt. 13. 44–end **ct**
8 Sunday	**THE SECOND SUNDAY OF ADVENT**			
P		Baruch ch. 5 *or* Mal. 3. 1–4 *Canticle*: Benedictus Phil. 1. 3–11 Luke 3. 1–6	Ps. 80 Isa. 64. 1–7 Matt. 11. 2–11	Ps. 75; [76] Isa. 40. 1–11 Luke 1. 1–25

	Calendar and Holy Communion	Morning Prayer	Evening Prayer	NOTES
	THE FIRST SUNDAY IN ADVENT Advent 1 Collect until Christmas Eve			
P	Mic. 4. 1–4, 6–7 Ps. 25. 1–9 Rom. 13. 8–14 Matt. 21. 1–13	Ps. 44 Isa. 51. 4–11 Rom. 13. 11–end	Ps. 9 (*or* 9. 1–8) Joel 3. 9–end Rev. 14.13 - 15.4	
P		Isa. 42. 18–end Rev. ch. 19	Isa. 25. 1–9 Matt. 12. 1–21	
P		Isa. 43. 1–13 Rev. ch. 20	Isa. 26. 1–13 Matt. 12. 22–37	
P		Isa. 43. 14–end Rev. 21. 1–8	Isa. 28. 1–13 Matt. 12. 38–end	
P		Isa. 44. 1–8 Rev. 21. 9–21	Isa. 28. 14–end Matt. 13. 1–23	
	Nicholas, Bishop of Myra, c. 326			
Pw	Com. Bishop	Isa. 44. 9–23 Rev. 21.22 - 22.5	Isa. 29. 1–14 Matt. 13. 24–43	
P		Isa. 44.24 - 45.13 Rev. 22. 6–end	Isa. 29. 15–end Matt. 13. 44–end **ct**	
	THE SECOND SUNDAY IN ADVENT			
P	2 Kings 22. 8–10; 23. 1–3 Ps. 50. 1–6 Rom. 15. 4–13 Luke 21. 25–33	Ps. 40 Isa. 64. 1–7 Luke 3. 1–6	Ps. 75 [76] Mal. 3. 1–4 Luke 1. 1–25	

		Sunday Principal Service Weekday Eucharist	Third Service Morning Prayer	Second Service Evening Prayer
9 Monday				
P		Isa. ch. 35 Ps. 85. 7–end Luke 5. 17–26	Ps. 44 *alt.* Ps. 27; ***30*** Isa. 45. 14–end 1 Thess. ch. 1	Ps. ***144***; 146 *alt.* Ps. 26; **28**; 29 Isa. 30. 1–18 Matt. 14. 1–12
10 Tuesday				
P		Isa. 40. 1–11 Ps. 96. 1, 10–end Matt. 18. 12–14	Ps. ***56***; 57 *alt.* Ps. 32; ***36*** Isa. ch. 46 1 Thess. 2. 1–12	Ps. ***11***; 12; 13 *alt.* Ps. 33 Isa. 30. 19–end Matt. 14. 13–end
11 Wednesday	Ember Day*			
P		Isa. 40. 25–end Ps. 103. 8–13 Matt. 11. 28–end	Ps. ***62***; 63 *alt.* Ps. 34 Isa. ch. 47 1 Thess. 2. 13–end	Ps. ***10***; 14 *alt.* Ps. 119. 33–56 Isa. ch. 31 Matt. 15. 1–20
12 Thursday				
P		Isa. 41. 13–20 Ps. 145. 1, 8–13 Matt. 11. 11–15	Ps. 53; ***54***; 60 *alt.* Ps. 37† Isa. 48. 1–11 1 Thess. ch. 3	Ps. 73 *alt.* Ps. 39; ***40*** Isa. ch. 32 Matt. 15. 21–28
13 Friday	**Lucy, Martyr at Syracuse, 304** Ember Day* *Samuel Johnson, Moralist, 1784*			
Pr	Com. Martyr *or* *also* Wisd. 3. 1–7 2 Cor. 4. 6–15	Isa. 48. 17–19 Ps. 1 Matt. 11. 16–19	Ps. 85; ***86*** *alt.* Ps. 31 Isa. 48. 12–end 1 Thess. 4. 1–12	Ps. 82; ***90*** *alt.* Ps. 35 Isa. 33. 1–22 Matt. 15. 29–end
14 Saturday	**John of the Cross, Poet, Teacher, 1591** Ember Day*			
Pw	Com. Teacher *or* *esp.* 1 Cor. 2. 1–10 *also* John 14. 18–23	Ecclus. 48. 1–4, 9–11 *or* 2 Kings 2. 9–12 Ps. 80. 1–4, 18–19 Matt. 17. 10–13	Ps. 145 *alt.* Ps. 41; ***42***; 43 Isa. 49. 1–13 1 Thess. 4. 13–end	Ps. 93; ***94*** *alt.* Ps. 45; ***46*** Isa. ch. 35 Matt. 16. 1–12 **ct**
15 Sunday	**THE THIRD SUNDAY OF ADVENT**			
P		Zeph. 3. 14–end *Canticle*: Isa. 12. 2–end *or* Ps. 146. 4–end Phil. 4. 4–7 Luke 3. 7–18	Ps. 12; 14 Isa. 25. 1–9 1 Cor. 4. 1–5	Ps. 50. 1–6; [62] Isa. ch. 35 Luke 1. 57–66 [67–end]
16 Monday				
P		Num. 24. 2–7, 15–17 Ps. 25. 3–8 Matt. 21. 23–27	Ps. 40 *alt.* Ps. 44 Isa. 49. 14–25 1 Thess. 5. 1–11	Ps. 25; ***26*** *alt.* Ps. ***47***; 49 Isa. 38. 1–8, 21–22 Matt. 16. 13–end

*For Ember Day provision, see p. 11.

	Calendar and Holy Communion	Morning Prayer	Evening Prayer	NOTES
P		Isa. 45. 14–end 1 Thess. ch. 1	Isa. 30. 1–18 Matt. 14. 1–12	
P		Isa. ch. 46 1 Thess. 2. 1–12	Isa. 30. 19–end Matt. 14. 13–end	
P		Isa. ch. 47 1 Thess. 2. 13–end	Isa. ch. 31 Matt. 15. 1–20	
P		Isa. 48. 1–11 1 Thess. ch. 3	Isa. ch. 32 Matt. 15. 21–28	
	Lucy, Martyr at Syracuse, 304			
Pr	Com. Virgin Martyr	Isa. 48. 12–end 1 Thess. 4. 1–12	Isa. 33. 1–22 Matt. 15. 29–end	
P		Isa. 49. 1–13 1 Thess. 4. 13–end	Isa. ch. 35 Matt. 16. 1–12 **ct**	
	THE THIRD SUNDAY IN ADVENT			
P	Isa. ch. 35 Ps. 80. 1–7 1 Cor. 4. 1–5 Matt. 11. 2–10	Ps. 12; 14 Isa. 25. 1–9 Luke 3. 7–18	Ps. 62 Zeph. 3. 14–end Luke 1. 57–66 [67–end]	
	O Sapientia			
P		Isa. 49. 14–25 1 Thess. 5. 1–11	Isa. 38. 1–8, 21–22 Matt. 16. 13–end	

		Sunday Principal Service Weekday Eucharist	Third Service Morning Prayer	Second Service Evening Prayer
17 Tuesday	O Sapientia *Eglantyne Jebb, Social Reformer, Founder of 'Save the Children', 1928*			
P		Gen. 49. 2, 8–10 Ps. 72. 1–5, 18–19 Matt. 1. 1–17	Ps. ***70***; 74 *alt.* Ps. ***48***; 52 Isa. ch. 50 1 Thess. 5. 12–end	Ps. ***50***; 54 *alt.* Ps. 50 Isa. 38. 9–20 Matt. 17. 1–13
18 Wednesday				
P		Jer. 23. 5–8 Ps. 72. 1–2, 12–13, 18–end Matt. 1. 18–24	Ps. ***75***; 96 *alt.* Ps. 119. 57–80 Isa. 51. 1–8 2 Thess. ch. 1	Ps. 25; ***82*** *alt.* Ps. ***59***; 60; (67) Isa. ch. 39 Matt. 17. 14–21
19 Thursday				
P		Judg. 13. 2–7, 24–end Ps. 71. 3–8 Luke 1. 5–25	Ps. 144; ***146*** Isa. 51. 9–16 2 Thess. ch. 2	Ps. 10; ***57*** Zeph. 1.1 – 2.3 Matt. 17. 22–end
20 Friday				
P		Isa. 7. 10–14 Ps. 24. 1–6 Luke 1. 26–38	Ps. ***46***; 95 Isa. 51. 17–end 2 Thess. ch. 3	Ps. ***4***; 9 Zeph. 3. 1–13 Matt. 18. 1–20
21 Saturday*				
P		Zeph. 3. 14–18 Ps. 33. 1–4, 11–12, 20–end Luke 1. 39–45	Ps. ***121***; 122; 123 Isa. 52. 1–12 Jude	Ps. 80; ***84*** Zeph. 3. 14–end Matt. 18. 21–end **ct**
22 Sunday	**THE FOURTH SUNDAY OF ADVENT**			
P		Mic. 5. 2–5a *Canticle*: Magnificat *or* Ps. 80. 1–8 Heb. 10. 5–10 Luke 1. 39–45 [46–55]	Ps. 144 Isa. 32. 1–8 Rev. 22. 6–end	Ps. 123; [131] Isa. 10.33 – 11.10 Matt. 1. 18–end
23 Monday				
P		Mal. 3. 1–4; 4. 5–end Ps. 25. 3–9 Luke 1. 57–66	Ps. 128; 129; ***130***; 131 Isa. 52.13 – 53.end 2 Pet. 1. 1–15	Ps. 89. 1–37 Mal. 1. 1, 6–end Matt. 19. 1–12
24 Tuesday	**CHRISTMAS EVE**			
P		*Morning Eucharist* 2 Sam. 7. 1–5, 8–11, 16 Ps. 89. 2, 19–27 Acts 13. 16–26 Luke 1. 67–79	Ps. ***45***; 113 Isa. ch. 54 2 Pet. 1.16 – 2.3	Ps. 85 Zech. ch. 2 Rev. 1. 1–8

*Thomas the Apostle may be celebrated on 21 December instead of 3 July.

	Calendar and Holy Communion	Morning Prayer	Evening Prayer	NOTES
P		Isa. ch. 50 1 Thess. 5. 12–end	Isa. 38. 9–20 Matt. 17. 1–13	
	Ember Day			
P	Ember CEG	Isa. 51. 1–8 2 Thess. ch. 1	Isa. ch. 39 Matt. 17. 14–21	
P		Isa. 51. 9–16 2 Thess. ch. 2	Zeph. 1.1 – 2.3 Matt. 17. 22–end	
	Ember Day			
P	Ember CEG	Isa. 51. 17–end 2 Thess. ch. 3	Zeph. 3. 1–13 Matt. 18. 1–20 *or First EP of Thomas* (Ps. 27) Isa. ch. 35 Heb. 10.35 – 11.1 **R ct**	
	THOMAS THE APOSTLE Ember Day			
R	Job 42. 1–6 Ps. 139. 1–11 Eph. 2. 19–end John 20. 24–end	(Ps. 92; 146) 2 Sam. 15. 17–21 *or* Ecclus. ch. 2 John 11. 1–16	(Ps. 139) Hab. 2. 1–4 1 Pet. 1. 3–12	
	THE FOURTH SUNDAY IN ADVENT			
P	Isa. 40. 1–9 Ps. 145. 17–end Phil. 4. 4–7 John 1. 19–28	Ps. 144 Isa. 32. 1–8 Rev. 22. 6–end	Ps. 123; [131] Isa. 10.33 – 11.10 Matt. 1. 18–end	
P		Isa. 52.13 – 53.end 2 Pet. 1. 1–15	Mal. 1. 1, 6–end Matt. 19. 1–12	
	CHRISTMAS EVE			
P	Collect (1) Christmas Eve (2) Advent 1 Mic. 5. 2–5a Ps. 24 Titus 3. 3–7 Luke 2. 1–14	Isa. ch. 54 2 Pet. 1.16 – 2.3	Zech. ch. 2 Rev. 1. 1–8	

		Sunday Principal Service Weekday Eucharist	Third Service Morning Prayer	Second Service Evening Prayer
25 Wednesday	**CHRISTMAS DAY**			
𝔚	*Any of the following sets of readings may be used on the evening of Christmas Eve and on Christmas Day. Set III should be used at some service during the celebration.*	*I* Isa. 9. 2–7 Ps. 96 Titus 2. 11–14 Luke 2. 1–14 [15–20] *II* Isa. 62. 6–end Ps. 97 Titus 3. 4–7 Luke 2. [1–7] 8–20 *III* Isa. 52. 7–10 Ps. 98 Heb. 1. 1–4 [5–12] John 1. 1–14	*MP*: Ps. ***110***; 117 Isa. 62. 1–5 Matt. 1. 18–end	*EP*: Ps. 8 Isa. 65. 17–25 Phil. 2. 5–11 *or* Luke 2. 1–20 *if it has not been used at the principal service of the day*
26 Thursday	**STEPHEN, DEACON, FIRST MARTYR**			
R		2 Chron. 24. 20–22 *or* Acts 7. 51–end Ps. 119. 161–168 Acts 7. 51–end *or* Gal. 2. 16b–20 Matt. 10. 17–22	*MP*: Ps. ***13***; 31. 1–8; 150 Jer. 26. 12–15 Acts ch. 6	*EP*: Ps. 57; ***86*** Gen. 4. 1–10 Matt. 23. 34–end
27 Friday	**JOHN, APOSTLE AND EVANGELIST**			
W		Exod. 33. 7–11a Ps. 117 1 John ch. 1 John 21. 19b–end	*MP*: Ps. ***21***; 147. 13–end Exod. 33. 12–end 1 John 2. 1–11	*EP*: Ps. 97 Isa. 6. 1–8 1 John 5. 1–12
28 Saturday	**THE HOLY INNOCENTS**			
R		Jer. 31. 15–17 Ps. 124 1 Cor. 1. 26–29 Matt. 2. 13–18	*MP*: Ps. ***36***; 146 Baruch 4. 21–27 *or* Gen. 37. 13–20 Matt. 18. 1–10	*EP*: Ps. 123; ***128*** Isa. 49. 14–25 Mark 10. 13–16
29 Sunday	**THE FIRST SUNDAY OF CHRISTMAS**			
W		1 Sam. 2. 18–20, 26 Ps. 148 (*or* 148. 7–end) Col. 3. 12–17 Luke 2. 41–end	Ps. 105. 1–11 Isa. 41.21 – 42.1 1 John 1. 1–7	Ps. 132 Isa. ch. 61 Gal. 3.27 – 4.7 *Gospel*: Luke 2. 15–21
30 Monday				
W		1 John 2. 12–17 Ps. 96. 7–10 Luke 2. 36–40	Ps. 111; 112; ***113*** Isa. 59. 1–15a John 1. 19–28	Ps. ***65***; 84 Jonah ch. 2 Col. 1. 15–23

	Calendar and Holy Communion	Morning Prayer	Evening Prayer
	CHRISTMAS DAY		
𝔚	Isa. 9. 2–7 Ps. 98 Heb. 1. 1–12 John 1. 1–14	Ps. 110; 117 Isa. 62. 1–5 Matt. 1. 18–end	Ps. 8 Isa. 65. 17–25 Phil. 2. 5–11 *or* Luke 2. 1–20
	STEPHEN, DEACON, FIRST MARTYR		
R	Collect (1) Stephen (2) Christmas 2 Chron. 24. 20–22 Ps. 119. 161–168 Acts 7. 55–end Matt. 23. 34–end	(Ps. 13; 31. 1–8; 150) Jer. 26. 12–15 Acts ch. 6	(Ps. 57; 86) Gen. 4. 1–10 Matt. 10. 17–22
	JOHN, APOSTLE AND EVANGELIST		
W	Collect (1) John (2) Christmas Exod. 33. 18–end Ps. 92. 11–end 1 John ch. 1 John 21. 19b–end	(Ps. 21; 147. 13–end) Exod. 33. 7–11a 1 John 2. 1–11	(Ps. 97) Isa. 6. 1–8 1 John 5. 1–12
	THE HOLY INNOCENTS		
R	Collect (1) Innocents (2) Christmas Jer. 31. 10–17 Ps. 123 Rev. 14. 1–5 Matt. 2. 13–18	(Ps. 36; 146) Baruch 4. 21–27 *or* Gen. 37. 13–20 Matt. 18. 1–10	(Ps. 124; 128) Isa. 49. 14–25 Mark 10. 13–16
	THE SUNDAY AFTER CHRISTMAS DAY		
W	Isa. 62. 10–12 Ps. 45. 1–7 Gal. 4. 1–7 Matt. 1. 18–end	Ps. 105. 1–11 Isa. 41.21 – 42.1 1 John 1. 1–7	Ps. 132 Isa. ch. 61 Luke 2. 15–21
W		Isa. 59. 1–15a John 1. 19–28	Jonah ch. 2 Col. 1. 15–23

NOTES

		Sunday Principal Service Weekday Eucharist	Third Service Morning Prayer	Second Service Evening Prayer
31 Tuesday	*John Wyclif, Reformer, 1384*			
W		1 John 2. 18–21 Ps. 96. 1, 11–end John 1. 1–18	Ps. 102 Isa. 59. 15b–end John 1. 29–34	Ps. ***90***; 148 Jonah chs 3 & 4 Col. 1.24 - 2.7 *or First EP of The Naming of Jesus* Ps. 148 Jer. 23. 1–6 Col. 2. 8–15 **ct**

January 2025

		Sunday Principal Service Weekday Eucharist	Third Service Morning Prayer	Second Service Evening Prayer
1 Wednesday	**THE NAMING AND CIRCUMCISION OF JESUS**			
W		Num. 6. 22–end Ps. 8 Gal. 4. 4–7 Luke 2.15–21	*MP*: Ps. ***103***; 150 Gen. 17. 1–13 Rom. 2. 17–end	*EP*: Ps. 115 Deut. 30. [1–10] 11–end Acts 3. 1–16
2 Thursday	**Basil the Great and Gregory of Nazianzus, Bishops, Teachers, 379 and 389** *Seraphim, Monk of Sarov, Spiritual Guide, 1833; Vedanayagam Samuel Azariah, Bishop in South India, Evangelist, 1945*			
W	Com. Teacher *or* *esp.* 2 Tim. 4. 1–8 Matt. 5. 13–19	1 John 2. 22–28 Ps. 98. 1–4 John 1. 19–28	Ps. 18. 1–30 Isa. 60. 1–12 John 1. 35–42	Ps. 45; ***46*** Ruth ch. 1 Col. 2. 8–end
3 Friday				
W		1 John 2.29 - 3.6 Ps. 98. 2–7 John 1. 29–34	Ps. ***127***; 128, 131 Isa. 60. 13–end John 1. 43–end	Ps. **2**; 110 Ruth ch. 2 Col. 3. 1–11
4 Saturday				
W		1 John 3. 7–10 Ps. 98. I, 8–end John 1. 35–42	Ps. 89. 1–37 Isa. ch. 61 John 2. 1–12	Ps. 85; ***87*** Ruth ch. 3 Col. 3.12 - 4.1 **ct** *or First EP of The Epiphany* Ps. 96; **97** Isa. 49. 1–13 John 4. 7–26 **𝔚 ct**
5 Sunday	**THE SECOND SUNDAY OF CHRISTMAS** *or* The Epiphany (see provision on 6 January)			
W		Jer. 31. 7–14 Ps. 147. 13–end *or* Ecclus. 24. 1–12 *Canticle*: Wisd. 10. 15–end Eph. 1. 3–14 John 1. [1–9] 10–18	Ps. 87 Isa. ch. 12 1 Thess. 2. 1–8	*First EP of The Epiphany* Ps. 96; **97** Isa. 49. 1–13 John 4. 7–26 **𝔚 ct**

	Calendar and Holy Communion	Morning Prayer	Evening Prayer	NOTES
	Silvester, Bishop of Rome, 335			
W	Com. Bishop	Isa. 59. 15b–end John 1. 29–34	Jonah chs 3 & 4 Col. 1.24 - 2.7 *or First EP of The Circumcision of Christ* (Ps. 148) Jer. 23. 1–6 Col. 2. 8–15 **ct**	
	THE CIRCUMCISION OF CHRIST			
W	Additional Collect Gen. 17. 3b–10 Ps. 98 Rom. 4. 8–13 *or* Eph. 2. 11–18 Luke 2. 15–21	(Ps. 103; 150) Gen. 17. 1–13 Rom. 2. 17–end	(Ps. 115) Deut. 30. [1–10] 11–20 Acts 3. 1–16	
W		Isa. 60. 1–12 John 1. 35–42	Ruth ch. 1 Col. 2. 8–end	
W		Isa. 60. 13–end John 1. 43–end	Ruth ch. 2 Col. 3. 1–11	
W		Isa. ch. 61 John 2. 1–12	Ruth ch. 3 Col. 3.12 - 4.1	
	THE SECOND SUNDAY AFTER CHRISTMAS			
W	Exod. 24. 12–18 Ps. 93 2 Cor. 8. 9 John 1. 14–18	Ps. 87 Isa. ch. 12 1 Thess. 2. 1–8	*First EP of The Epiphany* Ps. 96; 97 Isa. 49. 1–13 John 4. 7–26 **𝔚 ct**	

		Sunday Principal Service Weekday Eucharist	Third Service Morning Prayer	Second Service Evening Prayer
6 Monday	**THE EPIPHANY**			
𝔚		Isa. 60. 1–6 Ps. 72 (*or* 72. 10–15) Eph. 3. 1–12 Matt. 2. 1–12	*MP*: Ps. ***132***; 113 Jer. 31. 7–14 John 1. 29–34	*EP*: Ps. ***98***; 100 Baruch 4.36 – 5.end *or* Isa. 60. 1–9 John 2. 1–11
	or, if The Epiphany is celebrated on 5 January:			
W		1 John 3.22 – 4.6 Ps. 2. 7–end Matt. 4. 12–17, 23–end	Ps. 8; ***48*** *alt*. Ps. 71 Isa. ch. 62 John 2. 13–end	Ps. 96; ***97*** *alt*. Ps. ***72***; 75 Ruth 4. 1–17 Col. 4. 2–end
7 Tuesday				
W		1 John 3.22 – 4.6 Ps. 2. 7–end Matt. 4. 12–17, 23–end	Ps. ***99***; 147. 1–12 *alt*. Ps. 73 Isa. 63. 7–end 1 John ch. 3	Ps. 118 *alt*. Ps. 74 Baruch 1.15 – 2.10 *or* Jer. 23. 1–8 Matt. 20. 1–16
	or, if The Epiphany is celebrated on 5 January:	1 John 4. 7–10 Ps. 72. 1–8 Mark 6. 34–44	Ps. ***99***; 147. 1–12 *alt*. Ps. 73 Isa. 63. 7–end 1 John ch. 3	Ps. 118 *alt*. Ps. 74 Baruch 1.15 – 2.10 *or* Jer. 23. 1–8 Matt. 20. 1–16
8 Wednesday				
W		1 John 4. 7–10 Ps. 72. 1–8 Mark 6. 34–44	Ps. ***46***; 147. 13–end *alt*. Ps. 77 Isa. ch. 64 1 John 4. 7–end	Ps. 145 *alt*. Ps. 119. 81–104 Baruch 2. 11–end *or* Jer. 30. 1–17 Matt. 20. 17–28
	or, if The Epiphany is celebrated on 5 January:	1 John 4. 11–18 Ps. 72. 1, 10–13 Mark 6. 45–52	Ps. ***46***; 147. 13–end *alt*. Ps. 77 Isa. ch. 64 1 John 4. 7–end	Ps. 145 *alt*. Ps. 119. 81–104 Baruch 2. 11–end *or* Jer. 30. 1–17 Matt. 20. 17–28
9 Thursday				
W		1 John 4. 11–18 Ps. 72. 1, 10–13 Mark 6. 45–52	Ps. 2; ***148*** *alt*. Ps. 78. 1–39† Isa. 65. 1–16 1 John 5. 1–12	Ps. ***67***; 72 *alt*. Ps. 78. 40–end† Baruch 3. 1–8 *or* Jer. 30.18 – 31.9 Matt. 20. 29–end
	or, if The Epiphany is celebrated on 5 January:	1 John 4.19 – 5.4 Ps. 72. 1, 17–end Luke 4. 14–22	Ps. 2; ***148*** *alt*. Ps. 78. 1–39† Isa. 65. 1–16 1 John 5. 1–12	Ps. ***67***; 72 *alt*. Ps. 78. 40–end† Baruch 3. 1–8 *or* Jer. 30.18 – 31.9 Matt. 20. 29–end

	Calendar and Holy Communion	Morning Prayer	Evening Prayer	NOTES
	THE EPIPHANY			
𝔚	Isa. 60. 1–9 Ps. 100 Eph. 3. 1–12 Matt. 2. 1–12	Ps. 132; 113 Jer. 31. 7–14 John 1. 29–34	Ps. 72; 98 Baruch 4.36 - 5.end *or* Isa. 60. 1–9 John 2. 1–11	
W *or* **G**		Isa. 63. 7–end 1 John ch. 3	Baruch 1.15 - 2.10 *or* Jer. 23. 1–8 Matt. 20. 1–16	
	Lucian, Priest and Martyr, 290			
Wr *or* **Gr**	Com. Martyr	Isa. ch. 64 1 John 4. 7–end	Baruch 2. 11–end *or* Jer. 30. 1–17 Matt. 20. 17–28	
W *or* **G**		Isa. 65. 1–16 1 John 5. 1–12	Baruch 3. 1–8 *or* Jer. 30.18 - 31.9 Matt. 20. 29–end	

		Sunday Principal Service Weekday Eucharist	Third Service Morning Prayer	Second Service Evening Prayer
10 Friday	*William Laud, Archbishop of Canterbury, 1645*			
W		1 John 4.19 - 5.4 Ps. 72. 1, 17–end Luke 4. 14–22	Ps. 97; ***149*** *alt*. Ps. 55 Isa. 65. 17–end 1 John 5. 13–end	Ps. 27; ***29*** *alt*. Ps. 69 Baruch 3.9 - 4.4 *or* Jer. 31. 10–17 Matt. 23. 1–12
	or, if The Epiphany is celebrated on 5 January:	1 John 5. 5–13 Ps. 147. 13–end Luke 5. 12–16	Ps. 97; ***149*** *alt*. Ps. 55 Isa. 65. 17–end 1 John 5. 13–end	Ps. 27; ***29*** *alt*. Ps. 69 Baruch 3.9 - 4.4 *or* Jer. 31. 10–17 Matt. 23. 1–12
11 Saturday	*Mary Slessor, Missionary in West Africa, 1915*			
W		1 John 5. 5–13 Ps. 147. 13–end Luke 5. 12–16	Ps. 98; ***150*** *alt*. Ps. ***76***; 79 Isa. 66. 1–11 2 John	*First EP of The Baptism* Ps. 36 Isa. ch. 61 Titus 2. 11–14; 3. 4–7 **𝔚 ct**
	or, if The Epiphany is celebrated on 5 January:	1 John 5. 14–end Ps. 149. 1–5 John 3. 22–30	Ps. 98; ***150*** *alt*. Ps. ***76***; 79 Isa. 66. 1–11 2 John	*First EP of The Baptism* Ps. 36 Isa. ch. 61 Titus 2. 11–14; 3. 4–7 **𝔚 ct**
12 Sunday	**THE BAPTISM OF CHRIST (THE FIRST SUNDAY OF EPIPHANY)**			
𝔚		Isa. 43. 1–7 Ps. 29 Acts 8. 14–17 Luke 3. 15–17, 21–22	Ps. 89. 19–29 Isa. 42. 1–9 Acts 19. 1–7	Ps. 46; 47 Isa. 55. 1–11 Rom. 6. 1–11 *Gospel*: Mark 1. 4–11
13 Monday	**Hilary, Bishop of Poitiers, Teacher, 367** *Kentigern (Mungo), Missionary Bishop in Strathclyde and Cumbria, 603; George Fox, Founder of the Society of Friends (the Quakers), 1691*			
W **DEL 1**	Com. Teacher *or* *also* 1 John 2. 18–25 John 8. 25–32	Heb. 1. 1–6 Ps. 97. 1–2, 6–10 Mark 1. 14–20	Ps. **2**; 110 *alt*. Ps. ***80***; 82 Amos ch. 1 1 Cor. 1. 1–17	Ps. ***34***; 36 *alt*. Ps. ***85***; 86 Gen. 1. 1–19 Matt. 21. 1–17
14 Tuesday				
W		Heb. 2. 5–12 Ps. 8 Mark 1. 21–28	Ps. 8; ***9*** *alt*. Ps. 87; ***89. 1–18*** Amos ch. 2 1 Cor. 1. 18–end	Ps. ***45***; 46 *alt*. Ps. 89. 19–end Gen. 1.20 - 2.3 Matt. 21. 18–32
15 Wednesday				
W		Heb. 2. 14–end Ps. 105. 1–9 Mark 1. 29–39	Ps. 19; ***20*** *alt*. Ps. 119. 105–128 Amos ch. 3 1 Cor. ch. 2	Ps. ***47***; 48 *alt*. Ps. ***91***; 93 Gen. 2. 4–end Matt. 21. 33–end
16 Thursday				
W		Heb. 3. 7–14 Ps. 95. 1, 8–end Mark 1. 40–end	Ps. ***21***; 24 *alt*. Ps. 90; ***92*** Amos ch. 4 1 Cor. ch. 3	Ps. ***61***; 65 *alt*. Ps. 94 Gen. ch. 3 Matt. 22. 1–14

	Calendar and Holy Communion	Morning Prayer	Evening Prayer	NOTES
W *or* **G**		Isa. 65. 17–end 1 John 5. 13–end	Baruch 3.9 – 4.4 *or* Jer. 31. 10–17 Matt. 23. 1–12	
W *or* **G**		Isa. 66. 1–11 2 John	Baruch 4. 21–30 *or* Jer. 33. 14–end Matt. 23. 13–28 **ct**	
	THE FIRST SUNDAY AFTER THE EPIPHANY To celebrate The Baptism of Christ, see *Common Worship* provision.			
W *or* **G**	Zech. 8. 1–8 Ps. 72. 1–8 Rom. 12. 1–5 Luke 2. 41–end	Ps. 89. 19–29 Isa. 42. 1–9 Acts 19. 1–7	Ps. 46; 47 Isa. 55. 1–11 Rom. 6. 1–11	
	Hilary, Bishop of Poitiers, Teacher, 367			
W *or* **Gw**	Com. Doctor	Amos ch. 1 1 Cor. 1. 1–17	Gen. 1. 1–19 Matt. 21. 1–17	
W *or* **G**		Amos ch. 2 1 Cor. 1. 18–end	Gen. 1.20 – 2.3 Matt. 21. 18–32	
W *or* **G**		Amos ch. 3 1 Cor. ch. 2	Gen. 2. 4–end Matt. 21. 33–end	
W *or* **G**		Amos ch. 4 1 Cor. ch. 3	Gen. ch. 3 Matt. 22. 1–14	

		Sunday Principal Service Weekday Eucharist	Third Service Morning Prayer	Second Service Evening Prayer
17 Friday	**Antony of Egypt, Hermit, Abbot, 356** *Charles Gore, Bishop, Founder of the Community of the Resurrection, 1932*			
W	Com. Religious *or* *esp.* Phil. 3. 7–14 *also* Matt. 19. 16–26	Heb. 4. 1–5, 11 Ps. 78. 3–8 Mark 2. 1–12	Ps. ***67***; 72 *alt.* Ps. ***88***; (95) Amos 5. 1–17 1 Cor. ch. 4	Ps. 68 *alt.* Ps. 102 Gen. 4. 1–16, 25–26 Matt. 22. 15–33
18 Saturday	*Amy Carmichael, Founder of the Dohnavur Fellowship, Spiritual Writer, 1951* The Week of Prayer for Christian Unity until 25 January			
W		Heb. 4. 12–end Ps. 19. 7–end Mark 2. 13–17	Ps. 29; ***33*** *alt.* Ps. 96; ***97***; 100 Amos 5. 18–end 1 Cor. ch. 5	Ps. 84; ***85*** *alt.* Ps. 104 Gen. 6. 1–10 Matt. 22. 34–end **ct**
19 Sunday	**THE SECOND SUNDAY OF EPIPHANY**			
W		Isa. 62. 1–5 Ps. 36. 5–10 1 Cor. 12. 1–11 John 2. 1–11	Ps. 145. 1–13 Isa. 49. 1–7 Acts 16. 11–15	Ps. 96 1 Sam. 3. 1–20 Eph. 4. 1–16 *Gospel*: John 1. 29–42
20 Monday	*Richard Rolle of Hampole, Spiritual Writer, 1349*			
W **DEL 2**		Heb. 5. 1–10 Ps. 110. 1–4 Mark 2. 18–22	Ps. 145; ***146*** *alt.* Ps. ***98***; 99; 101 Amos ch. 6 1 Cor. 6. 1–11	Ps. 71 *alt.* Ps. ***105***† (*or* Ps. 103) Gen. 6.11 – 7.10 Matt. 24. 1–14
21 Tuesday	**Agnes, Child Martyr at Rome, 304**			
Wr	Com. Martyr *or* *also* Rev. 7. 13–end	Heb. 6. 10–end Ps. 111 Mark 2. 23–end	Ps. ***132***; 147. 1–12 *alt.* Ps. ***106***† (*or* Ps. 103) Amos ch. 7 1 Cor. 6. 12–end	Ps. 89. 1–37 *alt.* Ps. 107† Gen. 7. 11–end Matt. 24. 15–28
22 Wednesday	*Vincent of Saragossa, Deacon, first Martyr of Spain, 304*			
W		Heb. 7. 1–3, 15–17 Ps. 110. 1–4 Mark 3. 1–6	Ps. ***81***; 147. 13–end *alt.* Ps. 110; ***111***; 112 Amos ch. 8 1 Cor. 7. 1–24	Ps. ***97***; 98 *alt.* Ps. 119. 129–152 Gen. 8. 1–14 Matt. 24. 29–end
23 Thursday				
W		Heb. 7.25 – 8.6 Ps. 40. 7–10, 17–end Mark 3. 7–12	Ps. ***76***; 148 *alt.* Ps. 113; ***115*** Amos ch. 9 1 Cor. 7. 25–end	Ps. 99; 100; ***111*** *alt.* Ps. 114; ***116***; 117 Gen. 8.15 – 9.7 Matt. 25. 1–13
24 Friday	**Francis de Sales, Bishop of Geneva, Teacher, 1622**			
W	Com. Teacher *or* *also* Prov. 3. 13–18 John 3. 17–21	Heb. 8. 6–end Ps. 85. 7–end Mark 3. 13–19	Ps. ***27***; 149 *alt.* Ps. 139 Hos. 1.1 – 2.1 1 Cor. ch. 8	Ps. 73 *alt.* Ps. ***130***; 131; 137 Gen. 9. 8–19 Matt. 25. 14–30 *or First EP of The Conversion of Paul* Ps. 149 Isa. 49. 1–13 Acts 22. 3–16 **ct**

	Calendar and Holy Communion	Morning Prayer	Evening Prayer	NOTES
W *or* G		Amos 5. 1–17 1 Cor. ch. 4	Gen. 4. 1–16, 25–26 Matt. 22. 15–33	
	Prisca, Martyr at Rome, c. 265 For the Week of Prayer for Christian Unity, see *Common Worship* provision.			
Wr *or* **Gr**	Com. Virgin Martyr	Amos 5. 18–end 1 Cor. ch. 5	Gen. 6. 1–10 Matt. 22. 34–end **ct**	
	THE SECOND SUNDAY AFTER THE EPIPHANY			
W *or* **G**	2 Kings 4. 1–17 Ps. 107. 13–22 Rom. 12. 6–16a John 2. 1–11	Ps. 145. 1–13 Isa. 49. 1–7 Acts 16. 11–15	Ps. 96 1 Sam. 3. 1–20 Eph. 4. 1–16	
	Fabian, Bishop of Rome, Martyr, 250			
Wr *or* **Gr**	Com. Martyr	Amos ch. 6 1 Cor. 6. 1–11	Gen. 6.11 – 7.10 Matt. 24. 1–14	
	Agnes, Child Martyr at Rome, 304			
Wr *or* **Gr**	Com. Virgin Martyr	Amos ch. 7 1 Cor. 6. 12–end	Gen. 7. 11–end Matt. 24. 15–28	
	Vincent of Saragossa, Deacon, first Martyr of Spain, 304			
Wr *or* **Gr**	Com. Martyr	Amos ch. 8 1 Cor. 7. 1–24	Gen. 8. 1–14 Matt. 24. 29–end	
W *or* **G**		Amos ch. 9 1 Cor. 7. 25–end	Gen. 8.15 – 9.7 Matt. 25. 1–13	
W *or* **G**		Hos. 1.1 – 2.1 1 Cor. ch. 8	Gen. 9. 8–19 Matt. 25. 14–30 *or First EP of The Conversion of Paul* (Ps. 149) Isa. 49. 1–13 Acts 22. 3–16 **W ct**	

		Sunday Principal Service Weekday Eucharist	Third Service Morning Prayer	Second Service Evening Prayer
25 Saturday	**THE CONVERSION OF PAUL**			
W		Jer. 1. 4–10 *or* Acts 9. 1–22 Ps. 67 Acts 9. 1–22 *or* Gal. 1. 11–16a Matt. 19. 27–end	*MP*: Ps. 66; 147. 13–end Ezek. 3. 22–end Phil. 3. 1–14	*EP*: Ps. 119. 41–56 Ecclus. 39. 1–10 *or* Isa. 56. 1–8 Col. 1.24 - 2.7
26 Sunday	**THE THIRD SUNDAY OF EPIPHANY**			
W		Neh. 8. 1–3, 5–6, 8–10 Ps. 19 (*or* 19. 1–6) 1 Cor. 12. 12–31a Luke 4. 14–21	Ps. 113 Deut. 30. 11–15 3 John 1. 5–8	Ps. 33 (*or* 33. 1–12) Num. 9. 15–end 1 Cor. 7. 17–24 *Gospel*: Mark 1. 21–28
27 Monday				
W **DEL 3**		Heb. 9. 15, 24–end Ps. 98. 1–7 Mark 3. 22–30	Ps. 40; ***108*** *alt.* Ps. 123; 124; 125; ***126*** Hos. 2.18 - 3.end 1 Cor. 9. 15–end	Ps. ***138***; 144 *alt.* Ps. ***127***; 128; 129 Gen. 11.27 - 12.9 Matt. 26. 1–16
28 Tuesday	**Thomas Aquinas, Priest, Philosopher, Teacher, 1274**			
W	Com. Teacher *or* *esp.* Wisd. 7. 7–10, 15–16 1 Cor. 2. 9–end John 16. 12–15	Heb. 10. 1–10 Ps. 40. 1–4, 7–10 Mark 3. 31–end	Ps. 34; ***36*** *alt.* Ps. ***132***; 133 Hos. 4. 1–16 1 Cor. 10. 1–13	Ps. 145 *alt.* Ps. (134); ***135*** Gen. 13. 2–end Matt. 26. 17–35
29 Wednesday				
W		Heb. 10. 11–18 Ps. 110. 1–4 Mark 4. 1–20	Ps. 45; ***46*** *alt.* Ps. 119. 153–end Hos. 5. 1–7 1 Cor. 10.14 - 11.1	Ps. 21; ***29*** *alt.* Ps. 136 Gen. ch. 14 Matt. 26. 36–46
30 Thursday	**Charles, King and Martyr, 1649**			
Wr	Com. Martyr *or* *also* Ecclus. 2. 12–17 1 Tim. 6. 12–16	Heb. 10. 19–25 Ps. 24. 1–6 Mark 4. 21–25	Ps. ***47***; 48 *alt.* Ps. ***143***; 146 Hos. 5.8 - 6.6 1 Cor. 11. 2–16	Ps. ***24***; 33 *alt.* Ps. ***138***; 140; 141 Gen. ch. 15 Matt. 26. 47–56
31 Friday	*John Bosco, Priest, Founder of the Salesian Teaching Order, 1888*			
W		Heb. 10. 32–end Ps. 37. 3–6, 40–end Mark 4. 26–34	Ps. 61; ***65*** *alt.* Ps. 142; ***144*** Hos. 6.7 - 7.2 1 Cor. 11. 17–end	Ps. ***67***; 77 *alt. Ps.* ***145*** Gen. ch. 16 Matt. 26. 57–end

February 2025

1 Saturday	*Brigid, Abbess of Kildare, c. 525*			
W		Heb. 11. 1–2, 8–19 *Canticle*: Luke 1. 69–73 Mark 4. 35–end	Ps. 68 *alt.* Ps. 147 Hos. ch. 8 1 Cor. 12. 1–11	*First EP of The Presentation* Ps. 118 1 Sam. 1. 19b–end Heb. 4. 11–end **𝔚 ct**

	Calendar and Holy Communion	Morning Prayer	Evening Prayer
	THE CONVERSION OF PAUL		
W	Josh. 5. 13–end Ps. 67 Acts 9. 1–22 Matt. 19. 27–end	(Ps. 66; 147. 13–end) Ezek. 3. 22–end Phil. 3. 1–14	(Ps. 119. 41–56) Ecclus. 39. 1–10 *or* Isa. 56. 1–8 Col. 1.24 – 2.7
	THE THIRD SUNDAY AFTER THE EPIPHANY		
W *or* **G**	2 Kings 6. 14b–23 Ps. 102. 15–22 Rom. 12. 16b–end Matt. 8. 1–13	Ps. 113 Deut. 30. 11–15 3 John 1. 5–8	Ps. 33 (*or* 33. 1–12) Num. 9. 15–end 1 Cor. 7. 17–24
W *or* **G**		Hos. 2.18 – 3.end 1 Cor. 9. 15–end	Gen. 11.27 – 12.9 Matt. 26. 1–16
W *or* **G**		Hos. 4. 1–16 1 Cor. 10. 1–13	Gen. 13. 2–end Matt. 26. 17–35
W *or* **G**		Hos. 5. 1–7 1 Cor. 10.14 – 11.1	Gen. ch. 14 Matt. 26. 36–46
	Charles, King and Martyr, 1649		
Wr *or* **Gr**	Com. Martyr	Hos. 5.8 – 6.6 1 Cor. 11. 2–16	Gen. ch. 15 Matt. 26. 47–56
W *or* **G**		Hos. 6.7 – 7.2 1 Cor. 11. 17–end	Gen. ch. 16 Matt. 26. 57–end
W *or* **G**		Hos. ch. 8 1 Cor. 12. 1–11	*First EP of The Presentation* Ps. 118 1 Sam. 1. 19b–end Heb. 4. 11–end **W ct**

NOTES

		Sunday Principal Service Weekday Eucharist	Third Service Morning Prayer	Second Service Evening Prayer
2 Sunday	**THE PRESENTATION OF CHRIST IN THE TEMPLE (CANDLEMAS)**			
𝔚		Mal. 3. 1–5 Ps. 24 (*or* 24. 7–end) Heb. 2. 14–end Luke 2. 22–40	*MP*: Ps. ***48***; 146 Exod. 13. 1–16 Rom. 12. 1–5	*EP*: Ps. 122; ***132*** Hag. 2. 1–9 John 2. 18–22
3 Monday	**Anskar, Archbishop of Hamburg, Missionary in Denmark and Sweden, 865** Ordinary Time starts today*			
Gw **DEL 4**	Com. Missionary *or* *esp.* Isa. 52. 7–10 *also* Rom. 10. 11–15	Heb. 11. 32–end Ps. 31. 19–end Mark 5. 1–20	Ps. ***1***; 2; 3 Song of the Three 1–27 *or* Mal. 1. 1, 6–end John 13. 1–11	Ps. ***4***; 7 Lev. 22. 21–27; 23. 1–17 Phil. 1. 1–11
4 Tuesday	*Gilbert of Sempringham, Founder of the Gilbertine Order, 1189*			
G		Heb. 12. 1–4 Ps. 22. 25b–end Mark 5. 21–43	Ps. ***5***; 6; (8) Song of the Three 28–end *or* Mal. 2.17 – 3.12 John 13. 12–20	Ps. ***9***; 10† Exod. 29.38 – 30.16 Phil. 1. 12–end
5 Wednesday				
G		Heb. 12. 4–7, 11–15 Ps. 103. 1–2, 13–18 Mark 6. 1–6a	Ps. 119. 1–32 Susanna 1–27 *or* Mal. 2.17 – 3.12 John 13. 21–30	Ps. ***11***; 12; 13 Lev. ch. 8 Phil. 2. 1–13
6 Thursday	*The Martyrs of Japan, 1597*			
G		Heb. 12. 18–19, 21–24 Ps. 48. 1–3, 8–10 Mark 6. 7–13	Ps. 14; ***15***; 16 Susanna 28–end *or* Mal. 3.13 – 4.end John 13. 31–end	Ps. 18† Lev. ch. 9 Phil. 2. 14–end
7 Friday				
G		Heb. 13. 1–8 Ps. 27. 1–6, 9–12 Mark 6. 14–29	Ps. 17; ***19*** Bel and the Dragon *or* Nahum ch. 1 John 14. 1–14	Ps. 22 Lev. 16. 2–24 Phil. 3.1 – 4.1
8 Saturday				
G		Heb. 13. 15–17, 20–21 Ps. 23 Mark 6. 30–34	Ps. 20; 21; ***23*** Prayer of Manasseh *or* Obadiah John 14. 15–end	Ps. ***24***; 25 Lev. ch. 17 Phil. 4. 2–end **ct**
9 Sunday	**THE FOURTH SUNDAY BEFORE LENT (Proper 1)**			
G		Isa. 6. 1–8 [9–end] Ps. 138 1 Cor. 15. 1–11 Luke 5. 1–11	Ps. 3; 4 Jer. 26. 1–16 Acts 3. 1–10	Ps. [1]; 2 Wisd. 6. 1–21 *or* Hos. ch. 1 Col. 3. 1–22 *Gospel*: Matt. 5. 13–20
10 Monday	*Scolastica, sister of Benedict, Abbess of Plombariola, c. 543*			
G **DEL 5**		Gen. 1. 1–19 Ps. 104. 1–2, 6–13, 26 Mark 6. 53–end	Ps. 27; ***30*** Joel 1. 1–14 John 15. 1–11	Ps. 26; ***28***; 29 Lev. 19. 1–18, 30–end 1 Tim. 1. 1–17

*The Collect of 5 before Lent is used.

	Calendar and Holy Communion	Morning Prayer	Evening Prayer
	THE PRESENTATION OF CHRIST IN THE TEMPLE		
𝔚	Mal. 3. 1-5 Ps. 48. 1-7 Gal. 4. 1-7 Luke 2. 22-40	Ps. 48; 146 Exod. 13. 1-16 Rom. 12. 1-5	Ps. 122; 132 Hag. 2. 1-9 John 2. 18-22
	Blasius, Bishop of Sebastopol, Martyr, c. 316		
Gr	Com. Martyr	Song of the Three 1-27 *or* Mal. 1. 1, 6-end John 13. 1-11	Lev. 22. 21-27; 23. 1-17 Phil. 1. 1-11
G		Song of the Three 28-end *or* Mal. 2.17 - 3.12 John 13. 12-20	Exod. 29.38 - 30.16 Phil. 1. 12-end
	Agatha, Martyr in Sicily, 251		
Gr	Com. Virgin Martyr	Susanna 1-27 *or* Mal. 2.17 - 3.12 John 13. 21-30	Lev. ch. 8 Phil. 2. 1-13
G		Susanna 28-end *or* Mal. 3.13 - 4.end John 13. 31-end	Lev. ch. 9 Phil. 2. 14-end
G		Bel and the Dragon *or* Nahum ch. 1 John 14. 1-14	Lev. 16. 2-24 Phil. 3.1 - 4.1
G		Prayer of Manasseh *or* Obadiah John 14. 15-end	Lev. ch. 17 Phil. 4. 2-end **ct**
	THE FIFTH SUNDAY AFTER EPIPHANY		
G	Hos. 6. 4-6 Ps. 118. 14-21 Col. 3. 12-17 Matt. 13. 24b-30	Ps. 3; 4 Jer. 26. 1-16 Acts 3. 1-10	Ps. [1]; 2 Wisd. 6. 1-21 *or* Hos. ch. 1 Col. 3. 1-22
G		Joel 1. 1-14 John 15. 1-11	Lev. 19. 1-18, 30-end 1 Tim. 1. 1-17

NOTES

		Sunday Principal Service Weekday Eucharist	Third Service Morning Prayer	Second Service Evening Prayer
11 Tuesday				
G		Gen. 1.20 - 2.4a Ps. 8 Mark 7. 1–13	Ps. 32; ***36*** Joel 1. 15–end John 15. 12–17	Ps. 33 Lev. 23. 1–22 1 Tim. 1.18 - 2.end
12 Wednesday				
G		Gen. 2. 4b–9, 15–17 Ps. 104. 11–12, 29–32 Mark 7. 14–23	Ps. 34 Joel 2. 1–17 John 15. 18–end	Ps. 119. 33–56 Lev. 23. 23–end 1 Tim. ch. 3
13 Thursday				
G		Gen. 2. 18–end Ps. 128 Mark 7. 24–30	Ps. 37† Joel 2. 18–27 John 16. 1–15	Ps. 39; ***40*** Lev. 24. 1–9 1 Tim. ch. 4
14 Friday	**Cyril and Methodius, Missionaries to the Slavs, 869 and 885** *Valentine, Martyr at Rome, c. 269*			
Gw	Com. Missionaries *or* *esp.* Isa. 52. 7–10 *also* Rom. 10. 11–15	Gen. 3. 1–8 Ps. 32. 1–8 Mark 7. 31–end	Ps. 31 Joel 2. 28–end John 16. 16–22	Ps. 35 Lev. 25. 1–24 1 Tim. 5. 1–16
15 Saturday	*Sigfrid, Bishop, Apostle of Sweden, 1045; Thomas Bray, Priest, Founder of the SPCK and SPG, 1730*			
G		Gen. 3. 9–end Ps. 90. 1–12 Mark 8. 1–10	Ps. 41; ***42***; 43 Joel 3. 1–3, 9–end John 16. 23–end	Ps. 45; ***46*** Num. 6. 1–5, 21–end 1 Tim. 5. 17–end **ct**
16 Sunday	**THE THIRD SUNDAY BEFORE LENT (Proper 2)**			
G		Jer. 17. 5–10 Ps. 1 1 Cor. 15. 12–20 Luke 6. 17–26	Ps. 7 Jer. 30. 1–3, 10–22 Acts ch. 6	Ps. [5]; 6 Wisd. 11.21 - 12.11 *or* Hos. 10. 1–8, 12 Gal. 4. 8–20 *Gospel*: Matt. 5. 21–37
17 Monday	**Janani Luwum, Archbishop of Uganda, Martyr, 1977**			
Gr **DEL 6**	Com. Martyr *or* *also* Ecclus. 4. 20–28 John 12. 24–32	Gen. 4. 1–15, 25 Ps. 50. 1, 8, 16–end Mark 8. 11–13	Ps. 44 Eccles. ch. 1 John 17. 1–5	Ps. ***47***; 49 Gen. 24. 1–28 1 Tim. 6. 1–10
18 Tuesday				
G		Gen. 6. 5–8; 7. 1–5, 10 Ps. 29 Mark 8. 14–21	Ps. ***48***; 52 Eccles. ch. 2 John 17. 6–19	Ps. 50 Gen. 24. 29–end 1 Tim. 6. 11–end
19 Wednesday				
G		Gen. 8. 6–13, 20–end Ps. 116. 10–end Mark 8. 22–26	Ps. 119. 57–80 Eccles. 3. 1–15 John 17. 20–end	Ps. ***59***; 60; (67) Gen. 25. 7–11, 19–end 2 Tim. 1. 1–14
20 Thursday				
P		Gen. 9. 1–13 Ps. 102. 16–23 Mark 8. 27–33	Ps. 56; ***57***; (63†) Eccles. 3.16 - 4.end John 18. 1–11	Ps. 61; ***62***; 64 Gen. 26.34 - 27.40 2 Tim. 1.15 - 2.13
21 Friday				
G		Gen. 11. 1–9 Ps. 33. 10–15 Mark 8.34 - 9.1	Ps. ***51***; 54 Eccles. ch. 5 John 18. 12–27	Ps. 38 Gen. 27.41 - 28.end 2 Tim. 2. 14–end

	Calendar and Holy Communion	Morning Prayer	Evening Prayer	NOTES
G		Joel 1. 15–end John 15. 12–17	Lev. 23. 1–22 1 Tim. 1.18 - 2.end	
G		Joel 2. 1–17 John 15. 18–end	Lev. 23. 23–end 1 Tim. ch. 3	
G		Joel 2. 18–27 John 16. 1–15	Lev. 24. 1–9 1 Tim. ch. 4	
	Valentine, Martyr at Rome, c. 269			
Gr	Com. Martyr	Joel 2. 28–end John 16. 16–22	Lev. 25. 1–24 1 Tim. 5. 1–16	
G		Joel 3. 1–3, 9–end John 16. 23–end	Num. 6. 1–5, 21–end 1 Tim. 5. 17–end **ct**	
	SEPTUAGESIMA			
G	Gen. 1. 1–5 Ps. 9. 10–20 1 Cor. 9. 24–end Matt. 20. 1–16	Ps. 7 Jer. 30. 1–3, 10–22 Acts ch. 6	Ps. [5]; 6 Wisd. 11.21 - 12.11 *or* Hos. 10. 1–8, 12 Gal. 4. 8–20	
G		Eccles. ch. 1 John 17. 1–5	Gen. 24. 1–28 1 Tim. 6. 1–10	
G		Eccles. ch. 2 John 17. 6–19	Gen. 24. 29–end 1 Tim. 6. 11–end	
G		Eccles. 3. 1–15 John 17. 20–end	Gen. 25. 7–11, 19–end 2 Tim. 1. 1–14	
G		Eccles. 3.16 - 4.end John 18. 1–11	Gen. 26.34 - 27.40 2 Tim. 1.15 - 2.13	
G		Eccles. ch. 5 John 18. 12–27	Gen. 27.41 - 28.end 2 Tim. 2. 14–end	

		Sunday Principal Service Weekday Eucharist	Third Service Morning Prayer	Second Service Evening Prayer
22 Saturday				
G		Heb. 11. 1–7 Ps. 145. 1–10 Mark 9. 2–13	Ps. 68 Eccles. ch. 6 John 18. 28–end	Ps. 65; **66** Gen. 29. 1–30 2 Tim. ch. 3 **ct**
23 Sunday	**THE SECOND SUNDAY BEFORE LENT**			
G		Gen. 2. 4b–9, 15–end Ps. 65 Rev. ch. 4 Luke 8. 22–25	Ps. 104. 1–26 Job 28. 1–11 Acts 14. 8–17	Ps. 147 (*or* 147. 13–end) Gen. 1.1 – 2.3 Matt. 6. 25–end
24 Monday*				
G **DEL 7**		Ecclus. 1. 1–10 *or* James 1. 1–11 Ps. 93 *or* Ps. 119. 65–72 Mark 9. 14–29	Ps. 71 Eccles. 7. 1–14 John 19. 1–16	Ps. **72**; 75 Gen. 29.31 – 30.24 2 Tim. 4. 1–8
25 Tuesday				
G		Ecclus. 2. 1–11 *or* James 1. 12–18 Ps. 37. 3–6, 27–28 *or* Ps. 94. 12–18 Mark 9. 30–37	Ps. 73 Eccles. 7. 15–end John 19. 17–30	Ps. 74 Gen. 31. 1–24 2 Tim. 4. 9–end
26 Wednesday				
G		Ecclus. 4. 11–19 *or* James 1. 19–end Ps. 119. 161–168 *or* Ps. 15 Mark 9. 38–40	Ps. 77 Eccles. ch. 8 John 19. 31–end	Ps. 119. 81–104 Gen. 31.25 – 32.2 Titus ch. 1
27 Thursday	**George Herbert, Priest, Poet, 1633**			
Gw	Com. Pastor *or* *esp.* Mal. 2. 5–7 Matt. 11. 25–end *also* Rev. 19. 5–9	Ecclus. 5. 1–8 *or* James 2. 1–9 Ps. 1 *or* Ps. 34. 1–7 Mark 9. 41–end	Ps. 78. 1–39† Eccles. ch. 9 John 20. 1–10	Ps. 78. 40–end† Gen. 32. 3–30 Titus ch. 2
28 Friday				
G		Ecclus. 6. 5–17 *or* James 2. 14–24, 26 Ps. 119. 19–24 *or* Ps. 112 Mark 10. 1–12	Ps. 55 Eccles. 11. 1–8 John 20. 11–18	Ps. 69 Gen. 33. 1–17 Titus ch. 3

*Matthias may be celebrated on 24 February instead of 14 May.

	Calendar and Holy Communion	Morning Prayer	Evening Prayer	NOTES
G		Eccles. ch. 6 John 18. 28–end	Gen. 29. 1–30 2 Tim. ch. 3 **ct**	
	SEXAGESIMA			
G	Gen. 3. 9–19 Ps. 83. 1–2, 13–end 2 Cor. 11. 19–31 Luke 8. 4–15	Ps. 104. 1–26 Job 28. 1–11 Acts 14. 8–17	Ps. 147 (*or* 147. 13–end) Gen. 1.1 - 2.3 Matt. 6. 25–end *or First EP of Matthias* Ps. 147 Isa. 22. 15–22 Phil. 3.13b - 14.1 **R ct**	
	MATTHIAS THE APOSTLE			
R	1 Sam. 2. 27–35 Ps. 16. 1–7 Acts 1. 15–end Matt. 11. 25–end	(Ps. 15) Jonah 1. 1–9 Acts 2. 37–end	(Ps. 80) 1 Sam. 16. 1–13a Matt. 7. 15–27	
G		Eccles. 7. 15–end John 19. 17–30	Gen. 31. 1–24 2 Tim. 4. 9–end	
G		Eccles. ch. 8 John 19. 31–end	Gen. 31.25 - 32.2 Titus ch. 1	
G		Eccles. ch. 9 John 20. 1–10	Gen. 32. 3–30 Titus ch. 2	
G		Eccles. 11. 1–8 John 20. 11–18	Gen. 33. 1–17 Titus ch. 3	

March 2025

		Sunday Principal Service Weekday Eucharist	Third Service Morning Prayer	Second Service Evening Prayer
1 Saturday	**David, Bishop of Menevia, Patron of Wales, *c.* 601**			
Gw	Com. Bishop *or* *also* 2 Sam. 23. 1–4 Ps. 89. 19–22, 24	Ecclus. 17. 1–15 *or* James 3. 1–10 Ps. 103. 13–18 *or* Ps. 12. 1–7 Mark 10. 13–16	Ps. ***76***; 79 Eccles. 11.9 - 12.end John 20. 19–end	Ps. 81; ***84*** Gen. ch. 35 Philemon **ct**
2 Sunday	**THE SUNDAY NEXT BEFORE LENT**			
G		Exod. 34. 29–end Ps. 99 2 Cor. 3.12 - 4.2 Luke 9. 28–36 [37–43a]	Ps. 2 Exod. 33. 17–end 1 John 3. 1–3	Ps. 89. 1–18 (*or* 89. 5–12) Exod. 3. 1–6 John 12. 27–36a
3 Monday				
G **DEL 8**		Ecclus. 17. 24–29 *or* James 3. 13–end Ps. 32. 1–8 *or* Ps. 19. 7–end Mark 10. 17–27	Ps. ***80***; 82 Jer. ch. 1 John 3. 1–21	Ps. ***85***; 86 Gen. 37. 1–11 Gal. ch. 1
4 Tuesday				
G		Ecclus. 35. 1–12 *or* James 4. 1–10 Ps. 50. 1–6 *or* Ps. 55. 7–9, 24 Mark 10. 28–31	Ps. 87; ***89. 1–18*** Jer. 2. 1–13 John 3. 22–end	Ps. 89. 19–end Gen. 37. 12–end Gal. 2. 1–10
5 Wednesday	**ASH WEDNESDAY**			
P		Joel 2. 1–2, 12–17 *or* Isa. 58. 1–12 Ps. 51. 1–18 2 Cor. 5.20b - 6.10 Matt. 6. 1–6, 16–21 *or* John 8. 1–11	*MP*: Ps. 38 Dan. 9. 3–6, 17–19 1 Tim. 6. 6–19	*EP*: Ps. ***51*** *or* Ps. 102 (*or* 102. 1–18) Isa. 1. 10–18 Luke 15. 11–end
6 Thursday				
P		Deut. 30. 15–end Ps. 1 Luke 9. 22–25	Ps. 77 *alt.* Ps. 90; **92** Jer. 2. 14–32 John 4. 1–26	Ps. 74 *alt.* Ps. 94 Gen. ch. 39 Gal. 2. 11–end
7 Friday	**Perpetua, Felicity and their Companions, Martyrs at Carthage, 203**			
Pr	Com. Martyr *or* *esp.* Rev. 12. 10–12a *also* Wisd. 3. 1–7	Isa. 58. 1–9a Ps. 51. 1–5, 17–18 Matt. 9. 14–15	Ps. **3**; 7 *alt.* Ps. ***88***; (95) Jer. 3. 6–22 John 4. 27–42	Ps. 31 *alt.* Ps. 102 Gen. ch. 40 Gal. 3. 1–14
8 Saturday	**Edward King, Bishop of Lincoln, 1910** *Felix, Bishop, Apostle to the East Angles, 647; Geoffrey Studdert Kennedy, Priest, Poet, 1929*			
Pw	Com. Bishop *or* *also* Heb. 13. 1–8	Isa. 58. 9b–end Ps. 86. 1–7 Luke 5. 27–32	Ps. 71 *alt.* Ps. 96; **97**; 100 Jer. 4. 1–18 John 4. 43–end	Ps. 73 *alt.* Ps. 104 Gen. 41. 1–24 Gal. 3. 15–22 **ct**

	Calendar and Holy Communion	Morning Prayer	Evening Prayer
	David, Bishop of Menevia, Patron of Wales, c. 601		
Gw	Com. Bishop	Eccles. 11.9 – 12.end John 20. 19–end	Gen. ch. 35 Philemon **ct**
	QUINQUAGESIMA		
G	Gen. 9. 8–17 Ps. 77. 11–end 1 Cor. ch. 13 Luke 18. 31–43	Ps. 2 Exod. 33. 17–end Luke 9. 28–43	Ps. 89. 1–18 (*or* 89. 5–12) Exod. 3. 1–6 John 12. 27–36a
G		Jer. ch. 1 John 3. 1–21	Gen. 37. 1–11 Gal. ch. 1
G		Jer. 2. 1–13 John 3. 22–end	Gen. 37. 12–end Gal. 2. 1–10
	ASH WEDNESDAY		
P	Ash Wednesday Collect until 19 April Commination Joel 2. 12–17 Ps. 57 James 4. 1–10 Matt. 6. 16–21	Ps. 38 Dan. 9. 3–6, 17–19 1 Tim. 6. 6–19	Ps. 51 *or* Ps. 102 (*or* 102. 1–18) Isa. 1. 10–18 Luke 15. 11–end
P	Exod. 24. 12–end Matt. 8. 5–13	Jer. 2. 14–32 John 4. 1–26	Gen. ch. 39 Gal. 2. 11–end
	Perpetua, Martyr at Carthage, 203		
Pr	Com. Martyr *or* 1 Kings 19. 3b–8 Matt. 5.43 – 6.6	Jer. 3. 6–22 John 4. 27–42	Gen. ch. 40 Gal. 3. 1–14
P	Isa. 38. 1–6a Mark 6. 45–end	Jer. 4. 1–18 John 4. 43–end	Gen. 41. 1–24 Gal. 3. 15–22 **ct**

NOTES

		Sunday Principal Service Weekday Eucharist	Third Service Morning Prayer	Second Service Evening Prayer
9 Sunday	**THE FIRST SUNDAY OF LENT**			
P		Deut. 26. 1–11 Ps. 91. 1–2, 9–end (*or* 91. 1–11) Rom. 10. 8b–13 Luke 4. 1–13	Ps. 50. 1–15 Mic. 6. 1–8 Luke 5. 27–end	Ps. 119. 73–88 Jonah ch. 3 Luke 18. 9–14
10 Monday				
P		Lev. 19. 1–2, 11–18 Ps. 19. 7–end Matt. 25. 31–end	Ps. 10; ***11*** *alt.* Ps. ***98***; 99; 101 Jer. 4. 19–end John 5. 1–18	Ps. 12; ***13***; 14 *alt.* Ps. ***105***† (*or* 103) Gen. 41. 25–45 Gal. 3.23 - 4.7
11 Tuesday				
P		Isa. 55. 10–11 Ps. 34. 4–6, 21–22 Matt. 6. 7–15	Ps. 44 *alt.* Ps. ***106***† (*or* 103) Jer. 5. 1–19 John 5. 19–29	Ps. 46; ***49*** *alt.* Ps. 107† Gen. 41.46 - 42.5 Gal. 4. 8–20
12 Wednesday	Ember Day*			
P		Jonah ch. 3 Ps. 51. 1–5, 17–18 Luke 11. 29–32	Ps. ***6***; 17 *alt.* Ps. 110; ***111***; 112 Jer. 5. 20–end John 5. 30–end	Ps. 9; ***28*** *alt.* Ps. 119. 129–152 Gen. 42. 6–17 Gal. 4.21 - 5.1
13 Thursday				
P		Esther 14. 1–5, 12–14 *or* Isa. 55. 6–9 Ps. 138 Matt. 7. 7–12	Ps. ***42***; 43 *alt.* Ps. 113; ***115*** Jer. 6. 9–21 John 6. 1–15	Ps. 137; 138; ***142*** *alt.* Ps. 114; ***116***; 117 Gen. 42. 18–28 Gal. 5. 2–15
14 Friday	Ember Day*			
P		Ezek. 18. 21–28 Ps. 130 Matt. 5. 20–26	Ps. 22 *alt.* Ps. 139 Jer. 6. 22–end John 6. 16–27	Ps. 54; ***55*** *alt.* Ps. ***130***; 131; 137 Gen. 42. 29–end Gal. 5. 16–end
15 Saturday	Ember Day*			
P		Deut. 26. 16–end Ps. 119. 1–8 Matt. 5. 43–end	Ps. 59; ***63*** *alt.* Ps. 120; ***121***; 122 Jer. 7. 1–20 John 6. 27–40	Ps. ***4***; 16 *alt.* Ps. 118 Gen. 43. 1–15 Gal. ch. 6 **ct**
16 Sunday	**THE SECOND SUNDAY OF LENT**			
P		Gen. 15. 1–12, 17–18 Ps. 27 Phil. 3.17 - 4.1 Luke 13. 31–end	Ps. 119. 161–end Gen. 17. 1–7, 15–16 Rom. 11. 13–24	Ps. 135 (*or* 135. 1–14) Jer. 22. 1–9, 13–17 Luke 14. 27–33

*For Ember Day provision, see p. 11.

	Calendar and Holy Communion	Morning Prayer	Evening Prayer	NOTES
	THE FIRST SUNDAY IN LENT			
P	Collect (1) Lent 1 (2) Ash Wednesday Ember until 15 March Gen. 3. 1–6 Ps. 91. 1–12 2 Cor. 6. 1–10 Matt. 4. 1–11	Ps. 50. 1–15 Mic. 6. 1–8 Luke 5. 27–end	Ps. 119. 73–88 Jonah ch. 3 Luke 18. 9–14	
P	Ezek. 34. 11–16a Matt. 25. 31–end	Jer. 4. 19–end John 5. 1–18	Gen. 41. 25–45 Gal. 3.23 - 4.7	
P	Isa. 55. 6–11 Matt. 21. 10–16	Jer. 5. 1–19 John 5. 19–29	Gen. 41.46 - 42.5 Gal. 4. 8–20	
	Gregory the Great, Bishop of Rome, 604 Ember Day			
Pw	Ember CEG *or* Com. Doctor *or* Isa. 58. 1–9a Matt. 12. 38–end	Jer. 5. 20–end John 5. 30–end	Gen. 42. 6–17 Gal. 4.21 - 5.1	
P	Isa. 58. 9b–end John 8. 31–45	Jer. 6. 9–21 John 6. 1–15	Gen. 42. 18–28 Gal. 5. 2–15	
	Ember Day			
P	Ember CEG *or* Ezek. 18. 20–25 John 5. 2–15	Jer. 6. 22–end John 6. 16–27	Gen. 42. 29–end Gal. 5. 16–end	
	Ember Day			
P	Ember CEG *or* Ezek. 18. 26–end Matt. 17. 1–9 *or* Luke 4. 16–21 *or* John 10. 1–16	Jer. 7. 1–20 John 6. 27–40	Gen. 43. 1–15 Gal. ch. 6 **ct**	
	THE SECOND SUNDAY IN LENT			
P	Jer. 17. 5–10 Ps. 25. 13–end 1 Thess. 4. 1–8 Matt. 15. 21–28	Ps. 119. 161–end Gen. 17. 1–7, 15–16 Rom. 11. 13–24	Ps. 135 (*or* 135. 1–14) Jer. 22. 1–9, 13–17 Luke 14. 27–33	

		Sunday Principal Service Weekday Eucharist	Third Service Morning Prayer	Second Service Evening Prayer
17 Monday	**Patrick, Bishop, Missionary, Patron of Ireland, c. 460**			
Pw	Com. Missionary *or* *also* Ps. 91. 1–4, 13–end Luke 10. 1–12, 17–20	Dan. 9. 4–10 Ps. 79. 8–9, 12, 14 Luke 6. 36–38	Ps. 26; ***32*** *alt.* Ps. 123; 124; 125; ***126*** Jer. 7. 21–end John 6. 41–51	Ps. 70; ***74*** *alt.* Ps. ***127***; 128; 129 Gen. 43. 16–end Heb. ch. 1
18 Tuesday	*Cyril, Bishop of Jerusalem, Teacher, 386*			
P		Isa. 1. 10, 16–20 Ps. 50. 8, 16–end Matt. 23. 1–12	Ps. 50 *alt.* Ps. ***132***; 133 Jer. 8. 1–15 John 6. 52–59	Ps. ***52***; 53; 54 *alt.* Ps. (134); ***135*** Gen. 44. 1–17 Heb. 2. 1–9 *or First EP of Joseph* Ps. 132 Hos. 11. 1–9 Luke 2. 41–end **W ct**
19 Wednesday	**JOSEPH OF NAZARETH**			
W		2 Sam. 7. 4–16 Ps. 89. 26–36 Rom. 4. 13–18 Matt. 1. 18–end	*MP*: Ps. 25; 147. 1–12 Isa. 11. 1–10 Matt. 13. 54–end	*EP*: Ps. 1; 112 Gen. 50. 22–end Matt. 2. 13–end
20 Thursday	**Cuthbert, Bishop of Lindisfarne, Missionary, 687***			
Pw	Com. Missionary *or* *esp.* Ezek. 34. 11–16 *also* Matt. 18. 12–14	Jer. 17. 5–10 Ps. 1 Luke 16. 19–end	Ps. 34 *alt.* Ps. ***143***; 146 Jer. 9. 12–24 John 7. 1–13	Ps. 71 *alt.* Ps. ***138***; 140; 141 Gen. 45. 1–15 Heb. 3. 1–6
21 Friday	**Thomas Cranmer, Archbishop of Canterbury, Reformation Martyr, 1556**			
Pr	Com. Martyr *or*	Gen. 37. 3–4, 12–13, 17–28 Ps. 105. 16–22 Matt. 21. 33–43, 45–46	Ps. 40; ***41*** *alt.* Ps. 142; ***144*** Jer. 10. 1–16 John 7. 14–24	Ps. ***6***; 38 *alt.* Ps. 145 Gen. 45. 16–end Heb. 3. 7–end
22 Saturday				
P		Mic. 7. 4–15, 18–20 Ps. 103. 1–4, 9–12 Luke 15. 1–3, 11–end	Ps. 3; ***25*** *alt.* Ps. 147 Jer. 10. 17–24 John 7. 25–36	Ps. ***23***; 27 *alt.* Ps. ***148***; 149; 150 Gen. 46. 1–7, 28–end Heb. 4. 1–13 **ct**
23 Sunday	**THE THIRD SUNDAY OF LENT**			
P		Isa. 55. 1–9 Ps. 63. 1–9 1 Cor. 10. 1–13 Luke 13. 1–9	Ps. 26; 28 Deut. 6. 4–9 John 17. 1a, 11b–19	Ps. 12; 13 Gen. 28. 10–19a John 1. 35–end

*Cuthbert may be celebrated on 4 September instead of 20 March.

	Calendar and Holy Communion	Morning Prayer	Evening Prayer	NOTES
P	Heb. 2. 1–10 John 8. 21–30	Jer. 7. 21–end John 6. 41–51	Gen. 43. 16–end Heb. ch. 1	
	Edward, King of the W. Saxons, 978			
Pr	Com. Martyr *or* Heb. 2. 11–end Matt. 23. 1–12	Jer. 8. 1–15 John 6. 52–59	Gen. 44. 1–17 Heb. 2. 1–9	
	To celebrate Joseph, see *Common Worship* provision.			
P	Heb. 3. 1–6 Matt. 20. 17–28	Jer. 8.18 – 9.11 John 6. 60–end	Gen. 44. 18–end Heb. 2. 10–end	
P	Heb. 3. 7–end John 5. 30–end	Jer. 9. 12–24 John 7. 1–13	Gen. 45. 1–15 Heb. 3. 1–6	
	Benedict, Abbot of Monte Cassino, *c.* 550			
Pw	Com. Abbot *or* Heb. ch. 4 Matt. 21. 33–end	Jer. 10. 1–16 John 7. 14–24	Gen. 45. 16–end Heb. 3. 7–end	
P	Heb. ch. 5 Luke 15. 11–end	Jer. 10. 17–24 John 7. 25–36	Gen. 46. 1–7, 28–end Heb. 4. 1–13 **ct**	
	THE THIRD SUNDAY IN LENT			
P	Num. 22. 21–31 Ps. 9. 13–end Eph. 5. 1–14 Luke 11. 14–28	Ps. 26; 28 Deut. 6. 4–9 John 17. 1a, 11b–19	Ps. 12; 13 Gen. 28. 10–19a John 1. 35–end	

		Sunday Principal Service Weekday Eucharist	Third Service Morning Prayer	Second Service Evening Prayer
24 Monday*	*Walter Hilton of Thurgarton, Augustinian Canon, Mystic, 1396; Paul Couturier, Priest, Ecumenist, 1953; Oscar Romero, Archbishop of San Salvador, Martyr, 1980*			
P		2 Kings 5. 1–15 Ps. 42. 1–2; 34. 1–4 Luke 4. 24–30	Ps. ***5***; 7 *alt.* Ps. ***1***; 2; 3 Jer. 11. 1–17 John 7. 37–52	Ps. 11; ***17*** *alt.* Ps. ***4***; 7 Gen. 47. 1–27 Heb. 4.14 - 5.10 *or First EP of The Annunciation* Ps. 85 Wisd. 9. 1–12 *or* Gen. 3. 8–15 Gal. 4. 1–5 **𝔚 ct**
25 Tuesday	**THE ANNUNCIATION OF OUR LORD TO THE BLESSED VIRGIN MARY**			
𝔚		Isa. 7. 10–14 Ps. 40. 5–11 Heb. 10. 4–10 Luke 1. 26–38	*MP*: Ps. 111; 113 1 Sam. 2. 1–10 Rom. 5. 12–end	*EP*: Ps. 131; 146 Isa. 52. 1–12 Heb. 2. 5–end
26 Wednesday	*Harriet Monsell, Founder of the Community of St John the Baptist, Clewer, 1883*			
P		Deut. 4. 1, 5–9 Ps. 147. 13–end Matt. 5. 17–19	Ps. 38 *alt.* Ps. 119. 1–32 Jer. 13. 1–11 John 8. 12–30	Ps. 36; ***39*** *alt.* Ps. ***11***; 12; 13 Gen. 49. 1–32 Heb. 6. 13–end
27 Thursday				
P		Jer. 7. 23–28 Ps. 95. 1–2, 6–end Luke 11. 14–23	Ps. ***56***; 57 *alt.* Ps. 14; ***15***; 16 Jer. ch. 14 John 8. 31–47	Ps. ***59***; 60 *alt.* Ps. 18† Gen. 49.33 - 50.end Heb. 7. 1–10
28 Friday				
P		Hos. ch. 14 Ps. 81. 6–10, 13, 16 Mark 12. 28–34	Ps. 22 *alt.* Ps. 17; ***19*** Jer. 15. 10–end John 8. 48–end	Ps. 69 *alt.* Ps. 22 Exod. 1. 1–14 Heb. 7. 11–end
29 Saturday				
P		Hos. 5.15 - 6.6 Ps. 51. 1–2, 17–end Luke 18. 9–14	Ps. 31 *alt.* Ps. 20; 21; ***23*** Jer. 16.10 - 17.4 John 9. 1–17	Ps. ***116***; 130 *alt.* Ps. ***24***; 25 Exod. 1.22 - 2.10 Heb. ch. 8 **ct**

*The following readings may replace those provided for Holy Communion on any day (except The Annunciation) during the Third Week of Lent: Exod. 17. 1–7; Ps. 95. 1–2, 6–end; John 4. 5–42.

	Calendar and Holy Communion	Morning Prayer	Evening Prayer	NOTES
P	Heb. 6. 1–10 Luke 4. 23–30	Jer. 11. 1–17 John 7. 37–52	Gen. 47. 1–27 Heb. 4.14 - 5.10 *or First EP of The Annunciation* Ps. 85 Wisd. 9. 1–12 *or* Gen. 3. 8–15 Gal. 4. 1–5 **𝔚 ct**	
	THE ANNUNCIATION OF THE BLESSED VIRGIN MARY			
𝔚	Isa. 7. 10–14 [15] Ps. 113 Rom. 5. 12–19 Luke 1. 26–38	Ps. 111 1 Sam. 2. 1–10 Heb. 10. 4–10	Ps. 131; 146 Isa. 52. 1–12 Heb. 2. 5–end	
P	Heb. 7. 1–10 Matt. 15. 1–20	Jer. 13. 1–11 John 8. 12–30	Gen. 49. 1–32 Heb. 6. 13–end	
P	Heb. 7. 11–25 John 6. 26–35	Jer. ch. 14 John 8. 31–47	Gen. 49.33 - 50.end Heb. 7. 1–10	
P	Heb. 7. 26–end John 4. 5–26	Jer. 15. 10–end John 8. 48–end	Exod. 1. 1–14 Heb. 7. 11–end	
P	Heb. 8. 1–6 John 8. 1–11	Jer. 16.10 - 17.4 John 9. 1–17	Exod. 1.22 - 2.10 Heb. ch. 8 **ct**	

		Sunday Principal Service Weekday Eucharist	Third Service Morning Prayer	Second Service Evening Prayer
30 Sunday	**THE FOURTH SUNDAY OF LENT** (Mothering Sunday)			
P		Josh. 5. 9–12 Ps. 32 2 Cor. 5. 16–end Luke 15. 1–3, 11b–end	Ps. 84; 85 Gen. 37. 3–4, 12–end 1 Pet. 2. 16–end	Ps. 30 Prayer of Manasseh *or* Isa. 40.27 – 41.13 2 Tim. 4. 1–18 *Gospel*: John 11. 17–44 *If the Principal Service readings for The Fourth Sunday of Lent are displaced by Mothering Sunday provisions, they may be used at the Second Service.*
	or, for Mothering Sunday:	Exod. 2. 1–10 *or* 1 Sam. 1. 20–end Ps. 34. 11–20 *or* Ps. 127. 1–4 2 Cor. 1. 3–7 *or* Col. 3. 12–17 Luke 2. 33–35 *or* John 19. 25b–27		
31 Monday*	*John Donne, Priest, Poet, 1631*			
P		Isa. 65. 17–21 Ps. 30. 1–5, 8, 11–end John 4. 43–end	Ps. 70; ***77*** *alt*. Ps. 27; ***30*** Jer. 17. 5–18 John 9. 18–end	Ps. ***25***; 28 *alt*. Ps. 26; ***28***; 29 Exod. 2. 11–22 Heb. 9. 1–14

April 2025

1 Tuesday	*Frederick Denison Maurice, Priest, Teacher, 1872*			
P		Ezek. 47. 1–9, 12 Ps. 46. 1–8 John 5. 1–3, 5–16	Ps. 54; ***79*** *alt*. Ps. 32; ***36*** Jer. 18. 1–12 John 10. 1–10	Ps. ***80***; 82 *alt*. Ps. 33 Exod. 2.23 – 3.20 Heb. 9. 15–end
2 Wednesday				
P		Isa. 49. 8–15 Ps. 145. 8–18 John 5. 17–30	Ps. **63**; *90* *alt*. Ps. 34 Jer. 18. 13–end John 10. 11–21	Ps. 52; ***91*** *alt*. Ps. 119. 33–56 Exod. 4. 1–23 Heb. 10. 1–18
3 Thursday				
P		Exod. 32. 7–14 Ps. 106. 19–23 John 5. 31–end	Ps. 53; ***86*** *alt*. Ps. 37† Jer. 19. 1–13 John 10. 22–end	Ps. 94 *alt*. Ps. 39; ***40*** Exod. 4.27 – 6.1 Heb. 10. 19–25
4 Friday				
P		Wisd. 2. 1, 12–22 *or* Jer. 26. 8–11 Ps. 34. 15–end John 7. 1–2, 10, 25–30	Ps. 102 *alt*. Ps. 31 Jer. 19.14 – 20.6 John 11. 1–16	Ps. 13; ***16*** *alt*. Ps. 35 Exod. 6. 2–13 Heb. 10. 26–end

*The following readings may replace those provided for Holy Communion on any day during the Fourth Week of Lent: Mic. 7. 7–9; Ps. 27. 1, 9–10, 16–17; John ch. 9.

	Calendar and Holy Communion	Morning Prayer	Evening Prayer
	THE FOURTH SUNDAY IN LENT To celebrate Mothering Sunday, see *Common Worship* provision.		
P	Exod. 16. 2–7a Ps. 122 Gal. 4. 21–end *or* Heb. 12. 22–24 John 6. 1–14	Ps. 84; 85 Gen. 37. 3–4, 12–end 1 Pet. 2. 16–end	Ps. 30 Prayer of Manasseh *or* Isa. 40.27 - 41.13 2 Tim. 4. 1–18
P	Heb. 11. 1–6 John 2. 13–end	Jer. 17. 5–18 John 9. 18–end	Exod. 2. 11–22 Heb. 9. 1–14
P	Heb. 11. 13–16a John 7. 14–24	Jer. 18. 1–12 John 10. 1–10	Exod. 2.23 - 3.20 Heb. 9. 15–end
P	Heb. 12. 1–11 John 9. 1–17	Jer. 18. 13–end John 10. 11–21	Exod. 4. 1–23 Heb. 10. 1–18
	Richard, Bishop of Chichester, 1253		
Pw	Com. Bishop *or* Heb. 12. 12–17 John 5. 17–27	Jer. 19. 1–13 John 10. 22–end	Exod. 4.27 - 6.1 Heb. 10. 19–25
	Ambrose, Bishop of Milan, 397		
Pw	Com. Doctor *or* Heb. 12. 22–end John 11. 33–46	Jer. 19.14 - 20.6 John 11. 1–16	Exod. 6. 2–13 Heb. 10. 26–end

NOTES

		Sunday Principal Service Weekday Eucharist	Third Service Morning Prayer	Second Service Evening Prayer
5 Saturday				
P		Jer. 11. 18–20 Ps. 7. 1–2, 8–10 John 7. 40–52	Ps. 32 *alt.* Ps. 41; ***42***; 43 Jer. 20. 7–end John 11. 17–27	Ps. ***140***; 141; 142 *alt.* Ps. 45; ***46*** Exod. 7. 8–end Heb. 11. 1–16 **ct**
6 Sunday	**THE FIFTH SUNDAY OF LENT (Passiontide begins)**			
P		Isa. 43. 16–21 Ps. 126 Phil. 3. 4b–14 John 12. 1–8	Ps. 111; 112 Isa. ch. 35 Rom. 7.21 - 8.4	Ps. 35 (*or* 35. 1–9) 2 Chron. 35. 1–6, 10–16 Luke 22. 1–13
7 Monday*				
P		Susanna 1–9, 15–17, 19–30, 33–62 (*or* 41b–62) *or* Josh. 2. 1–14 Ps. 23 John 8. 1–11	Ps. ***73***; 121 *alt.* Ps. 44 Jer. 21. 1–10 John 11. 28–44	Ps. ***26***; 27 *alt.* Ps. ***47***; 49 Exod. 8. 1–19 Heb. 11. 17–31
8 Tuesday				
P		Num. 21. 4–9 Ps. 102. 1–3, 16–23 John 8. 21–30	Ps. ***35***; 123 *alt.* Ps. ***48***; 52 Jer. 22. 1–5, 13–19 John 11. 45–end	Ps. ***61***; 64 *alt.* Ps. 50 Exod. 8. 20–end Heb. 11.32 - 12.2
9 Wednesday	*Dietrich Bonhoeffer, Lutheran Pastor, Martyr, 1945*			
P		Dan. 3. 14–20, 24–25, 28 *Canticle*: Bless the Lord John 8. 31–42	Ps. ***55***; 124 *alt.* Ps. 119. 57–80 Jer. 22.20 - 23.8 John 12. 1–11	Ps. 56; ***62*** *alt.* Ps. ***59***; 60 (67) Exod. 9. 1–12 Heb. 12. 3–13
10 Thursday	**William Law, Priest, Spiritual Writer, 1761** *William of Ockham, Friar, Philosopher, Teacher, 1347*			
Pw	Com. Teacher *or* *esp.* 1 Cor. 2. 9–end *also* Matt. 17. 1–9	Gen. 17. 3–9 Ps. 105. 4–9 John 8. 51–end	Ps. ***40***; 125 *alt.* Ps. 56; ***57***; (63†) Jer. 23. 9–32 John 12. 12–19	Exod. 9. 13–end Heb. 12. 14–end
11 Friday	*George Augustus Selwyn, first Bishop of New Zealand, 1878*			
P		Jer. 20. 10–13 Ps. 18. 1–6 John 10. 31–end	Ps. ***22***; 126 *alt.* Ps. ***51***; 54 Jer. ch. 24 John 12. 20–36a	Ps. 31 *alt.* Ps. 38 Exod. ch. 10 Heb. 13. 1–16
12 Saturday				
P		Ezek. 37. 21–end *Canticle*: Jer. 31. 10–13 *or* Ps. 121 John 11. 45–end	Ps. ***23***; 127 *alt.* Ps. 68 Jer. 25. 1–14 John 12. 36b–end	Ps. 128; 129; ***130*** *alt.* Ps. 65; ***66*** Exod. ch. 11 Heb. 13. 17–end **ct**

*The following readings may replace those provided for Holy Communion on any day during the Fifth Week of Lent: 2 Kings 4. 18–21, 32–37; Ps. 17. 1–8, 16; John 11. 1–45.

	Calendar and Holy Communion	Morning Prayer	Evening Prayer	NOTES
P	Heb. 13. 17–21 John 8. 12–20	Jer. 20. 7–end John 11. 17–27	Exod. 7. 8–end Heb. 11. 1–16 **ct**	
	THE FIFTH SUNDAY IN LENT			
P	Exod. 24. 4–8 Ps. 143 Heb. 9. 11–15 John 8. 46–end	Ps. 111; 112 Isa. ch. 35 Rom. 7.21 - 8.4	Ps. 35 (*or* 35. 1–9) 2 Chron. 35. 1–6, 10–16 Luke 22. 1–13	
P	Col. 1. 13–23a John 7. 1–13	Jer. 21. 1–10 John 11. 28–44	Exod. 8. 1–19 Heb. 11. 17–31	
P	Col. 2. 8–12 John 7. 32–39	Jer. 22. 1–5, 13–19 John 11. 45–end	Exod. 8. 20–end Heb. 11.32 - 12.2	
P	Col. 2. 13–19 John 7. 40–end	Jer. 22.20 - 23.8 John 12. 1–11	Exod. 9. 1–12 Heb. 12. 3–13	
P	Col. 3. 8–11 John 10. 22–38	Jer. 23. 9–32 John 12. 12–19	Exod. 9. 13–end Heb. 12. 14–end	
P	Col. 3. 12–17 John 11. 47–54	Jer. ch. 24 John 12. 20–36a	Exod. ch. 10 Heb. 13. 1–16	
P	Col. 4. 2–6 John 6. 53–end	Jer. 25. 1–14 John 12. 36b–end	Exod. ch. 11 Heb. 13. 17–end **ct**	

		Sunday Principal Service Weekday Eucharist	Third Service Morning Prayer	Second Service Evening Prayer
13 Sunday	**PALM SUNDAY**			
R	*Liturgy of the Palms* Luke 19. 28–40 Ps. 118. 1–2, 19–end (*or* 118. 19–end)	*Liturgy of the Passion* Isa. 50. 4–9a Ps. 31. 9–16 (*or* 31. 9–18) Phil. 2. 5–11 Luke 22.14 - 23.end *or* Luke 23. 1–49	Ps. 61; 62 Zech. 9. 9–12 1 Cor. 2. 1–12	Ps. 69. 1–20 Isa. 5. 1–7 Luke 20. 9–19
14 Monday	**MONDAY OF HOLY WEEK**			
R		Isa. 42. 1–9 Ps. 36. 5–11 Heb. 9. 11–15 John 12. 1–11	*MP*: Ps. 41 Lam. 1. 1–12a Luke 22. 1–23	*EP*: Ps. 25 Lam. 2. 8–19 Col. 1. 18–23
15 Tuesday	**TUESDAY OF HOLY WEEK**			
R		Isa. 49. 1–7 Ps. 71. 1–14 (*or* 71. 1–8) 1 Cor. 1. 18–31 John 12. 20–36	*MP*: Ps. 27 Lam. 3. 1–18 Luke 22. [24–38] 39–53	*EP*: Ps. 55. 13–24 Lam. 3. 40–51 Gal. 6. 11–end
16 Wednesday	**WEDNESDAY OF HOLY WEEK**			
R		Isa. 50. 4–9a Ps. 70 Heb. 12. 1–3 John 13. 21–32	*MP*: Ps. 102 (*or* 102. 1–18) Wisd. 1.16 - 2.1, 12–22 *or* Jer. 11. 18–20 Luke 22. 54–end	*EP*: Ps. 88 Isa. 63. 1–9 Rev. 14.18 - 15.4
17 Thursday	**MAUNDY THURSDAY**			
W(HC)R		Exod. 12. 1–4 [5–10] 11–14 Ps. 116. 1, 10–end (*or* 116. 9–end) 1 Cor. 11. 23–26 John 13. 1–17, 31b–35	*MP*: Ps. 42; 43 Lev. 16. 2–24 Luke 23. 1–25	*EP*: Ps. 39 Exod. ch. 11 Eph. 2. 11–18
18 Friday	**GOOD FRIDAY**			
R		Isa. 52.13 - 53.end Ps. 22 (*or* 22. 1–11 *or* 22. 1–21) Heb. 10. 16–25 *or* Heb. 4. 14–16; 5. 7–9 John 18.1 - 19.end	*MP*: Ps. 69 Gen. 22. 1–18 *A part of* John 18 - 19 *if not read at the Principal Service* *or* Heb. 10. 1–10	*EP*: Ps. 130; 143 Lam. 5. 15–end *A part of* John 18 - 19 *if not read at the Principal Service, especially* John 19. 38–end *or* Col. 1. 18–23
19 Saturday	**Easter Eve**			
	These readings are for use at services other than the Easter Vigil.	Job 14. 1–14 *or* Lam. 3. 1–9, 19–24 Ps. 31. 1–4, 15–16 (*or* 31. 1–5) 1 Pet. 4. 1–8 Matt. 27. 57–end *or* John 19. 38–end	Ps. 142 Hos. 6. 1–6 John 2. 18–22	Ps. 116 Job 19. 21–27 1 John 5. 5–12

	Calendar and Holy Communion	Morning Prayer	Evening Prayer
	THE SUNDAY NEXT BEFORE EASTER (PALM SUNDAY)		
R	Zech. 9. 9-12 Ps. 73. 22-end Phil. 2. 5-11 Passion acc. to Matthew Matt. 27. 1-54 *or* Matt. 26.1 - 27.61 *or* Matt. 21. 1-13	Ps. 61; 62 Isa. 42. 1-9 1 Cor. 2. 1-12	Ps. 69. 1-20 Isa. 5. 1-7 Luke 20. 9-19
	MONDAY IN HOLY WEEK		
R	Isa. 63. 1-19 Ps. 55. 1-8 Gal. 6. 1-11 Mark ch. 14	Ps. 41 Lam. 1. 1-12a John 12. 1-11	Ps. 25 Lam. 2. 8-19 Col. 1. 18-23
	TUESDAY IN HOLY WEEK		
R	Isa. 50. 5-11 Ps. 13 Rom. 5. 6-19 Mark 15. 1-39	Ps. 27 Lam. 3. 1-18 John 12. 20-36	Ps. 55. 13-24 Lam. 3. 40-51 Gal. 6. 11-end
	WEDNESDAY IN HOLY WEEK		
R	Isa. 49. 1-9a Ps. 54 Heb. 9. 16-end Luke ch. 22	Ps. 102 (*or* 102. 1-18) Wisd. 1.16 - 2.1, 12-22 *or* Jer. 11. 18-20 John 13. 21-32	Ps. 88 Isa. 63. 1-9 Rev. 14.18 - 15.4
	MAUNDY THURSDAY		
W **(HC)** **R**	Exod. 12. 1-11 Ps. 43 1 Cor. 11. 17-end Luke 23. 1-49	Ps. 42; 43 Lev. 16. 2-24 John 13. 1-17, 31b-35	Ps. 39 Exod. ch. 11 Eph. 2. 11-18
	GOOD FRIDAY		
R	Alt. Collect Passion acc. to John Alt. Gospel, if Passion is read Num. 21. 4-9 Ps. 140. 1-9 Heb. 10. 1-25 John 19. 1-37 *or* John 19. 38-end	Ps. 69 Gen. 22. 1-18 John ch. 18	Ps. 130; 143 Lam. 5. 15-end John 19. 38-end
	Easter Eve		
	Job 14. 1-14 1 Pet. 3. 17-22 Matt. 27. 57-end	Ps. 142 Hos. 6. 1-6 John 2. 18-22	Ps. 116 Job 19. 21-27 1 John 5. 5-12

NOTES

		Sunday Principal Service Weekday Eucharist	Third Service Morning Prayer	Second Service Evening Prayer
20 Sunday	**EASTER DAY**			
𝔴	*The following readings and psalms (or canticles) are provided for use at the Easter Vigil. A minimum of three Old Testament readings should be chosen. The reading from* Exodus ch. 14 *should always be used.*	Gen. 1.1 - 2.4a & Ps. 136. 1-9, 23-end Gen. 7. 1-5, 11-18; 8. 6-18; 9. 8-13 & Ps. 46 Gen. 22. 1-18 & Ps. 16 Exod. 14. 10-end; 15. 20-21 & *Canticle*: Exod. 15. 1b-13, 17-18 Isa. 55. 1-11 & *Canticle*: Isa. 12. 2-end Baruch 3.9-15, 32 - 4.4 & Ps. 19 *or* Prov. 8. 1-8, 19-21; 9. 4b-6 & Ps. 19 Ezek. 36. 24-28 & Ps. 42; 43 Ezek. 37. 1-14 & Ps. 143 Zeph. 3. 14-end & Ps. 98 Rom. 6. 3-11 & Ps. 114 Luke 24. 1-12		
𝔴	*Easter Day Services The reading from Acts must be used as either the first or second reading at the Principal Service.*	Acts 10. 34-43 *or* Isa. 65. 17-end Ps. 118. 1-2, 14-24 (*or* 118. 14-24) 1 Cor. 15. 19-26 *or* Acts 10. 34-43 John 20. 1-18 *or* Luke 24. 1-12	*MP*: Ps. 114; 117 Ezek. 47. 1-12 John 2. 13-22	*EP*: Ps. 105 *or* Ps. 66. 1-11 Isa. 43. 1-21 1 Cor. 15. 1-11 *or* John 20. 19-23
21 Monday	**MONDAY OF EASTER WEEK**			
W		Acts 2. 14, 22-32 Ps. 16. 1-2, 6-end Matt. 28. 8-15	Ps. ***111***; 117; 146 Song of Sol. 1.9 - 2.7 Mark 16. 1-8	Ps. 135 Exod. 12. 1-14 1 Cor. 15. 1-11
22 Tuesday	**TUESDAY OF EASTER WEEK**			
W		Acts 2. 36-41 Ps. 33. 4-5, 18-end John 20. 11-18	Ps. ***112***; 147. 1-12 Song of Sol. 2. 8-end Luke 24. 1-12	Ps. 136 Exod. 12. 14-36 1 Cor. 15. 12-19
23 Wednesday	**WEDNESDAY OF EASTER WEEK** (George transferred to 28 April)			
W		Acts 3. 1-10 Ps. 105. 1-9 Luke 24. 13-35	Ps. ***113***; 147. 13-end Song of Sol. ch. 3 Matt. 28. 16-end	Ps. 105 Exod. 12. 37-end 1 Cor. 15. 20-28
24 Thursday	**THURSDAY OF EASTER WEEK**			
W		Acts 3. 11-end Ps. 8 Luke 24. 35-48	Ps. ***114***; 148 Song of Sol. 5.2 - 6.3 Luke 7. 11-17	Ps. 106 Exod. 13. 1-16 1 Cor. 15. 29-34
25 Friday	**FRIDAY OF EASTER WEEK** (Mark transferred to 29 April)			
W		Acts 4. 1-12 Ps. 118. 1-4, 22-26 John 21. 1-14	Ps. ***115***; 149 Song of Sol. 7.10 - 8.4 Luke 8. 41-end	Ps. 107 Exod. 13.17 - 14.14 1 Cor. 15. 35-50
26 Saturday	**SATURDAY OF EASTER WEEK**			
W		Acts 4. 13-21 Ps. 118. 1-4, 14-21 Mark 16. 9-15	Ps. ***116***; 150 Song of Sol. 8. 5-7 John 11. 17-44	Ps. 145 Exod. 14. 15-end 1 Cor. 15. 51-end **ct**

	Calendar and Holy Communion	Morning Prayer	Evening Prayer	NOTES
	EASTER DAY			
𝔴	Exod. 12. 21–28 Ps. 111 Col. 3. 1–7 John 20. 1–10	Ps. 114; 117 Ezek. 47. 1–12 John 2. 13–22	Ps. 105 *or* Ps. 66. 1–11 Isa. 43. 1–21 1 Cor. 15. 1–11 *or* John 20. 19–23	
	MONDAY IN EASTER WEEK			
W	Hos. 6. 1–6 Easter Anthems Acts 10. 34–43 Luke 24. 13–35	Song of Sol. 1.9 – 2.7 Mark 16. 1–8	Exod. 12. 1–14 1 Cor. 15. 1–11	
	TUESDAY IN EASTER WEEK			
W	1 Kings 17. 17–end Ps. 16. 9–end Acts 13. 26–41 Luke 24. 36b–48	Song of Sol. 2. 8–end Luke 24. 1–12	Exod. 12. 14–36 1 Cor. 15. 12–19	
W	Isa. 42. 10–16 Ps. 111 Acts 3. 12–18 John 20. 11–18	Song of Sol. ch. 3 Matt. 28. 16–end	Exod. 12. 37–end 1 Cor. 15. 20–28	
W	Isa. 43. 16–21 Ps. 113 Acts 8. 26–end John 21. 1–14	Song of Sol. 5.2 – 6.3 Luke 7. 11–17	Exod. 13. 1–16 1 Cor. 15. 29–34	
	(Mark transferred to 29 April)			
W	Ezek. 37. 1–14 Ps. 116. 1–9 1 Pet. 3. 18–end Matt. 28. 16–end	Song of Sol. 7.10 – 8.4 Luke 8. 41–end	Exod. 13.17 – 14.14 1 Cor. 15. 35–50	
W	Zech. 8. 1–8 Ps. 118. 14–21 1 Pet. 2. 1–10 John 20. 24–end	Song of Sol. 8. 5–7 John 11. 17–44	Exod. 14. 15–end 1 Cor. 15. 51–end **ct**	

		Sunday Principal Service Weekday Eucharist	Third Service Morning Prayer	Second Service Evening Prayer
27 Sunday	**THE SECOND SUNDAY OF EASTER**			
W	*The reading from Acts must be used as either the first or second reading at the Eucharist.*	Acts 5. 27–32 [*or* Exod. 14. 10–end; 15. 20–21] Ps. 118. 14–end *or* Ps. 150 Rev. 1. 4–8 John 20. 19–end	Ps. 136. 1–16 Exod. 12. 1–13 1 Pet. 1. 3–12	Ps. 16 Isa. 52.13 – 53.12 *or* 53. 1–6, 9–12 Luke 24. 13–35 *or First EP of George* Ps. 111; 116 Jer. 15. 15–end Heb. 11.32 – 12.2 **R ct**
28 Monday	**GEORGE, MARTYR, PATRON OF ENGLAND, c. 304** (transferred from 23 April)			
R		1 Macc. 2. 59–64 *or* Rev. 12. 7–12 Ps. 126 2 Tim. 2. 3–13 John 15. 18–21	*MP*: Ps. 5; 146 Josh. 1. 1–9 Eph. 6. 10–20	*EP*: Ps. 3; 11 Isa. 43. 1–7 John 15. 1–8 *or First EP of Mark* Ps. 19 Isa. 52. 7–10 Mark 1. 1–15 **ct**
29 Tuesday	**MARK THE EVANGELIST** (transferred from 25 April)			
R		Prov. 15. 28–end *or* Acts 15. 35–end Ps. 119. 9–16 Eph. 4. 7–16 Mark 13. 5–13	*MP*: Ps. 37. 23–end; 148 Isa. 62. 6–10 *or* Ecclus. 51. 13–end Acts 12.25 – 13.13	*EP*: Ps. 45 Ezek. 1. 4–14 2 Tim. 4. 1–11
30 Wednesday	*Pandita Mary Ramabai, Translator of the Scriptures, 1922*			
W		Acts 5. 17–26 Ps. 34. 1–8 John 3. 16–21	Ps. 16; ***30*** *alt.* Ps. 119. 1–32 Deut. 3. 18–end John 20. 19–end	Ps. 33 *alt.* Ps. ***11***; 12; 13 Exod. 16. 11–end Col. 2. 1–15 *or First EP of Philip and James* Ps. 25 Isa. 40. 27–end John 12. 20–26 **R ct**

May 2025

1 Thursday	**PHILIP AND JAMES, APOSTLES**			
R		Isa. 30. 15–21 Ps. 119. 1–8 Eph. 1. 3–10 John 14. 1–14	*MP*: Ps. 139; 146 Prov. 4. 10–18 James 1. 1–12	*EP*: Ps. 149 Job 23. 1–12 John 1. 43–end
2 Friday	**Athanasius, Bishop of Alexandria, Teacher, 373**			
W	Com. Teacher *or* *also* Ecclus. 4. 20–28 Matt. 10. 24–27	Acts 5. 34–42 Ps. 27. 1–5, 16–17 John 6. 1–15	Ps. 57; ***61*** *alt.* Ps. 17; ***19*** Deut. 4. 15–31 John 21. 15–19	Ps. 118 *alt.* Ps. 22 Exod. 18. 1–12 Col. 3.12 – 4.1

	Calendar and Holy Communion	Morning Prayer	Evening Prayer	NOTES
	THE FIRST SUNDAY AFTER EASTER			
W	Ezek. 37. 1–10 Ps. 81. 1–4 1 John 5. 4–12 John 20. 19–23	Ps. 136. 1–16 Exod. 12. 1–13 1 Pet. 1. 3–12	Ps. 16 Isa. 52.13 - 53.12 *or* 53. 1–6, 9–12 Luke 24. 13–35	
W		Deut. 1. 3–18 John 20. 1–10	Exod. 15. 1–21 Col. 1. 1–14 *or First EP of Mark* (Ps. 19) Isa. 52. 7–10 Mark 1. 1–15 **R ct**	
	MARK THE EVANGELIST (transferred from 25 April)			
R	Prov. 15. 28–end Ps. 119. 9–16 Eph. 4. 7–16 John 15. 1–11	(Ps. 37. 23–end; 148) Isa. 62. 6–10 *or* Ecclus. 51. 13–end Acts 12.25 - 13.13	(Ps. 45) Ezek. 1. 4–14 2 Tim. 4. 1–11	
W		Deut. 3. 18–end John 20. 19–end	Exod. 16. 11–end Col. 2. 1–15 *or First EP of Philip and James* (Ps. 119. 1–8) Isa. 40. 27–end John 12. 20–26 **R ct**	
	PHILIP AND JAMES, APOSTLES			
R	Prov. 4. 10–18 Ps. 25. 1–9 James 1. [1] 2–12 John 14. 1–14	(Ps. 139; 146) Isa. 30. 1–5 John 12. 20–26	(Ps. 149) Job 23. 1–12 John 1. 43–end	
W		Deut. 4. 15–31 John 21. 15–19	Exod. 18. 1–12 Col. 3.12 - 4.1	

		Sunday Principal Service Weekday Eucharist	Third Service Morning Prayer	Second Service Evening Prayer
3 Saturday				
W		Acts 6. 1–7 Ps. 33. 1–5, 18–19 John 6. 16–21	Ps. 63; ***84*** *alt.* Ps. 20; 21; ***23*** Deut. 4. 32–40 John 21. 20–end	Ps. 66 *alt.* Ps. ***24***; 25 Exod. 18. 13–end Col. 4. 2–end **ct**
4 Sunday	**THE THIRD SUNDAY OF EASTER**			
W	*The reading from Acts must be used as either the first or second reading at the Eucharist.*	Acts 9. 1–6 [7–20] [or Zeph. 3. 14–end] Ps. 30 Rev. 5. 11–end John 21. 1–19	Ps. 80. 1–8 Exod. 15. 1–2, 9–18 John 10. 1–19	Ps. 86 Isa. 38. 9–20 John 11. [17–26] 27–44
5 Monday				
W		Acts 6. 8–15 Ps. 119. 17–24 John 6. 22–29	Ps. ***96***; 97 *alt.* Ps. 27; ***30*** Deut. 5. 1–22 Eph. 1. 1–14	Ps. ***61***; 65 *alt.* Ps. 26; ***28***; 29 Exod. ch. 19 Luke 1. 1–25
6 Tuesday				
W		Acts 7.51 - 8.1a Ps. 31. 1–5, 16 John 6. 30–35	Ps. ***98***; 99; 100 *alt.* Ps. 32; ***36*** Deut. 5. 22–end Eph. 1. 15–end	Ps. 71 *alt.* Ps. 33 Exod. 20. 1–21 Luke 1. 26–38
7 Wednesday				
W		Acts 8. 1b–8 Ps. 66. 1–6 John 6. 35–40	Ps. 105 *alt.* Ps. 34 Deut. ch. 6 Eph. 2. 1–10	Ps. 67; ***72*** *alt.* Ps. 119. 33–56 Exod. ch. 24 Luke 1. 39–56
8 Thursday	**Julian of Norwich, Spiritual Writer, c. 1417**			
W	Com. Religious *or* *also* 1 Cor. 13. 8–end Matt. 5. 13–16	Acts 8. 26–end Ps. 66. 7–8, 14–end John 6. 44–51	Ps. 136 *alt.* Ps. 37† Deut. 7. 1–11 Eph. 2. 11–end	Ps. 73 *alt.* Ps. 39; ***40*** Exod. 25. 1–22 Luke 1. 57–end
9 Friday				
W		Acts 9. 1–20 Ps. 117 John 6. 52–59	Ps. 107 *alt.* Ps. 31 Deut. 7. 12–end Eph. 3. 1–13	Ps. 77 *alt.* Ps. 35 Exod. 28. 1–4a, 29–38 Luke 2. 1–20
10 Saturday				
W		Acts 9. 31–42 Ps. 116. 10–15 John 6. 60–69	Ps. 108; ***110***; 111 *alt.* Ps. 41; ***42***; 43 Deut. ch. 8 Eph. 3. 14–end	Ps. 23; ***27*** *alt.* Ps. 45; ***46*** Exod. 29. 1–9 Luke 2. 21–40 **ct**
11 Sunday	**THE FOURTH SUNDAY OF EASTER**			
W	*The reading from Acts must be used as either the first or second reading at the Eucharist.*	Acts 9. 36–end [or Gen. 7. 1–5, 11–18; 8. 6–18; 9. 8–13] Ps. 23 Rev. 7. 9–end John 10. 22–30	Ps. 146 1 Kings 17. 17–end Luke 7. 11–23	Ps. 113; 114 Isa. 63. 7–14 Luke 24. 36–49

	Calendar and Holy Communion	Morning Prayer	Evening Prayer	NOTES
	The Invention of the Cross			
Wr		Deut. 4. 32–40 John 21. 20–end	Exod. 18. 13–end Col. 4. 2–end	
			ct	
	THE SECOND SUNDAY AFTER EASTER			
W	Ezek. 34. 11–16a Ps. 23 1 Pet. 2. 19–end John 10. 11–16	Ps. 80. 1–8 Exod. 15. 1–2, 9–18 John 21. 1–19	Ps. 86 Isa. 38. 9–20 John 11. [17–26] 27–44	
W		Deut. 5. 1–22 Eph. 1. 1–14	Exod. ch. 19 Luke 1. 1–25	
	John the Evangelist, ante Portam Latinam			
W	CEG of 27 December	Deut. 5. 22–end Eph. 1. 15–end	Exod. 20. 1–21 Luke 1. 26–38	
W		Deut. ch. 6 Eph. 2. 1–10	Exod. ch. 24 Luke 1. 39–56	
W		Deut. 7. 1–11 Eph. 2. 11–end	Exod. 25. 1–22 Luke 1. 57–end	
W		Deut. 7. 12–end Eph. 3. 1–13	Exod. 28. 1–4a, 29–38 Luke 2. 1–20	
W		Deut. ch. 8 Eph. 3. 14–end	Exod. 29. 1–9 Luke 2. 21–40	
			ct	
	THE THIRD SUNDAY AFTER EASTER			
W	Gen. 45. 3–10 Ps. 57 1 Pet. 2. 11–17 John 16. 16–22	Ps. 146 1 Kings 17. 17–end Luke 7. 11–23	Ps. 113; 114 Isa. 63. 7–14 Luke 24. 36–49	

		Sunday Principal Service Weekday Eucharist	Third Service Morning Prayer	Second Service Evening Prayer
12 Monday	*Gregory Dix, Priest, Monk, Scholar, 1952*			
W		Acts 11. 1–18 Ps. 42. 1–2; 43. 1–4 John 10. 1–10 (*or* 11–18)	Ps. 103 *alt.* Ps. 44 Deut. 9. 1–21 Eph. 4. 1–16	Ps. 112; 113; ***114*** *alt.* Ps. ***47***; 49 Exod. 32. 1–14 Luke 2. 41–end
13 Tuesday				
W		Acts 11. 19–26 Ps. 87 John 10. 22–30	Ps. 139 *alt.* ***48***; 52 Deut. 9.23 – 10.5 Eph. 4. 17–end	Ps. 115; ***116*** *alt.* Ps. 50 Exod. 32. 15–34 Luke 3. 1–14 *or First EP of Matthias* Ps. 147 Isa. 22. 15–22 Phil. 3.13b – 4.1 **R ct**
14 Wednesday	**MATTHIAS THE APOSTLE***			
R		Isa. 22. 15–end *or* Acts 1. 15–end Ps. 15 Acts 1. 15–end *or* 1 Cor. 4. 1–7 John 15. 9–17	*MP*: Ps. 16; 147. 1–12 1 Sam. 2. 27–35 Acts 2. 37–end	*EP*: Ps. 80 1 Sam. 16. 1–13a Matt. 7. 15–27
	or, if Matthias is celebrated on 24 February:			
W		Acts 12.24 – 13.5 Ps. 67 John 12. 44–end	Ps. 135 *alt.* Ps. 119. 57–80 Deut. 10. 12–end Eph. 5. 1–14	Ps. ***47***; 48 *alt.* Ps. ***59***; 60 (67) Exod. ch. 33 Luke 3. 15–22
15 Thursday				
W		Acts 13. 13–25 Ps. 89. 1–2, 20–26 John 13. 16–20	Ps. 118 *alt.* 56; ***57***; (63†) Deut. 11. 8–end Eph. 5. 15–end	Ps. 81; ***85*** *alt.* Ps. 61; ***62***; 64 Exod. 34. 1–10, 27–end Luke 4. 1–13
16 Friday	*Caroline Chisholm, Social Reformer, 1877*			
W		Acts 13. 26–33 Ps. 2 John 14. 1–6	Ps. 33 *alt.* Ps. ***51***; 54 Deut. 12. 1–14 Eph. 6. 1–9	Ps. ***36***; 40 *alt.* Ps. 38 Exod. 35.20 – 36.7 Luke 4. 14–30
17 Saturday				
W		Acts 13. 44–end Ps. 98. 1–5 John 14. 7–14	Ps. 34 *alt.* Ps. 68 Deut. 15. 1–18 Eph. 6. 10–end	Ps. ***84***; 86 *alt.* Ps. 65; ***66*** Exod. 40. 17–end Luke 4. 31–37 **ct**
18 Sunday	**THE FIFTH SUNDAY OF EASTER**			
W	*The reading from Acts must be used as either the first or second reading at the Eucharist.*	Acts 11. 1–18 [*or* Baruch 3.9–15, 32 – 4.4 *or* Gen. 22. 1–18] Ps. 148 (*or* 148. 1–6) Rev. 21. 1–6 John 13. 31–35	Ps. 16 2 Sam. 7. 4–13 Acts 2. 14a, 22–32 [33–36]	Ps. 98 Dan. 6. [1–5] 6–23 Mark 15.46 – 16.8

*Matthias may be celebrated on 24 February instead of 14 May.

	Calendar and Holy Communion	Morning Prayer	Evening Prayer
W		Deut. 9. 1–21 Eph. 4. 1–16	Exod. 32. 1–14 Luke 2. 41–end
W		Deut. 9.23 – 10.5 Eph. 4. 17–end	Exod. 32. 15–34 Luke 3. 1–14
W		Deut. 10. 12–end Eph. 5. 1–14	Exod. ch. 33 Luke 3. 15–22
W		Deut. 11. 8–end Eph. 5. 15–end	Exod. 34. 1–10, 27–end Luke 4. 1–13
W		Deut. 12. 1–14 Eph. 6. 1–9	Exod. 35.20 – 36.7 Luke 4. 14–30
W		Deut. 15. 1–18 Eph. 6. 10–end	Exod. 40. 17–end Luke 4. 31–37 **ct**
	THE FOURTH SUNDAY AFTER EASTER		
W	Job 19. 21–27a Ps. 66. 14–end James 1. 17–21 John 16. 5–15	Ps. 16 2 Sam. 7. 4–13 Acts 2. 14a, 22–32 [33–36]	Ps. 98 Dan. 6. [1–5] 6–23 Mark 15.46 – 16.8

NOTES

		Sunday Principal Service Weekday Eucharist	Third Service Morning Prayer	Second Service Evening Prayer
19 Monday	**Dunstan, Archbishop of Canterbury, Restorer of Monastic Life, 988**			
W	Com. Bishop *or* *esp.* Matt. 24. 42–46 *also* Exod. 31. 1–5	Acts 14. 5–18 Ps. 118. 1–3, 14–15 John 14. 21–26	Ps. 145 *alt.* Ps. 71 Deut. 16. 1–20 1 Pet. 1. 1–12	Ps. 105 *alt.* Ps. ***72***; 75 Num. 9. 15–end; 10. 33–end Luke 4. 38–end
20 Tuesday	**Alcuin of York, Deacon, Abbot of Tours, 804**			
W	Com. Religious *or* *also* Col. 3. 12–16 John 4. 19–24	Acts 14. 19–end Ps. 145. 10–end John 14. 27–end	Ps. ***19***; 147. 1–12 *alt.* Ps. 73 Deut. 17. 8–end 1 Pet. 1. 13–end	Ps. 96; ***97*** *alt.* Ps. 74 Num. 11. 1–33 Luke 5. 1–11
21 Wednesday	*Helena, Protector of the Holy Places, 330*			
W		Acts 15. 1–6 Ps. 122. 1–5 John 15. 1–8	Ps. 30; 147. 13–end *alt.* Ps. 77 Deut. 18. 9–end 1 Pet. 2. 1–10	Ps. 98; ***99***; 100 *alt.* Ps. 119. 81–104 Num. ch. 12 Luke 5. 12–26
22 Thursday				
W		Acts 15. 7–21 Ps. 96. 1–3, 7–10 John 15. 9–11	Ps. ***57***; 148 *alt.* Ps. 78. 1–39† Deut. ch. 19 1 Pet. 2. 11–end	Ps. 104 *alt.* Ps. 78. 40–end† Num. 13. 1–3, 17–end Luke 5. 27–end
23 Friday				
W		Acts 15. 22–31 Ps. 57. 8–end John 15. 12–17	Ps. ***138***; 149 *alt.* Ps. 55 Deut. 21.22 - 22.8 1 Pet. 3. 1–12	Ps. 66 *alt.* Ps. 69 Num. 14. 1–25 Luke 6. 1–11
24 Saturday	**John and Charles Wesley, Evangelists, Hymn Writers, 1791 and 1788**			
W	Com. Pastor *or* *also* Eph. 5. 15–20	Acts 16. 1–10 Ps. 100 John 15. 18–21	Ps. ***146***; 150 *alt.* Ps. ***76***; 79 Deut. 24. 5–end 1 Pet. 3. 13–end	Ps. 118 *alt.* Ps. 81; ***84*** Num. 14. 26–end Luke 6. 12–26 **ct**
25 Sunday	**THE SIXTH SUNDAY OF EASTER**			
W	*The reading from Acts must be used as either the first or second reading at the Eucharist.*	Acts 16. 9–15 [or Ezek. 37. 1–14] Ps. 67 Rev. 21.10, 22 - 22.5 John 14. 23–29 *or* John 5. 1–9	Ps. 40. 1–9 Gen. 1. 26–28 [29–end] Col. 3. 1–11	Ps. 126; 127 Zeph. 3. 14–end Matt. 28. 1–10, 16–end
26 Monday	**Augustine, first Archbishop of Canterbury, 605** Rogation Day* *John Calvin, Reformer, 1564; Philip Neri, Founder of the Oratorians, Spiritual Guide, 1595*			
W	Com. Bishop *or* *also* 1 Thess. 2. 2b–8 Matt. 13. 31–33	Acts 16. 11–15 Ps. 149. 1–5 John 15.26 - 16.4	Ps. ***65***; 67 *alt.* Ps. ***80***; 82 Deut. ch. 26 1 Pet. 4. 1–11	Ps. ***121***; 122; 123 *alt.* Ps. ***85***; 86 Num. 16. 1–35 Luke 6. 27–38

*For Rogation Day provision, see p. 11.

	Calendar and Holy Communion	Morning Prayer	Evening Prayer	NOTES
	Dunstan, Archbishop of Canterbury, Restorer of Monastic Life, 988			
W	Com. Bishop	Deut. 16. 1–20 1 Pet. 1. 1–12	Num. 9. 15–end; 10. 33–end Luke 4. 38–end	
W		Deut. 17. 8–end 1 Pet. 1. 13–end	Num. 11. 1–33 Luke 5. 1–11	
W		Deut. 18. 9–end 1 Pet. 2. 1–10	Num. ch. 12 Luke 5. 12–26	
W		Deut. ch. 19 1 Pet. 2. 11–end	Num. 13. 1–3, 17–end Luke 5. 27–end	
W		Deut. 21.22 – 22.8 1 Pet. 3. 1–12	Num. 14. 1–25 Luke 6. 1–11	
W		Deut. 24. 5–end 1 Pet. 3. 13–end	Num. 14. 26–end Luke 6. 12–26 **ct**	
	THE FIFTH SUNDAY AFTER EASTER Rogation Sunday			
W	Joel 2. 21–26 Ps. 66. 1–8 James 1. 22–end John 16. 23b–end	Ps. 40. 1–9 Gen. 1. 26–28 [29–end] John 5. 1–9	Ps. 126; 127 Zeph. 3. 14–end Matt. 28. 1–10, 16–end	
	Augustine, first Archbishop of Canterbury, 605 Rogation Day			
W	Com. Bishop *or* Job 28. 1–11 Ps. 107. 1–9 James 5. 7–11 Luke 6. 36–42	Deut. ch. 26 1 Pet. 4. 1–11	Num. 16. 1–35 Luke 6. 27–38	

		Sunday Principal Service Weekday Eucharist	Third Service Morning Prayer	Second Service Evening Prayer
27 Tuesday	Rogation Day*			
W		Acts 16. 22–34 Ps. 138 John 16. 5–11	Ps. 124; 125; ***126***; 127 *alt.* Ps. 87; ***89. 1–18*** Deut. 28. 1–14 1 Pet. 4. 12–end	Ps. ***128***; 129; 130; 131 *alt.* Ps. 89. 19–end Num. 16. 36–end Luke 6. 39–end
28 Wednesday	Rogation Day* *Lanfranc, Prior of Le Bec, Archbishop of Canterbury, Scholar, 1089*			
W		Acts 17.15, 22 - 18.1 Ps. 148. 1–2, 11–end John 16. 12–15	Ps. ***132***; 133 *alt.* Ps. 119. 105–128 Deut. 28. 58–end 1 Pet. ch. 5	*First EP of Ascension Day* Ps. 15; 24 2 Sam. 23. 1–5 Col. 2.20 - 3.4 **𝔚 ct**
29 Thursday	**ASCENSION DAY**			
𝔚	*The reading from Acts must be used as either the first or second reading at the Eucharist.*	Acts 1. 1–11 *or* Dan. 7. 9–14 Ps. 47 *or* Ps. 93 Eph. 1. 15–end *or* Acts 1. 1–11 Luke 24. 44–end	*MP*: Ps. 110; 150 Isa. 52. 7–end Heb. 7. [11–25] 26–end	*EP*: Ps. 8 Song of the Three 29–37 *or* 2 Kings 2. 1–15 Rev. ch. 5 *Gospel*: Matt. 28. 16–end
30 Friday	**Josephine Butler, Social Reformer, 1906** *Joan of Arc, Visionary, 1431; Apolo Kivebulaya, Evangelist in Central Africa, 1933*			
W	Com. Saint *or* *esp.* Isa. 58. 6–11 *also* 1 John 3. 18–23 Matt. 9. 10–13	Acts 18. 9–18 Ps. 47. 1–6 John 16. 20–23	Ps. 20; ***81*** *alt.* Ps. ***88***; (95) Deut. 29. 2–15 1 John 1.1 - 2.6 [Exod. 35.30 - 36.1 Gal. 5. 13–end]**	Ps. 145 *alt.* Ps. 102 Num. 20. 1–13 Luke 7. 11–17 *or First EP of the Visit of Mary to Elizabeth* Ps. 45 Song of Sol. 2. 8–14 Luke 1. 26–38 **W ct**
31 Saturday	**THE VISIT OF THE BLESSED VIRGIN MARY TO ELIZABETH*** **			
W		Zeph. 3. 14–18 Ps. 113 Rom. 12. 9–16 Luke 1. 39–49 [50–56]	*MP*: Ps. 85; 150 1 Sam. 2. 1–10 Mark 3. 31–end	*EP*: Ps. 122; 127; 128 Zech. 2. 10–end John 3. 25–30
	or, if The Visitation is celebrated on 2 July:			
W		Acts 18. 22–end Ps. 47. 1–2, 7–end John 16. 23–28	Ps. 21; ***47*** *alt.* Ps. 96; ***97***; 100 Deut. ch. 30 1 John 2. 7–17 [Num. 11. 16–17, 24–29 1 Cor. ch. 2]**	Ps. 84; ***85*** *alt.* Ps. 104 Num. 21. 4–9 Luke 7. 18–35 **ct**

*For Rogation Day provision, see p. 11.
**The alternative readings in square brackets may be used at one of the offices, in preparation for the Day of Pentecost.
***The Visit of the Blessed Virgin Mary to Elizabeth may be celebrated on 2 July instead of 31 May.

	Calendar and Holy Communion	Morning Prayer	Evening Prayer	NOTES
	The Venerable Bede, Monk at Jarrow, Scholar, Historian, 735 Rogation Day			
W	Com. Religious *or* Deut. 8. 1–10 Ps. 121 James 5. 16–end Luke 11. 5–13	Deut. 28. 1–14 1 Pet. 4. 12–end	Num. 16. 36–end Luke 6. 39–end	
	Rogation Day			
W	Deut. 34. 1–7 Ps. 108. 1–6 Eph. 4. 7–13 John 17. 1–11	Deut. 28. 58–end 1 Pet. ch. 5	*First EP of Ascension Day* Ps. 15; 24 2 Sam. 23. 1–5 Col. 2.20 – 3.4 **𝔚 ct**	
	ASCENSION DAY			
𝔚	Dan. 7. 13–14 Ps. 68. 1–6 Acts 1. 1–11 Mark 16. 14–end *or* Luke 24. 44–end	Ps. 110; 150 Isa. 52. 7–end Heb. 7. [11–25] 26–end	Ps. 8 Song of the Three 29–37 *or* 2 Kings 2. 1–15 Rev. ch. 5	
	Ascension CEG			
W		Deut. 29. 2–15 1 John 1.1 – 2.6	Num. 20. 1–13 Luke 7. 11–17	
	Ascension CEG			
W		Deut. ch. 30 1 John 2. 7–17 [Num. 11. 16–17, 24–29 1 Cor. ch. 2]	Num. 21. 4–9 Luke 7. 18–35 **ct**	

		Sunday Principal Service Weekday Eucharist	Third Service Morning Prayer	Second Service Evening Prayer
June 2025				
1 Sunday	**THE SEVENTH SUNDAY OF EASTER (SUNDAY AFTER ASCENSION DAY)**			
W	*The reading from Acts must be used as either the first or second reading at the Principal Service.*	Acts 16. 16–34 [or Ezek. 36. 24–28] Ps. 97 Rev. 22. 12–14, 16–17, 20–end John 17. 20–end	Ps. 99 Deut. ch. 34 Luke 24. 44–end *or* Acts 1. 1–8	Ps. 68 (*or* 68. 1–13, 18–19) Isa. 44. 1–8 Eph. 4. 7–16 *Gospel*: Luke 24. 44–end
2 Monday				
W		Acts 19. 1–8 Ps. 68. 1–6 John 16. 29–end	Ps. ***93***; 96; 97 *alt.* Ps. ***98***; 99; 101 Deut. 31. 1–13 1 John 2. 18–end [Num. 27. 15–end 1 Cor. ch. 3]*	Ps. 18 *alt.* Ps. ***105***† (*or* 103) Num. 22. 1–35 Luke 7. 36–end
3 Tuesday	*The Martyrs of Uganda, 1885–87 and 1977*			
W		Acts 20. 17–27 Ps. 68. 9–10, 18–19 John 17. 1–11	Ps. 98; ***99***; 100 *alt.* Ps. ***106***† (*or* 103) Deut. 31. 14–29 1 John 3. 1–10 [1 Sam. 10. 1–10 1 Cor. 12. 1–13]*	Ps. 68 *alt.* Ps. 107† Num. 22.36 - 23.12 Luke 8. 1–15
4 Wednesday	*Petroc, Abbot of Padstow, 6th century*			
W		Acts 20. 28–end Ps. 68. 27–28, 32–end John 17. 11–19	Ps. 2; ***29*** *alt.* Ps. 110; ***111***; 112 Deut. 31.30 - 32.14 1 John 3. 11–end [1 Kings 19. 1–18 Matt. 3. 13–end]*	Ps. 36; ***46*** *alt.* Ps. 119. 129–152 Num. 23. 13–end Luke 8. 16–25
5 Thursday	**Boniface (Wynfrith) of Crediton, Bishop, Apostle of Germany, Martyr, 754**			
Wr	Com. Martyr *or* *also* Acts 20. 24–28	Acts 22. 30; 23. 6–11 Ps. 16. 1, 5–end John 17. 20–end	Ps. ***24***; 72 *alt.* Ps. 113; ***115*** Deut. 32. 15–47 1 John 4. 1–6 [Ezek. 11. 14–20 Matt. 9.35 - 10.20]*	Ps. 139 *alt.* Ps. 114; ***116***; 117 Num. ch. 24 Luke 8. 26–39
6 Friday	*Ini Kopuria, Founder of the Melanesian Brotherhood, 1945*			
W		Acts 25. 13–21 Ps. 103. 1–2, 11–12, 19–20 John 21. 15–19	Ps. ***28***; 30 *alt.* Ps. 139 Deut. ch. 33 1 John 4. 7–end [Ezek. 36. 22–28 Matt. 12. 22–32]*	Ps. 147 *alt.* Ps. ***130***; 131; 137 Num. 27. 12–end Luke 8. 40–end
7 Saturday				
W		Acts 28. 16–20, 30–end Ps. 11. 4–end John 21. 20–end	Ps. 42; ***43*** *alt.* Ps. 120; ***121***; 122 Deut. 32. 48–end; ch. 34 1 John ch. 5 [Mic. 3. 1–8 Eph. 6. 10–20]*	*First EP of Pentecost* Ps. 48 Deut. 16. 9–15 John 7. 37–39 **R ct**

*The alternative readings in square brackets may be used at one of the offices, in preparation for the Day of Pentecost.

	Calendar and Holy Communion	Morning Prayer	Evening Prayer	NOTES
	THE SUNDAY AFTER ASCENSION DAY			
W	2 Kings 2. 9–15 Ps. 68. 32–end 1 Pet. 4. 7–11 John 15.26 – 16.4a	Ps. 99 Deut. ch. 34 Luke 24. 44–end *or* Acts 1. 1–8	Ps. 68 (*or* 68. 1–13, 18–19) Isa. 44. 1–8 Eph. 4. 7–16	
W		Deut. 31. 1–13 1 John 2. 18–end [Num. 27. 15–end 1 Cor. ch. 3]	Num. 22. 1–35 Luke 7. 36–end	
W		Deut. 31. 14–29 1 John 3. 1–10 [1 Sam. 10. 1–10 1 Cor. 12. 1–13]	Num. 22.36 – 23.12 Luke 8. 1–15	
W		Deut. 31.30 – 32.14 1 John 3. 11–end [1 Kings 19. 1–18 Matt. 3. 13–end]	Num. 23. 13–end Luke 8. 16–25	
	Boniface (Wynfrith) of Crediton, Bishop, Apostle of Germany, Martyr, 754			
Wr	Com. Martyr	Deut. 32. 15–47 1 John 4. 1–6 [Ezek. 11. 14–20 Matt. 9.35 – 10.20]	Num. ch. 24 Luke 8. 26–39	
W		Deut. ch. 33 1 John 4. 7–end [Ezek. 36. 22–28 Matt. 12. 22–32]	Num. 27. 12–end Luke 8. 40–end	
W		Deut. 32. 48–end; ch. 34 1 John ch. 5 [Mic. 3. 1–8 Eph. 6. 10–20]	*First EP of Whit Sunday* Ps. 48 Deut. 16. 9–15 John 7. 37–39 **R ct**	

		Sunday Principal Service Weekday Eucharist	Third Service Morning Prayer	Second Service Evening Prayer
8 Sunday	**DAY OF PENTECOST (Whit Sunday)**			
R	*The reading from Acts must be used as either the first or second reading at the Principal Service.*	Acts 2. 1–21 *or* Gen. 11. 1–9 Ps. 104. 26–36, 37b (or 104. 26–end) Rom. 8. 14–17 *or* Acts 2. 1–21 John 14. 8–17 [25–27]	*MP*: Ps. 36. 5–10; 150 Isa. 40. 12–23 *or* Wisd. 9. 9–17 1 Cor. 2. 6–end	*EP*: Ps. 33. 1–12 Exod. 33. 7–20 2 Cor. 3. 4–end *Gospel*: John 16. 4b–15
9 Monday	**Columba, Abbot of Iona, Missionary, 597** *Ephrem of Syria, Deacon, Hymn Writer, Teacher, 373* Ordinary Time resumes today			
Gw **DEL 10**	Com. Missionary *or* *also* Titus 3. 11–end	2 Cor. 1. 1–7 Ps. 34. 1–8 Matt. 5. 1–12	Ps. 123; 124; 125; ***126*** Job ch. 1 Rom. 1. 1–17	Ps. ***127***; 128; 129 Josh. ch. 1 Luke 9. 18–27
10 Tuesday				
G		2 Cor. 1. 18–22 Ps. 119. 129–136 Matt. 5. 13–16	Ps. ***132***; 133 Job ch. 2 Rom. 1. 18–end	Ps. (134); ***135*** Josh. ch. 2 Luke 9. 28–36 *or First EP of Barnabas* Ps. 1; 15 Isa. 42. 5–12 Acts 14. 8–end **R ct**
11 Wednesday	**BARNABAS THE APOSTLE**			
R		Job 29. 11–16 *or* Acts 11. 19–end Ps. 112 Acts 11. 19–end *or* Gal. 2. 1–10 John 15. 12–17	*MP*: Ps. 100; 101; 117 Jer. 9. 23–24 Acts 4. 32–end	*EP*: Ps. 147 Eccles. 12. 9–end *or* Tobit 4. 5–11 Acts 9. 26–31
12 Thursday				
G		2 Cor. 3.15 – 4.1, 3–6 Ps. 78. 36–40 Matt. 5. 20–26	Ps. ***143***; 146 Job ch. 4 Rom. 2. 17–end	Ps. ***138***; 140; 141 Josh. 4.1 – 5.1 Luke 9. 51–end
13 Friday				
G		2 Cor. 4. 7–15 Ps. 99 Matt. 5. 27–32	Ps. ***142***; 144 Job ch. 5 Rom. 3. 1–20	Ps. 145 Josh. 5. 2–end Luke 10. 1–16
14 Saturday	*Richard Baxter, Puritan Divine, 1691*			
G		2 Cor. 5. 14–end Ps. 103. 1–12 Matt. 5. 33–37	Ps. 147 Job ch. 6 Rom. 3. 21–end	*First EP of Trinity Sunday* Ps. 97; 98 Isa. 40. 12–end Mark 1. 1–13 **W ct**
15 Sunday	**TRINITY SUNDAY**			
W		Prov. 8. 1–4, 22–31 Ps. 8 Rom. 5. 1–5 John 16. 12–15	*MP*: Ps. 29 Isa. 6. 1–8 Rev. ch. 4	*EP*: Ps. 73. 1–3, 16–end Exod. 3. 1–15 John 3. 1–17

	Calendar and Holy Communion	Morning Prayer	Evening Prayer
	WHIT SUNDAY		
R	Deut. 16. 9–12 Ps. 122 Acts 2. 1–11 John 14. 15–31a	Ps. 36. 5–10; 150 Isa. 40. 12–23 *or* Wisd. 9. 9–17 1 Cor. 2. 6–end	Ps. 33. 1–12 Exod. 33. 7–20 2 Cor. 3. 4–end
	Monday in Whitsun Week		
R	Acts 10. 34–end John 3. 16–21	Ezek. 11. 14–20 Acts 2. 12–36	Exod. 35.30 - 36.1 Acts 2. 37–end
	Tuesday in Whitsun Week		
R	Acts 8. 14–17 John 10. 1–10	Ezek. 37. 1–14 1 Cor. 12. 1–13	2 Sam. 23. 1–5 1 Cor. 12.27 - 13.end *or First EP of Barnabas* (Ps. 1; 15) Isa. 42. 5–12 Acts 14. 8–end **R ct**
	BARNABAS THE APOSTLE Ember Day		
R	Job 29. 11–16 Ps. 112 Acts 11. 22–end John 15. 12–16	(Ps. 100; 101; 117) Jer. 9. 23–24 Acts 4. 32–end	(Ps. 147) Eccles. 12. 9–end *or* Tobit 4. 5–11 Acts 9. 26–31
R	Acts 2. 22–28 Luke 9. 1–6	Job ch. 4 Rom. 2. 17–end	Josh. 4.1 - 5.1 Luke 9. 51–end
	Ember Day		
R	Ember CEG *or* Acts 8. 5–8 Luke 5. 17–26	Job ch. 5 Rom. 3. 1–20	Josh. 5. 2–end Luke 10. 1–16
	Ember Day		
R	Ember CEG *or* Acts 13. 44–end Matt. 20. 29–end	Job ch. 6 Rom. 3. 21–end	*First EP of Trinity Sunday* Ps. 97; 98 Isa. 40. 12–end Mark 1. 1–13 **𝔚 ct**
	TRINITY SUNDAY		
𝔚	Isa. 6. 1–8 Ps. 8 Rev. 4. 1–11 John 3. 1–15	Ps. 29 Prov. 8. 1–4, 22–31 Rom. 5. 1–5	Ps. 73. 1–3, 16–end Exod. 3. 1–15 Matt. 28. 16–end

NOTES

		Sunday Principal Service Weekday Eucharist	Third Service Morning Prayer	Second Service Evening Prayer
16 Monday	**Richard, Bishop of Chichester, 1253** *Joseph Butler, Bishop of Durham, Philosopher, 1752*			
Gw **DEL 11**	Com. Bishop *or* *also* John 21. 15–19	2 Cor. 6. 1–10 Ps. 98 Matt. 5. 38–42	Ps. ***1***; 2; 3 Job ch. 7 Rom. 4. 1–12	Ps. **4**; 7 Josh. 7. 1–15 Luke 10. 25–37
17 Tuesday	*Samuel and Henrietta Barnett, Social Reformers, 1913 and 1936*			
G		2 Cor. 8. 1–9 Ps. 146 Matt. 5. 43–end	Ps. ***5***; 6; (8) Job ch. 8 Rom. 4. 13–end	Ps. **9**; 10† Josh. 7. 16–end Luke 10. 38–end
18 Wednesday	*Bernard Mizeki, Apostle of the MaShona, Martyr, 1896*			
G		2 Cor. 9. 6–11 Ps. 112 Matt. 6. 1–6, 16–18	Ps. 119. 1–32 Job ch. 9 Rom. 5. 1–11	Ps. ***11***; 12; 13 Josh. 8. 1–29 Luke 11. 1–13 *or First EP of Corpus Christi* Ps. 110; 111 Exod. 16. 2–15 John 6. 22–35 **W ct**
19 Thursday	**DAY OF THANKSGIVING FOR HOLY COMMUNION (CORPUS CHRISTI)** *Sundar Singh of India, Sadhu (holy man), Evangelist, Teacher, 1929*			
W		Gen. 14. 18–20 Ps. 116. 10–end 1 Cor. 11. 23–26 John 6. 51–58	*MP*: Ps. 147 Deut. 8. 2–16 1 Cor. 10. 1–17	*EP*: Ps. 23; 42; 43 Prov. 9. 1–5 Luke 9. 11–17
	or the ferial readings for the day:			
G		2 Cor. 11. 1–11 Ps. 111 Matt. 6. 7–15	Ps. 14; ***15***; 16 Job ch. 10 Rom. 5. 12–end	Ps. 18† Josh. 8. 30–end Luke 11. 14–28
20 Friday				
G		2 Cor. 11. 18, 21b–30 Ps. 34. 1–6 Matt. 6. 19–23	Ps. 17; ***19*** Job ch. 11 Rom. 6. 1–14	Ps. 22 Josh. 9. 3–26 Luke 11. 29–36
21 Saturday				
G		2 Cor. 12. 1–10 Ps. 89. 20–33 Matt. 6. 24–end	Ps. 20; 21; **23** Job ch. 12 Rom. 6. 15–end	Ps. **24**; 25 Josh. 10. 1–15 Luke 11. 37–end **ct**
22 Sunday	**THE FIRST SUNDAY AFTER TRINITY (Proper 7)**			
G	*Track 1* 1 Kings 19. 1–4 [5–7] 8–15a Ps. 42; 43 (*or* Ps. 42 *or* 43) Gal. 3. 23–end Luke 8. 26–39	*Track 2* Isa. 65. 1–9 Ps. 22. 19–28 Gal. 3. 23–end Luke 8. 26–39	Ps. 55. 1–16, 18–21 Deut. 11. 1–15 Acts 27. 1–12	Ps. [50]; 57 Gen. 24. 1–27 Mark 5. 21–end

	Calendar and Holy Communion	Morning Prayer	Evening Prayer
G		Job ch. 7 Rom. 4. 1–12	Josh. 7. 1–15 Luke 10. 25–37
	Alban, first Martyr of Britain, c. 250		
Gr	Com. Martyr	Job ch. 8 Rom. 4. 13–end	Josh. 7. 16–end Luke 10. 38–end
G		Job ch. 9 Rom. 5. 1–11	Josh. 8. 1–29 Luke 11. 1–13
	To celebrate Corpus Christi, see *Common Worship* provision.		
G		Job ch. 10 Rom. 5. 12–end	Josh. 8. 30–end Luke 11. 14–28
	Translation of Edward, King of the West Saxons, 979		
Gr	Com. Martyr	Job ch. 11 Rom. 6. 1–14	Josh. 9. 3–26 Luke 11. 29–36
G		Job ch. 12 Rom. 6. 15–end	Josh. 10. 1–15 Luke 11. 37–end **ct**
	THE FIRST SUNDAY AFTER TRINITY		
G	2 Sam. 9. 6–end Ps. 41. 1–4 1 John 4. 7–end Luke 16. 19–31	Ps. 52; 53 Deut. 11. 1–15 Acts 27. 1–12	Ps. [50]; 57 Gen. 24. 1–27 Mark 5. 21–end

NOTES

		Sunday Principal Service Weekday Eucharist	Third Service Morning Prayer	Second Service Evening Prayer
23 Monday	**Etheldreda, Abbess of Ely, c. 678**			
Gw **DEL 12**	Com. Religious *or* *also* Matt. 25. 1–13	Gen. 12. 1–9 Ps. 33. 12–end Matt. 7. 1–5	Ps. 27; ***30*** Job ch. 13 Rom. 7. 1–6	Ps. 26; **28**; 29 Josh. ch. 14 Luke 12. 1–12 *or First EP of The Birth of John the Baptist* Ps. 71 Judges 13. 2–7, 24–end Luke 1. 5–25 **W ct**
24 Tuesday	**THE BIRTH OF JOHN THE BAPTIST**			
W		Isa. 40. 1–11 Ps. 85. 7–end Acts 13. 14b–26 *or* Gal. 3. 23–end Luke 1. 57–66, 80	*MP*: Ps. 50; 149 Ecclus. 48. 1–10 *or* Mal. 3. 1–6 Luke 3. 1–17	*EP*: Ps. 80; 82 Mal. ch. 4 Matt. 11. 2–19
25 Wednesday	Ember Day*			
G *or* **R**		Gen. 15. 1–12, 17–18 Ps. 105. 1–9 Matt. 7. 15–20	Ps. 34 Job ch. 15 Rom. 8. 1–11	Ps. 119. 33–56 Josh. 22. 9–end Luke 12. 22–31
26 Thursday				
G		Gen. 16. 1–12, 15–16 Ps. 106. 1–5 Matt. 7. 21–end	Ps. 37† Job 16.1 – 17.2 Rom. 8. 12–17	Ps. 39; ***40*** Josh. ch. 23 Luke 12. 32–40
27 Friday	Ember Day* *Cyril, Bishop of Alexandria, Teacher, 444*			
G *or* **R**		Gen. 17. 1, 9–10, 15–22 Ps. 128 Matt. 8. 1–4	Ps. 31 Job 17. 3–end Rom. 8. 18–30	Ps. 35 Josh. 24. 1–28 Luke 12. 41–48
28 Saturday	**Irenaeus, Bishop of Lyons, Teacher, c. 200** Ember Day*			
Gw *or* **Rw**	Com. Teacher *or* *also* 2 Pet. 1. 16–21	Gen. 18. 1–15 *Canticle*: Luke 1. 46b–55 Matt. 8. 5–17	Ps. 41; **42**; 43 Job ch. 18 Rom. 8. 31–end	Ps. 45; ***46*** Josh. 24. 29–end Luke 12. 49–end **ct** *or First EP of Peter and Paul* Ps. 66; 67 Ezek. 3. 4–11 Gal. 1.13 – 2.8 *or, for Peter alone*: Acts 9. 32–end **R ct**

*For Ember Day provision, see p. 11.

	Calendar and Holy Communion	Morning Prayer	Evening Prayer	NOTES
G		Job ch. 13 Rom. 7. 1–6	Josh. ch. 14 Luke 12. 1–12 *or First EP of The Nativity of John the Baptist* (Ps. 71) Judges 13. 2–7, 24–end Luke 1. 5–25 **W ct**	
	THE NATIVITY OF JOHN THE BAPTIST			
W	Isa. 40. 1–11 Ps. 80. 1–7 Acts 13. 22–26 Luke 1. 57–80	(Ps. 50; 149) Ecclus. 48. 1–10 *or* Mal. 3. 1–6 Luke 3. 1–17	(Ps. 82) Mal. ch. 4 Matt. 11. 2–19	
G		Job ch. 15 Rom. 8. 1–11	Josh. 22. 9–end Luke 12. 22–31	
G		Job 16.1 – 17.2 Rom. 8. 12–17	Josh. ch. 23 Luke 12. 32–40	
G		Job 17. 3–end Rom. 8. 18–30	Josh. 24. 1–28 Luke 12. 41–48	
G		Job ch. 18 Rom. 8. 31–end	Josh. 24. 29–end Luke 12. 49–end **ct** *or First EP of Peter* (Ps. 66; 67) Ezek. 3. 4–11 Acts 9. 32–end **R ct**	

		Sunday Principal Service Weekday Eucharist	Third Service Morning Prayer	Second Service Evening Prayer
29 Sunday	**PETER AND PAUL, APOSTLES** (or transferred to 30 June)			
R		Zech. 4. 1–6a, 10b–end *or* Acts 12. 1–11 Ps. 125 Acts 12. 1–11 *or* 2 Tim. 4. 6–8, 17–18 Matt. 16. 13–19	*MP*: Ps. 71; 113 Isa. 49. 1–6 Acts 11. 1–18	*EP*: Ps. 124; 138 Ezek. 34. 11–16 John 21. 15–22
	or, if Peter is commemorated alone:			
R		Ezek. 3. 22–end *or* Acts 12. 1–11 Ps. 125 Acts 12. 1–11 *or* 1 Pet. 2. 19–end Matt. 16. 13–19	*MP*: Ps. 71; 113 Isa. 49. 1–6 Acts 11. 1–18	*EP*: Ps. 124; 138 Ezek. 34. 11–16 John 21. 15–22
	or, for the Second Sunday after Trinity (Proper 8):			
G	*Track 1* 2 Kings 2. 1–2, 6–14 Ps. 77. 1–2, 11–end (*or* 77. 11–end) Gal. 5. 1, 13–25 Luke 9. 51–end	*Track 2* 1 Kings 19. 15–16, 19–end Ps. 16 Gal. 5. 1, 13–25 Luke 9. 51–end	Ps. 64 Deut. 15. 1–11 Acts 27. [13–32] 33–end	Ps. [59. 1–6, 18–end]; 60 Gen. 27. 1–40 Mark 6. 1–6
30 Monday				
G **DEL 13**		Gen. 18. 16–end Ps. 103. 6–17 Matt. 8. 18–22	Ps. 44 Job ch. 19 Rom. 9. 1–18	Ps. ***47***; 49 Judg. ch. 2 Luke 13. 1–9
July 2025				
1 Tuesday	*Henry, John and Henry Venn the Younger, Priests, Evangelical Divines, 1797, 1813 and 1873*			
G		Gen. 19. 15–29 Ps. 26 Matt. 8. 23–27	Ps. ***48***; 52 Job ch. 21 Rom. 9. 19–end	Ps. 50 Judg. 4. 1–23 Luke 13. 10–21
2 Wednesday*				
G		Gen. 21. 5, 8–20 Ps. 34. 1–12 Matt. 8. 28–end	Ps. 119. 57–80 Job ch. 22 Rom. 10. 1–10	Ps. ***59***; 60; (67) Judg. ch. 5 Luke 13. 22–end *or First EP of Thomas* Ps. 27 Isa. ch. 35 Heb. 10.35 – 11.1 **R ct**
3 Thursday	**THOMAS THE APOSTLE***			
R		Hab. 2. 1–4 Ps. 31. 1–6 Eph. 2. 19–end John 20. 24–29	*MP*: Ps. 92; 146 2 Sam. 15. 17–21 *or* Ecclus. ch. 2 John 11. 1–16	*EP*: Ps. 139 Job 42. 1–6 1 Pet. 1. 3–12
	or, if Thomas is not celebrated:			
G		Gen. 22. 1–19 Ps. 116. 1–7 Matt. 9. 1–8	Ps. 56; ***57***; (63†) Job ch. 23 Rom. 10. 11–end	Ps. 61; ***62***; 64 Judg. 6. 1–24 Luke 14. 1–11

*The Visit of the Blessed Virgin Mary to Elizabeth may be celebrated on 2 July instead of 31 May.
****Common Worship** Morning and Evening Prayer provision for 31 May may be used.
***Thomas the Apostle may be celebrated on 22 December instead of 3 July.

	Calendar and Holy Communion	Morning Prayer	Evening Prayer	NOTES
	PETER THE APOSTLE			
R	Ezek. 3. 4–11 Ps. 125 Acts 12. 1–11 Matt. 16. 13–19	Ps. 71; 113 Isa. 49. 1–6 Acts 11. 1–18	Ps. 124; 138 Ezek. 34. 11–16 John 21. 15–22	
	or, for the Second Sunday after Trinity:			
G	Gen. 12. 1–4 Ps. 120 1 John 3. 13–end Luke 14. 16–24	Ps. 64 Deut. 15. 1–11 Acts 27. [13–32] 33–end	Ps. [59. 1–6, 18–end]; 60 Gen. 27. 1–40 Mark 6. 1–6	
G		Job ch. 19 Rom. 9. 1–18	Judg. ch. 2 Luke 13. 1–9	
G		Job ch. 21 Rom. 9. 19–end	Judg. 4. 1–23 Luke 13. 10–21	
	The Visitation of the Blessed Virgin Mary**			
Gw	1 Sam. 2. 1–3 Ps. 113 Gal. 4. 1–5 Luke 1. 39–45	Job ch. 22 Rom. 10. 1–10	Judg. ch. 5 Luke 13. 22–end	
G		Job ch. 23 Rom. 10. 11–end	Judg. 6. 1–24 Luke 14. 1–11	

		Sunday Principal Service Weekday Eucharist	Third Service Morning Prayer	Second Service Evening Prayer
4 Friday				
G		Gen. 23. 1–4, 19; 24. 1–8, 62–end Ps. 106. 1–5 Matt. 9. 9–13	Ps. ***51***; 54 Job ch. 24 Rom. 11. 1–12	Ps. 38 Judg. 6. 25–end Luke 14. 12–24
5 Saturday				
G		Gen. 27. 1–5a, 15–29 Ps. 135. 1–6 Matt. 9. 14–17	Ps. 68 Job chs 25 & 26 Rom. 11. 13–24	Ps. 65; ***66*** Judg. ch. 7 Luke 14. 25–end **ct**
6 Sunday	**THE THIRD SUNDAY AFTER TRINITY (Proper 9)**			
G	*Track 1* 2 Kings 5. 1–14 Ps. 30 Gal. 6. [1–6] 7–16 Luke 10. 1–11, 16–20	*Track 2* Isa. 66. 10–14 Ps. 66. 1–8 Gal. 6. [1–6] 7–16 Luke 10. 1–11, 16–20	Ps. 74 Deut. 24. 10–end Acts 28. 1–16	Ps. 65; [70] Gen. 29. 1–20 Mark 6. 7–29
7 Monday*				
G **DEL 14**		Gen. 28. 10–end Ps. 91. 1–10 Matt. 9. 18–26	Ps. 71 Job ch. 27 Rom. 11. 25–end	Ps. **72**; 75 Judg. 8. 22–end Luke 15. 1–10
8 Tuesday				
G		Gen. 32. 22–end Ps. 17. 1–8 Matt. 9. 32–end	Ps. 73 Job ch. 28 Rom. 12. 1–8	Ps. 74 Judg. 9. 1–21 Luke 15. 11–end
9 Wednesday				
G		Gen. 41. 55–end; 42. 5–7, 17–end Ps. 33. 1–4, 18–end Matt. 10. 1–7	Ps. 77 Job ch. 29 Rom. 12. 9–end	Ps. 119. 81–104 Judg. 9. 22–end Luke 16. 1–18
10 Thursday				
G		Gen. 44. 18–21, 23–29; 45. 1–5 Ps. 105. 11–17 Matt. 10. 7–15	Ps. 78. 1–39† Job ch. 30 Rom. 13. 1–7	Ps. 78. 40–end† Judg. 11. 1–11 Luke 16. 19–end
11 Friday	**Benedict of Nursia, Abbot of Monte Cassino, Father of Western Monasticism, c. 550**			
Gw	Com. Religious *or* *also* 1 Cor. 3. 10–11 Luke 18. 18–22	Gen. 46. 1–7, 28–30 Ps. 37. 3–6, 27–28 Matt. 10. 16–23	Ps. 55 Job ch. 31 Rom. 13. 8–end	Ps. 69 Judg. 11. 29–end Luke 17. 1–10
12 Saturday				
G		Gen. 49. 29–end; 50. 15–25 Ps. 105. 1–7 Matt. 10. 24–33	Ps. ***76***; 79 Job ch. 32 Rom. 14. 1–12	Ps. 81; ***84*** Judg. 12. 1–7 Luke 17. 11–19 **ct**

*Thomas Becket may be celebrated on 7 July instead of 29 December.

	Calendar and Holy Communion	Morning Prayer	Evening Prayer	NOTES
	Translation of Martin, Bishop of Tours, c. 397			
Gw	Com. Bishop	Job ch. 24 Rom. 11. 1–12	Judg. 6. 25–end Luke 14. 12–24	
G		Job chs 25 & 26 Rom. 11. 13–24	Judg. ch. 7 Luke 14. 25–end **ct**	
	THE THIRD SUNDAY AFTER TRINITY			
G	2 Chron. 33. 9–13 Ps. 55. 17–23 1 Pet. 5. 5b–11 Luke 15. 1–10	Ps. 73 Deut. 24. 10–end Acts 28. 1–16	Ps. 65; [70] Gen. 29. 1–20 Mark 6. 7–29	
G		Job ch. 27 Rom. 11. 25–end	Judg. 8. 22–end Luke 15. 1–10	
G		Job ch. 28 Rom. 12. 1–8	Judg. 9. 1–21 Luke 15. 11–end	
G		Job ch. 29 Rom. 12. 9–end	Judg. 9. 22–end Luke 16. 1–18	
G		Job ch. 30 Rom. 13. 1–7	Judg. 11. 1–11 Luke 16. 19–end	
G		Job ch. 31 Rom. 13. 8–end	Judg. 11. 29–end Luke 17. 1–10	
G		Job ch. 32 Rom. 14. 1–12	Judg. 12. 1–7 Luke 17. 11–19 **ct**	

		Sunday Principal Service Weekday Eucharist	Third Service Morning Prayer	Second Service Evening Prayer
13 Sunday	**THE FOURTH SUNDAY AFTER TRINITY (Proper 10)**			
G	*Track 1* Amos 7. 7–end Ps. 82 Col. 1. 1–14 Luke 10. 25–37	*Track 2* Deut. 30. 9–14 Ps. 25. 1–10 Col. 1. 1–14 Luke 10. 25–37	Ps. 76 Deut. 28. 1–14 Acts 28. 17–end	Ps. 77 (*or* 77. 1–12) Gen. 32. 9–30 Mark 7. 1–23
14 Monday	**John Keble, Priest, Tractarian, Poet, 1866**			
Gw **DEL 15**	Com. Pastor *or* *also* Lam. 3. 19–26 Matt. 5. 1–8	Exod. 1. 8–14, 22 Ps. 124 Matt. 10.34 – 11.1	Ps. ***80***; 82 Job ch. 33 Rom. 14. 13–end	Ps. ***85***; 86 Judg. 13. 1–24 Luke 17. 20–end
15 Tuesday	**Swithun, Bishop of Winchester, c. 862** *Bonaventure, Friar, Bishop, Teacher, 1274*			
Gw	Com. Bishop *or* *also* James 5. 7–11, 13–18	Exod. 2. 1–15 Ps. 69. 1–2, 31–end Matt. 11. 20–24	Ps. 87; ***89. 1–18*** Job ch. 39 Rom. 15. 14–21	Ps. 89. 19–end Judg. 15.1 – 16.3 Luke 18. 15–30
16 Wednesday	*Osmund, Bishop of Salisbury, 1099*			
G		Exod. 3. 1–6, 9–12 Ps. 103. 1–7 Matt. 11. 25–27	Ps. 119. 105–128 Job ch. 39 Rom. 15. 14–21	Ps. ***91***; 93 Judg. 15.1 – 16.3 Luke 18. 15–30
17 Thursday				
G		Exod. 3. 13–20 Ps. 105. 1, 5, 8–9, 24–27 Matt. 11. 28–end	Ps. 90; **92** Job ch. 40 Rom. 15. 22–end	Ps. 94 Judg. 16. 4–end Luke 18. 31–end
18 Friday	*Elizabeth Ferard, first Deaconess of the Church of England, Founder of the Community of St Andrew, 1883*			
G		Exod. 11.10 – 12.14 Ps. 116. 10–end Matt. 12. 1–8	Ps. ***88***; (95) Job ch. 41 Rom. 16. 1–16	Ps. 102 Judg. ch. 17 Luke 19. 1–10
19 Saturday	**Gregory, Bishop of Nyssa, and his sister Macrina, Deaconess, Teachers, c. 394 and c. 379**			
Gw	Com. Teacher *or* *esp.* 1 Cor. 2. 9–13 *also* Wisd. 9. 13–17	Exod. 12. 37–42 Ps. 136. 1–4, 10–15 Matt. 12. 14–21	Ps. 96; ***97***; 100 Job ch. 42 Rom. 16. 17–end	Ps. 104 Judg. 18. 1–20, 27–end Luke 19. 11–27 **ct**
20 Sunday	**THE FIFTH SUNDAY AFTER TRINITY (Proper 11)**			
G	*Track 1* Amos 8. 1–12 Ps. 52 Col. 1. 15–28 Luke 10. 38–end	*Track 2* Gen. 18. 1–10a Ps. 15 Col. 1. 15–28 Luke 10. 38–end	Ps. 82; 100 Deut. 30. 1–10 1 Pet. 3. 8–18	Ps. 81 Gen. 41. 1–16, 25–37 1 Cor. 4. 8–13 *Gospel*: John 4. 31–35
21 Monday				
G **DEL 16**		Exod. 14. 5–18 Ps. 136. 1–4, 10–15 *or Canticle*: Exod. 15. 1–6 Matt. 12. 38–42	Ps. ***98***; 99; 101 Ezek. 1. 1–14 2 Cor. 1. 1–14	Ps. ***105***† (*or* 103) 1 Sam. 1. 1–20 Luke 19. 28–40 *or First EP of Mary Magdalene* Ps. 139 Isa. 25. 1–9 2 Cor. 1. 3–7 **W ct**

	Calendar and Holy Communion	Morning Prayer	Evening Prayer	NOTES
	THE FOURTH SUNDAY AFTER TRINITY			
G	Gen. 3. 17–19 Ps. 79. 8–10 Rom. 8. 18–23 Luke 6. 36–42	Ps. 76 Deut. 28. 1–14 Acts 28. 17–end	Ps. 77 (*or* 77. 1–12) Gen. 32. 9–30 Mark 7. 1–23	
G		Job ch. 33 Rom. 14. 13–end	Judg. 13. 1–24 Luke 17. 20–end	
	Swithun, Bishop of Winchester, c. 862			
Gw	Com. Bishop	Job ch. 39 Rom. 15. 14–21	Judg. 15.1 - 16.3 Luke 18. 15–30	
G		Job ch. 39 Rom. 15. 14–21	Judg. 15.1 - 16.3 Luke 18. 15–30	
G		Job ch. 40 Rom. 15. 22–end	Judg. 16. 4–end Luke 18. 31–end	
G		Job ch. 41 Rom. 16. 1–16	Judg. ch. 17 Luke 19. 1–10	
G		Job ch. 42 Rom. 16. 17–end	Judg. 18. 1–20, 27–end Luke 19. 11–27 **ct**	
	THE FIFTH SUNDAY AFTER TRINITY			
G	1 Kings 19. 19–21 Ps. 84. 8–end 1 Pet. 3. 8–15a Luke 5. 1–11	Ps. 82; 100 Deut. 30. 1–10 1 Pet. 3. 8–18	Ps. 81 Gen. 41. 1–16, 25–37 1 Cor. 4. 8–13	
G		Ezek. 1. 1–14 2 Cor. 1. 1–14	1 Sam. 1. 1–20 Luke 19. 28–40 *or First EP of Mary Magdalene* (Ps. 139) Isa. 25. 1–9 2 Cor. 1. 3–7 **W ct**	

		Sunday Principal Service Weekday Eucharist	Third Service Morning Prayer	Second Service Evening Prayer
22 Tuesday	**MARY MAGDALENE**			
W		Song of Sol. 3. 1–4 Ps. 42. 1–10 2 Cor. 5. 14–17 John 20. 1–2, 11–18	*MP*: Ps. 30; 32; 150 1 Sam. 16. 14–end Luke 8. 1–3	*EP*: Ps. 63 Zeph. 3. 14–end Mark 15.40 – 16.7
23 Wednesday	*Bridget of Sweden, Abbess of Vadstena, 1373*			
G		Exod. 16. 1–5, 9–15 Ps. 78. 17–31 Matt. 13. 1–9	Ps. 110; ***111***; 112 Ezek. 2.3 – 3.11 2 Cor. 2. 5–end	Ps. 119. 129–152 1 Sam. 2. 12–26 Luke 20. 1–8
24 Thursday				
G		Exod. 19. 1–2, 9–11, 16–20 *Canticle*: Bless the Lord Matt. 13. 10–17	Ps. 113; ***115*** Ezek. 3. 12–end 2 Cor. ch. 3	Ps. 114; ***116***; 117 1 Sam. 2. 27–end Luke 20. 9–19 *or First EP of James* Ps. 144 Deut. 30. 11–end Mark 5. 21–end **R ct**
25 Friday	**JAMES THE APOSTLE**			
R		Jer. 45. 1–5 *or* Acts 11.27 – 12.2 Ps. 126 Acts 11.27 – 12.2 *or* 2 Cor. 4. 7–15 Matt. 20. 20–28	*MP*: Ps. 7; 29; 117 2 Kings 1. 9–15 Luke 9. 46–56	*EP*: Ps. 94 Jer. 26. 1–15 Mark 1. 14–20
26 Saturday	**Anne and Joachim, Parents of the Blessed Virgin Mary**			
Gw	Zeph. 3. 14–18a *or* Ps. 127 Rom. 8. 28–30 Matt. 13. 16–17	Exod. 24. 3–8 Ps. 50. 1–6, 14–15 Matt. 13. 24–30	Ps. 120; ***121***; 122 Ezek. ch. 9 2 Cor. ch. 5	Ps. 118 1 Sam. 4. 1b–end Luke 20. 27–40 **ct**
27 Sunday	**THE SIXTH SUNDAY AFTER TRINITY (Proper 12)**			
G	*Track 1* Hos. 1. 2–10 Ps. 85 (*or* 85. 1–7) Col. 2. 6–15 [16–19] Luke 11. 1–13	*Track 2* Gen. 18. 20–32 Ps. 138 Col. 2. 6–15 [16–19] Luke 11. 1–13	Ps. 95 Song of Sol. ch. 2 *or* 1 Macc. 2. [1–14] 15–22 1 Pet. 4. 7–14	Ps. 88 (*or* 88. 1–10) Gen. 42. 1–25 1 Cor. 10. 1–24 *Gospel*: Matt. 13. 24–30 [31–43]
28 Monday				
G **DEL 17**		Exod. 32. 15–24, 30–34 Ps. 106. 19–23 Matt. 13. 31–35	Ps. 123; 124; 125; ***126*** Ezek. 10. 1–19 2 Cor. 6.1 – 7.1	Ps. ***127***; 128; 129 1 Sam. ch. 5 Luke 20.41 – 21.4
29 Tuesday	**Mary, Martha and Lazarus, Companions of Our Lord**			
Gw	Isa. 25. 6–9 *or* Ps. 49. 5–10, 16 Heb. 2. 10–15 John 12. 1–8	Exod. 33. 7–11; 34. 5–9, 28 Ps. 103. 8–12 Matt. 13. 36–43	Ps. ***132***; 133 Ezek. 11. 14–end 2 Cor. 7. 2–end	Ps. (134); ***135*** 1 Sam. 6. 1–16 Luke 21. 5–19
30 Wednesday	**William Wilberforce, Social Reformer, Olaudah Equiano and Thomas Clarkson, Anti-Slavery Campaigners, 1833, 1797 and 1846**			
Gw	Com. Saint *or* *also* Job 31. 16–23 Gal. 3. 26–end; 4. 6–7 Luke 4. 16–21	Exod. 34. 29–end Ps. 99 Matt. 13. 44–46	Ps. 119. 153–end Ezek. 12. 1–16 2 Cor. 8. 1–15	Ps. 136 1 Sam. ch. 7 Luke 21. 20–28

	Calendar and Holy Communion	Morning Prayer	Evening Prayer	NOTES
	MARY MAGDALENE			
W	Zeph. 3. 14–end Ps. 30. 1–5 2 Cor. 5. 14–17 John 20. 11–18	(Ps. 30; 32; 150) 1 Sam. 16. 14–end Luke 8. 1–3	(Ps. 63) Song of Sol. 3. 1–4 Mark 15.40 – 16.7	
G		Ezek. 2.3 – 3.11 2 Cor. 2. 5–end	1 Sam. 2. 12–26 Luke 20. 1–8	
G		Ezek. 3. 12–end 2 Cor. ch. 3	1 Sam. 2. 27–end Luke 20. 9–19 *or First EP of James* (Ps. 144) Deut. 30. 11–end Mark 5. 21–end **R ct**	
	JAMES THE APOSTLE			
R	2 Kings 1. 9–15 Ps. 15 Acts 11.27 – 12.3a Matt. 20. 20–28	(Ps. 7; 29; 117) Jer. 45. 1–5 Luke 9. 46–56	(Ps. 94) Jer. 26. 1–15 Mark 1. 14–20	
	Anne, Mother of the Blessed Virgin Mary			
Gw	Com. Saint	Ezek. ch. 9 2 Cor. ch. 5	1 Sam. 4. 1b–end Luke 20. 27–40 **ct**	
	THE SIXTH SUNDAY AFTER TRINITY			
G	Gen. 4. 2b–15 Ps. 90. 12–end Rom. 6. 3–11 Matt. 5. 20–26	Ps. 96 Song of Sol. ch. 2 *or* 1 Macc. 2. [1–14] 15–22 1 Pet. 4. 7–14	Ps. 88 (*or* 88. 1–10) Gen. 42. 1–25 1 Cor. 9. 16–end	
G		Ezek. 10. 1–19 2 Cor. 6.1 – 7.1	1 Sam. ch. 5 Luke 20.41 – 21.4	
G		Ezek. 11. 14–end 2 Cor. 7. 2–end	1 Sam. 6. 1–16 Luke 21. 5–19	
G		Ezek. 12. 1–16 2 Cor. 8. 1–15	1 Sam. ch. 7 Luke 21. 20–28	

		Sunday Principal Service Weekday Eucharist	Third Service Morning Prayer	Second Service Evening Prayer
31 Thursday	*Ignatius of Loyola, Founder of the Society of Jesus, 1556*			
G		Exod. 40. 16–21, 34–end Ps. 84. 1–6 Matt. 13. 47–53	Ps. ***143***; 146 Ezek. 12. 17–end 2 Cor. 8.16 – 9.5	Ps. ***138***; 140; 141 1 Sam. ch. 8 Luke 21. 29–end

August 2025

		Sunday Principal Service Weekday Eucharist	Third Service Morning Prayer	Second Service Evening Prayer
1 Friday				
G		Lev. 23. 1, 4–11, 15–16, 27, 34–37 Ps. 81. 1–8 Matt. 13. 54–end	Ps. 142; ***144*** Ezek. 13. 1–16 2 Cor. 9. 6–end	Ps. 145 1 Sam. 9. 1–14 Luke 22. 1–13
2 Saturday				
G		Lev. 25. 1, 8–17 Ps. 67 Matt. 14. 1–12	Ps. 147 Ezek. 14. 1–11 2 Cor. ch. 10	Ps. ***148***; 149; 150 1 Sam. 9.15 – 10.1 Luke 22. 14–23 **ct**
3 Sunday	**THE SEVENTH SUNDAY AFTER TRINITY (Proper 13)**			
G	*Track 1* Hos. 11. 1–11 Ps. 107. 1–9, 43 (*or* 107. 1–9) Col. 3. 1–11 Luke 12. 13–21	*Track 2* Eccles. 1. 2, 12–14; 2. 18–23 Ps. 49. 1–12 (*or* 49. 1–9) Col. 3. 1–11 Luke 12. 13–21	Ps. 106. 1–10 Song of Sol. 5. 2–end *or* 1 Macc. 3. 1–12 2 Pet. 1. 1–15	Ps. 107. 1–32 (*or* 107. 1–16) Gen. 50. 4–end 1 Cor. 14. 1–19 *Gospel*: Mark 6. 45–52
4 Monday	*Jean-Baptiste Vianney, Curé d'Ars, Spiritual Guide, 1859*			
G **DEL 18**		Num. 11. 4–15 Ps. 81. 11–end Matt. 14. 13–21 (*or* 14. 22–end)	Ps. ***1***; 2; 3 Ezek. 14. 12–end 2 Cor. 11. 1–15	Ps. ***4***; 7 1 Sam. 10. 1–16 Luke 22. 24–30
5 Tuesday	**Oswald, King of Northumbria, Martyr, 642**			
Gr	Com. Martyr *or* *esp.* 1 Pet. 4. 12–end	Num. 12. 1–13 Ps. 51. 1–8 Matt. 14. 22–end *or* Matt. 15. 1–2, 10–14	Ps. ***5***; 6; (8) Ezek. 18. 1–20 2 Cor. 11. 16–end	Ps. ***9***; 10† 1 Sam. 10. 17–end Luke 22. 31–38 *or First EP of The Transfiguration* Ps. 99; 110 Exod. 24. 12–end John 12. 27–36a **W ct**
6 Wednesday	**THE TRANSFIGURATION OF OUR LORD**			
W		Dan. 7. 9–10, 13–14 Ps. 97 2 Pet. 1. 16–19 Luke 9. 28–36	*MP*: Ps. 27; 150 Ecclus. 48. 1–10 *or* 1 Kings 19. 1–16 1 John 3. 1–3	*EP*: Ps. 72 Exod. 34. 29–end 2 Cor. ch. 3
7 Thursday	*John Mason Neale, Priest, Hymn Writer, 1866*			
G		Num. 20. 1–13 Ps. 95. 1, 8–end Matt. 16. 13–23	Ps. 14; ***15***; 16 Ezek. 20. 1–20 2 Cor. ch. 13	Ps. 18† 1 Sam. ch. 12 Luke 22. 47–62

	Calendar and Holy Communion	Morning Prayer	Evening Prayer	NOTES
G		Ezek. 12. 17–end 2 Cor. 8.16 – 9.5	1 Sam. ch. 8 Luke 21. 29–end	
	Lammas Day			
G		Ezek. 13. 1–16 2 Cor. 9. 6–end	1 Sam. 9. 1–14 Luke 22. 1–13	
G		Ezek. 14. 1–11 2 Cor. ch. 10	1 Sam. 9.15 – 10.1 Luke 22. 14–23 **ct**	
	THE SEVENTH SUNDAY AFTER TRINITY			
G	1 Kings 17. 8–16 Ps. 34. 11–end Rom. 6. 19–end Mark 8. 1–10a	Ps. 106. 1–10 Song of Sol. 5. 2–end *or* 1 Macc. 3. 1–12 2 Pet. 1. 1–15	Ps. 107. 1–32 (*or* 107. 1–16) Gen. 50. 4–end 1 Cor. 14. 1–19	
G		Ezek. 14. 12–end 2 Cor. 11. 1–15	1 Sam. 10. 1–16 Luke 22. 24–30	
G		Ezek. 18. 1–20 2 Cor. 11. 16–end	1 Sam. 10. 17–end Luke 22. 31–38 *or First EP of The Transfiguration* (Ps. 99; 110) Exod. 24. 12–end John 12. 27–36a **W ct**	
	THE TRANSFIGURATION OF OUR LORD			
W	Exod. 24. 12–end Ps. 84. 1–7 1 John 3. 1–3 Mark 9. 2–7	(Ps. 27; 150) Ecclus. 48. 1–10 *or* 1 Kings 19. 1–16 2 Pet. 1. 16–19	(Ps. 72) Exod. 34. 29–end 2 Cor. ch. 3	
	The Name of Jesus			
Gw	Jer. 14. 7–9 Ps. 8 Acts 4. 8–12 Matt. 1. 20–23	Ezek. 20. 1–20 2 Cor. ch. 13	1 Sam. ch. 12 Luke 22. 47–62	

		Sunday Principal Service Weekday Eucharist	Third Service Morning Prayer	Second Service Evening Prayer
8 Friday	**Dominic, Priest, Founder of the Order of Preachers, 1221**			
Gw	Com. Religious *or* *also* Ecclus. 39. 1-10	Deut. 4. 32–40 Ps. 77. 11–end Matt. 16. 24–end	Ps. 17; ***19*** Ezek. 20. 21–38 James 1. 1–11	Ps. 22 1 Sam. 13. 5–18 Luke 22. 63–end
9 Saturday	**Mary Sumner, Founder of the Mothers' Union, 1921**			
Gw	Com. Saint *or* *also* Heb. 13. 1-5	Deut. 6. 4–13 Ps. 18. 1–2, 48–end Matt. 17. 14–20	Ps. 20; 21; ***23*** Ezek. 24. 15–end James 1. 12–end	Ps. ***24***; 25 1 Sam. 13.19 - 14.15 Luke 23. 1–12 **ct**
10 Sunday	**THE EIGHTH SUNDAY AFTER TRINITY (Proper 14)**			
G	*Track 1* Isa. 1. 1, 10–20 Ps. 50. 1–8, 23–end (*or* 50. 1–7) Heb. 11. 1–3, 8–16 Luke 12. 32–40	*Track 2* Gen. 15. 1–6 Ps. 33. 12–end (*or* 33. 12–21) Heb. 11. 1–3, 8–16 Luke 12. 32–40	Ps. 115 Song of Sol. 8. 5–7 *or* 1 Macc. 14. 4–15 2 Pet. 3. 8–13	Ps. 108; [116] Isa. 11.10 - 12.end 2 Cor. 1. 1–22 *Gospel*: Mark 7. 24–30
11 Monday	**Clare of Assisi, Founder of the Minoresses (Poor Clares), 1253** *John Henry Newman, Priest, Tractarian, 1890*			
Gw **DEL 19**	Com. Religious *or* *esp.* Song of Sol. 8. 6–7	Deut. 10. 12–end Ps. 147. 13–end Matt. 17. 22–end	Ps. 27; ***30*** Ezek. 28. 1–19 James 2. 1–13	Ps. 26; ***28***; 29 1 Sam. 14. 24–46 Luke 23. 13–25
12 Tuesday				
G		Deut. 31. 1–8 Ps. 107. 1–3, 42–end *or Canticle*: Deut. 32. 3–4, 7–9 Matt. 18. 1–5, 10, 12–14	Ps. 32; ***36*** Ezek. 33. 1–20 James 2. 14–end	Ps. 33 1 Sam. 15. 1–23 Luke 23. 26–43
13 Wednesday	**Jeremy Taylor, Bishop of Down and Connor, Teacher, 1667** *Florence Nightingale, Nurse, Social Reformer, 1910; Octavia Hill, Social Reformer, 1912*			
Gw	Com. Teacher *or* *also* Titus 2. 7–8, 11–14	Deut. ch. 34 Ps. 66. 14–end Matt. 18. 15–20	Ps. 34 Ezek. 33. 21–end James ch. 3	Ps. 119. 33–56 1 Sam. ch. 16 Luke 23. 44–56a
14 Thursday	*Maximilian Kolbe, Friar, Martyr, 1941*			
G		Josh. 3. 7–11, 13–17 Ps. 114 Matt. 18.21 - 19.1	Ps. 37† Ezek. 34. 1–16 James 4. 1–12	Ps. 39; ***40*** 1 Sam. 17. 1–30 Luke 23.56b - 24.12 *or First EP of The Blessed Virgin Mary* Ps. 72 Prov. 8. 22–31 John 19. 23–27 **W ct**

	Calendar and Holy Communion	Morning Prayer	Evening Prayer	NOTES
G		Ezek. 20. 21–38 James 1. 1–11	1 Sam. 13. 5–18 Luke 22. 63–end	
G		Ezek. 24. 15–end James 1. 12–end	1 Sam. 13.19 - 14.15 Luke 23. 1–12 **ct**	
	THE EIGHTH SUNDAY AFTER TRINITY			
G	Jer. 23. 16–24 Ps. 31. 1–6 Rom. 8. 12–17 Matt. 7. 15–21	Ps. 115 Song of Sol. 8. 5–7 *or* 1 Macc. 14. 4–15 2 Pet. 3. 8–13	Ps. 108; [116] Isa. 11.10 - 12.end 2 Cor. 1. 1–22	
G		Ezek. 28. 1–19 James 2. 1–13	1 Sam. 14. 24–46 Luke 23. 13–25	
G		Ezek. 33. 1–20 James 2. 14–end	1 Sam. 15. 1–23 Luke 23. 26–43	
G		Ezek. 33. 21–end James ch. 3	1 Sam. ch. 16 Luke 23. 44–56a	
G		Ezek. 34. 1–16 James 4. 1–12	1 Sam. 17. 1–30 Luke 23.56b - 24.12	

			Sunday Principal Service Weekday Eucharist	Third Service Morning Prayer	Second Service Evening Prayer
15 Friday		**THE BLESSED VIRGIN MARY***			
	W		Isa. 61. 10–end *or* Rev. 11.19 – 12.6, 10 Ps. 45. 10–end Gal. 4. 4–7 Luke 1. 46–55	*MP*: Ps. 98; 138; 147. 1–12 Isa. 7. 10–15 Luke 11. 27–28	*EP*: Ps. 132 Song of Sol. 2. 1–7 Acts 1. 6–14
		or, if The Blessed Virgin Mary is celebrated on 8 September:			
	G		Josh. 24. 1–13 Ps. 136. 1–3, 16–22 Matt. 19. 3–12	Ps. 31 Ezek. 34. 17–end James 4.13 – 5.6	Ps. 35 1 Sam. 17. 31–54 Luke 24. 13–35
16 Saturday					
	G		Josh. 24. 14–29 Ps. 16. 1, 5–end Matt. 19. 13–15	Ps. 41; ***42***; 43 Ezek. 36. 16–36 James 5. 7–end	Ps. 45; ***46*** 1 Sam. 17.55 – 18.16 Luke 24. 36–end **ct**
17 Sunday		**THE NINTH SUNDAY AFTER TRINITY (Proper 15)**			
	G	*Track 1* Isa. 5. 1–7 Ps. 80. 1–2, 9–end (*or* 80. 9–end) Heb. 11.29 – 12.2 Luke 12. 49–56	*Track 2* Jer. 23. 23–29 Ps. 82 Heb. 11.29 – 12.2 Luke 12. 49–56	Ps. 119. 33–48 Jonah ch. 1 *or* Ecclus. 3. 1–15 2 Pet. 3. 14–end	Ps. 119. 17–32 (*or* 119. 17–24) Isa. 28. 9–22 2 Cor. 8. 1–9 *Gospel*: Matt. 20. 1–16
18 Monday					
	G **DEL 20**		Judg. 2. 11–19 Ps. 106. 34–42 Matt. 19. 16–22	Ps. 44 Ezek. 37. 1–14 Mark 1. 1–13	Ps. ***47***; 49 1 Sam. 19. 1–18 Acts 1. 1–14
19 Tuesday					
	G		Judg. 6. 11–24 Ps. 85. 8–end Matt. 19. 23–end	Ps. ***48***; 52 Ezek. 37. 15–end Mark 1. 14–20	Ps. 50 1 Sam. 20. 1–17 Acts 1. 15–end
20 Wednesday		**Bernard, Abbot of Clairvaux, Teacher, 1153** *William and Catherine Booth, Founders of the Salvation Army, 1912 and 1890*			
	Gw	Com. Religious *or* esp. Rev. 19. 5–9	Judg. 9. 6–15 Ps. 21. 1–6 Matt. 20. 1–16	Ps. 119. 57–80 Ezek. 39. 21–end Mark 1. 21–28	Ps. ***59***; 60; (67) 1 Sam. 20. 18–end Acts 2. 1–21
21 Thursday					
	G		Judg. 11. 29–end Ps. 40. 4–11 Matt. 22. 1–14	Ps. 56; ***57***; (63†) Ezek. 43. 1–12 Mark 1. 29–end	Ps. 61; ***62***; 64 1 Sam. 21.1 – 22.5 Acts 2. 22–36
22 Friday					
	G		Ruth 1. 1, 3–6, 14–16, 22 Ps. 146 Matt. 22. 34–40	Ps. ***51***; 54 Ezek. 44. 4–16 Mark 2. 1–12	Ps. 38 1 Sam. 22. 6–end Acts 2. 37–end

*The Blessed Virgin Mary may be celebrated on 8 September instead of 15 August.

	Calendar and Holy Communion	Morning Prayer	Evening Prayer	NOTES
	To celebrate The Blessed Virgin Mary, see *Common Worship* provision.			
G		Ezek. 34. 17–end James 4.13 – 5.6	1 Sam. 17. 31–54 Luke 24. 13–35	
G		Ezek. 36. 16–36 James 5. 7–end	1 Sam. 17.55 – 18.16 Luke 24. 36–end **ct**	
	THE NINTH SUNDAY AFTER TRINITY			
G	Num. 10.35 – 11.3 Ps. 95 1 Cor. 10. 1–13 Luke 16. 1–9 *or* Luke 15. 11–end	Ps. 119. 33–48 Jonah ch. 1 *or* Ecclus. 3. 1–15 2 Pet. 3. 14–end	Ps. 119. 17–32 (*or* 119. 17–24) Isa. 28. 9–22 2 Cor. 8. 1–9	
G		Ezek. 37. 1–14 Mark 1. 1–13	1 Sam. 19. 1–18 Acts 1. 1–14	
G		Ezek. 37. 15–end Mark 1. 14–20	1 Sam. 20. 1–17 Acts 1. 15–end	
G		Ezek. 39. 21–end Mark 1. 21–28	1 Sam. 20. 18–end Acts 2. 1–21	
G		Ezek. 43. 1–12 Mark 1. 29–end	1 Sam. 21.1 – 22.5 Acts 2. 22–36	
G		Ezek. 44. 4–16 Mark 2. 1–12	1 Sam. 22. 6–end Acts 2. 37–end	

		Sunday Principal Service Weekday Eucharist	Third Service Morning Prayer	Second Service Evening Prayer
23 Saturday				
G		Ruth 2. 1–3, 1–11; 4. 13–17 Ps. 128 Matt. 23. 1–12	Ps. 68 Ezek. 47. 1–12 Mark 2. 13–22	Ps. 65; **66** 1 Sam. ch. 23 Acts 3. 1–10 **ct** *or First EP of Bartholomew* Ps. 97 Isa. 61. 1–9 2 Cor. 6. 1–10 **R ct**
24 Sunday	**BARTHOLOMEW THE APOSTLE** (or transferred to 25 August)			
R		Isa. 43. 8–13 *or* Acts 5. 12–16 Ps. 145. 1–7 Acts 5. 12–16 *or* 1 Cor. 4. 9–15 Luke 22. 24–30	*MP*: Ps. 86; 117 Gen. 28. 10–17 John 1. 43–end	*EP*: Ps. 91; 116 Ecclus. 39. 1–10 *or* Deut. 18. 15–19 Matt. 10. 1–22
	or, for The Tenth Sunday after Trinity (Proper 16):			
G	*Track 1* Jer. 1. 4–10 Ps. 71. 1–6 Heb. 12. 18–end Luke 13. 10–17	*Track 2* Isa. 58. 9b–end Ps. 103. 1–8 Heb. 12. 18–end Luke 13. 10–17	Ps. 119. 73–88 Jonah ch. 2 *or* Ecclus. 3. 17–29 Rev. ch. 1	Ps. 119. 49–72 (*or* 119. 49–56) Isa. 30. 8–21 2 Cor. ch. 9 *Gospel*: Matt. 21. 28–32
25 Monday				
G **DEL 21**		1 Thess. 1. 1–5, 8–end Ps. 149. 1–5 Matt. 23. 13–22	Ps. 71 Prov. 1. 1–19 Mark 2.23 - 3.6	Ps. ***72***; 75 1 Sam. ch. 24 Acts 3. 11–end
26 Tuesday				
G		1 Thess. 2. 1–8 Ps. 139. 1–9 Matt. 23. 23–26	Ps. 73 Prov. 1. 20–end Mark 3. 7–19a	Ps. 74 1 Sam. ch. 26 Acts 4. 1–12
27 Wednesday	**Monica, Mother of Augustine of Hippo, 387**			
Gw	Com. Saint *or* *also* Ecclus. 26. 1–3, 13–16	1 Thess. 2. 9–13 Ps. 126 Matt. 23. 27–32	Ps. 77 Prov. ch. 2 Mark 3. 19b–end	Ps. 119. 81–104 1 Sam. 28. 3–end Acts 4. 13–31
28 Thursday	**Augustine, Bishop of Hippo, Teacher, 430**			
Gw	Com. Teacher *or* *esp.* Ecclus. 39. 1–10 *also* Rom. 13. 11–13	1 Thess. 3. 7–end Ps. 90. 13–end Matt. 24. 42–end	Ps. 78. 1–39† Prov. 3. 1–26 Mark 4. 1–20	Ps. 78. 40–end† 1 Sam. ch. 31 Acts 4.32 - 5.11
29 Friday	**The Beheading of John the Baptist**			
Gr	Jer. 1. 4–10 *or* Ps. 11 Heb. 11.32 - 12.2 Matt. 14. 1–12	1 Thess. 4. 1–8 Ps. 97 Matt. 25. 1–13	Ps. 55 Prov. 3.27 - 4.19 Mark 4. 21–34	Ps. 69 2 Sam. ch. 1 Acts 5. 12–26
30 Saturday	**John Bunyan, Spiritual Writer, 1688**			
Gw	Com. Teacher *or* *also* Heb. 12. 1–2 Luke 21. 21, 34–36	1 Thess. 4. 9–12 Ps. 98. 1–2, 8–end Matt. 25. 14–30	Ps. ***76***; 79 Prov. 6. 1–19 Mark 4. 35–end	Ps. 81; ***84*** 2 Sam. 2. 1–11 Acts 5. 27–end **ct**

	Calendar and Holy Communion	Morning Prayer	Evening Prayer
G		Ezek. 47. 1–12 Mark 2. 13–22	1 Sam. ch. 23 Acts 3. 1–10 **ct** *or First EP of Bartholomew* (Ps. 97) Isa. 61. 1–9 2 Cor. 6. 1–10 **R ct**
	BARTHOLOMEW THE APOSTLE		
R	Gen. 28. 10–17 Ps. 15 Acts 5. 12–16 Luke 22. 24–30	Ps. 86; 117 Isa. 43. 8–13 John 1. 43–end	Ps. 91; 116 Ecclus. 39. 1–10 *or* Deut. 18. 15–19 Matt. 10. 1–22
	or, for The Tenth Sunday after Trinity:		
G	Jer. 7. 9–15 Ps. 17. 1–8 1 Cor. 12. 1–11 Luke 19. 41–47a	Ps. 119. 73–88 Jonah ch. 2 *or* Ecclus. 3. 17–29 Rev. ch. 1	Ps. 119. 49–72 (*or* 119. 49–56) Isa. 30. 8–21 2 Cor. ch. 9
G		Prov. 1. 1–19 Mark 2.23 - 3.6	1 Sam. ch. 24 Acts 3. 11–end
G		Prov. 1. 20–end Mark 3. 7–19a	1 Sam. ch. 26 Acts 4. 1–12
G		Prov. ch. 2 Mark 3. 19b–end	1 Sam. 28. 3–end Acts 4. 13–31
	Augustine, Bishop of Hippo, Teacher, 430		
Gw	Com. Doctor	Prov. 3. 1–26 Mark 4. 1–20	1 Sam. ch. 31 Acts 4.32 - 5.11
	The Beheading of John the Baptist		
Gr	2 Chron. 24. 17–21 Ps. 92. 11–end Heb. 11.32 - 12.2 Matt. 14. 1–12	Prov. 3.27 - 4.19 Mark 4. 21–34	2 Sam. ch. 1 Acts 5. 12–26
G		Prov. 6. 1–19 Mark 4. 35–end	2 Sam. 2. 1–11 Acts 5. 27–end **ct**

NOTES

		Sunday Principal Service Weekday Eucharist	Third Service Morning Prayer	Second Service Evening Prayer
31 Sunday	**THE ELEVENTH SUNDAY AFTER TRINITY (Proper 17)**			
G	*Track 1* Jer. 2. 4-13 Ps. 81. 1, 10-end (*or* 81. 1-11) Heb. 13. 1-8, 15-16 Luke 14. 1, 7-14	*Track 2* Ecclus. 10. 12-18 *or* Prov. 25. 6-7 Ps. 112 Heb. 13. 1-8, 15-16 Luke 14. 1, 7-14	Ps. 119. 161-end Jonah 3. 1-9 *or* Ecclus. 11. [7-17] 18-28 Rev. 3. 14-22	Ps. 119. 81-96 (*or* 119. 81-88) Isa. 33. 13-22 John 3. 22-36

September 2025

1 Monday	*Giles of Provence, Hermit, c. 710*			
G **DEL 22**		1 Thess. 4. 13-end Ps. 96 Luke 4. 16-30	Ps. ***80***; 82 Prov. 8. 1-21 Mark 5. 1-20	Ps. ***85***; 86 2 Sam. 3. 12-end Acts ch. 6
2 Tuesday	*The Martyrs of Papua New Guinea, 1901 and 1942*			
G		1 Thess. 5. 1-6, 9-11 Ps. 27. 1-8 Luke 4. 31-37	Ps. 87; ***89. 1-18*** Prov. 8. 22-end Mark 5. 21-34	Ps. 89. 19-end 2 Sam. 5. 1-12 Acts 7. 1-16
3 Wednesday	**Gregory the Great, Bishop of Rome, Teacher, 604**			
Gw	Com. Teacher *or* *also* 1 Thess. 2. 3-8	Col. 1. 1-8 Ps. 34. 11-18 Luke 4. 38-end	Ps. 119. 105-128 Prov. ch. 9 Mark 5. 35-end	Ps. ***91***; 93 2 Sam. 6. 1-19 Acts 7. 17-43
4 Thursday	*Birinus, Bishop of Dorchester (Oxon), Apostle of Wessex, 650**			
G		Col. 1. 9-14 Ps. 98. 1-5 Luke 5. 1-11	Ps. 90; **92** Prov. 10. 1-12 Mark 6. 1-13	Ps. 94 2 Sam. 7. 1-17 Acts 7. 44-53
5 Friday				
G		Col. 1. 15-20 Ps. 89. 19b-28 Luke 5. 33-end	Ps. ***88***; (95) Prov. 11. 1-12 Mark 6. 14-29	Ps. 102 2 Sam. 7. 18-end Acts 7.54 - 8.3
6 Saturday	*Allen Gardiner, Founder of the South American Mission Society, 1851*			
G		Col. 1. 21-23 Ps. 117 Luke 6. 1-5	Ps. 96; ***97***; 100 Prov. 12. 10-end Mark 6. 30-44	Ps. 104 2 Sam. ch. 9 Acts 8. 4-25 **ct**
7 Sunday	**THE TWELFTH SUNDAY AFTER TRINITY (Proper 18)**			
G	*Track 1* Jer. 18. 1-11 Ps. 139. 1-5, 12-18 (*or* 139. 1-7) Philemon 1-21 Luke 14. 25-33	*Track 2* Deut. 30. 15-end Ps. 1 Philemon 1-21 Luke 14. 25-33	Ps. 122; 123 Jonah 3.10 - 4.end *or* Ecclus. 27.30 - 28.9 Rev. 8. 1-5	Ps. [120]; 121 Isa. 43.14 - 44.5 John 5. 30-end

*Cuthbert may be celebrated on 4 September instead of 20 March.

	Calendar and Holy Communion	Morning Prayer	Evening Prayer	NOTES
	THE ELEVENTH SUNDAY AFTER TRINITY			
G	1 Kings 3. 5–15 Ps. 28 1 Cor. 15. 1–11 Luke 18. 9–14	Ps. 119. 161–end Jonah 3. 1–9 *or* Ecclus. 11. [7–17] 18–28 Rev. 3. 14–22	Ps. 119. 81–96 (*or* 119. 81–88) Isa. 33. 13–22 John 3. 22–36	
	Giles of Provence, Hermit, *c.* 710			
Gw	Com. Abbot	Prov. 8. 1–21 Mark 5. 1–20	2 Sam. 3. 12–end Acts ch. 6	
G		Prov. 8. 22–end Mark 5. 21–34	2 Sam. 5. 1–12 Acts 7. 1–16	
G		Prov. ch. 9 Mark 5. 35–end	2 Sam. 6. 1–19 Acts 7. 17–43	
G		Prov. 10. 1–12 Mark 6. 1–13	2 Sam. 7. 1–17 Acts 7. 44–53	
G		Prov. 11. 1–12 Mark 6. 14–29	2 Sam. 7. 18–end Acts 7.54 - 8.3	
G		Prov. 12. 10–end Mark 6. 30–44	2 Sam. ch. 9 Acts 8. 4–25 **ct**	
	THE TWELFTH SUNDAY AFTER TRINITY			
G	Exod. 34. 29–end Ps. 34. 1–10 2 Cor. 3. 4–9 Mark 7. 31–37	Ps. 122; 123 Jonah 3.10 - 4.end *or* Ecclus. 27.30 - 28.9 Rev. 8. 1–5	Ps. [120]; 121 Isa. 43.14 - 44.5 John 5. 30–end	

		Sunday Principal Service Weekday Eucharist	Third Service Morning Prayer	Second Service Evening Prayer
8 Monday	**The Birth of the Blessed Virgin Mary*** (The Accession of King Charles III may be observed on 8 September, and Collect, Readings and Post-Communion for the sovereign used.)			
Gw **DEL 23**	Com. BVM *or*	Col. 1.24 – 2.3 Ps. 62. 1–7 Luke 6. 6–11	Ps. ***98***; 99; 101 Prov. 14.31 – 15.17 Mark 6. 45–end	Ps. ***105***† (*or* 103) 2 Sam. ch. 11 Acts 8. 26–end
9 Tuesday	*Charles Fuge Lowder, Priest, 1880*			
G		Col. 2. 6–15 Ps. 8 Luke 6. 12–19	Ps. ***106***† (*or* 103) Prov. 15. 18–end Mark 7. 1–13	Ps. 107† 2 Sam. 12. 1–25 Acts 9. 1–19a
10 Wednesday				
G		Col. 3. 1–11 Ps. 15 Luke 6. 20–26	Ps. 110; ***111***; 112 Prov. 18. 10–end Mark 7. 14–23	Ps. 119. 129–152 2 Sam. 15. 1–12 Acts 9. 19b–31
11 Thursday				
G		Col. 3. 12–17 Ps. 149. 1–5 Luke 6. 27–38	Ps. 113; ***115*** Prov. 20. 1–22 Mark 7. 24–30	Ps. 114; ***116***; 117 2 Sam. 15. 13–end Acts 9. 32–end
12 Friday				
G		1 Tim. 1. 1–2, 12–14 Ps. 16 Luke 6. 39–42	Ps. 139 Prov. 22. 1–16 Mark 7. 31–end	Ps. ***130***; 131; 137 2 Sam. 16. 1–14 Acts 10. 1–16
13 Saturday	**John Chrysostom, Bishop of Constantinople, Teacher, 407**			
Gw	Com. Teacher *or* *esp.* Matt. 5. 13–19 *also* Jer. 1. 4–10	1 Tim. 1. 15–17 Ps. 113 Luke 6. 43–end	Ps. 120; ***121***; 122 Prov. 24. 23–end Mark 8. 1–10	Ps. 118 2 Sam. 17. 1–23 Acts 10. 17–33 **ct** *or First EP of Holy Cross Day* Ps. 66 Isa, 52.13 – 53.end Eph. 2. 11–end **R ct**
14 Sunday	**HOLY CROSS DAY** (or transferred to 15 September)			
R		Num. 21. 4–9 Ps. 22. 23–28 Phil. 2. 6–11 John 3. 13–17	*MP*: Ps. 2; 8; 146 Gen. 3. 1–15 John 12. 27–36a	*EP*: Ps. 110; 150 Isa. 63. 1–16 1 Cor. 1. 18–25
G	*or, for The Thirteenth Sunday after Trinity (Proper 19):*			
	Track 1 Jer. 4. 11–12, 22–28 Ps. 14 1 Tim. 1. 12–17 Luke 15. 1–10	*Track 2* Exod. 32. 7–14 Ps. 51. 1–11 1 Tim. 1. 12–17 Luke 15. 1–10	Ps. 126; 127 Isa. 44.24 – 45.8 Rev. 12. 1–12	Ps. 124; 125 Isa. ch. 60 John 6. 51–69

*The Blessed Virgin Mary may be celebrated on 8 September instead of 15 August.

	Calendar and Holy Communion	Morning Prayer	Evening Prayer
	The Birth of the Blessed Virgin Mary The Accession of King Charles III, 2022		
Gw	Gen. 3. 9–15 Ps. 45. 11–18 Rom. 5. 12–17 Luke 11. 27–28		
G	*For Accession Service*: Ps. 20; 101; 121; Josh. 1. 1–9; Prov. 8. 1–16; Rom. 13. 1–10; Rev. 21.22 - 22.4		
	For The Accession: 1 Pet. 2. 11–17 Matt. 22. 16–22	Prov. 14.31 - 15.17 Mark 6. 45–end	2 Sam. ch. 11 Acts 8. 26–end
G		Prov. 15. 18–end Mark 7. 1–13	2 Sam. 12. 1–25 Acts 9. 1–19a
G		Prov. 18. 10–end Mark 7. 14–23	2 Sam. 15. 1–12 Acts 9. 19b–31
G		Prov. 20. 1–22 Mark 7. 24–30	2 Sam. 15. 13–end Acts 9. 32–end
G		Prov. 22. 1–16 Mark 7. 31–end	2 Sam. 16. 1–14 Acts 10. 1–16
G		Prov. 24. 23–end Mark 8. 1–10	2 Sam. 17. 1–23 Acts 10. 17–33 **ct**
	THE THIRTEENTH SUNDAY AFTER TRINITY (Proper 19) To celebrate Holy Cross Day, see *Common Worship* provision.		
G	Lev. 19. 13–18 Ps. 74. 20–end Gal. 3. 16–22 *or* Heb. 13. 1–6 Luke 10. 23b–37	Ps. 126; 127 Isa. 44.24 - 45.8 Rev. 12. 1–12	Ps. 124; 125 Isa. ch. 60 John 6. 51–69

NOTES

		Sunday Principal Service Weekday Eucharist	Third Service Morning Prayer	Second Service Evening Prayer
15 Monday	**Cyprian, Bishop of Carthage, Martyr, 258**			
Gr **DEL 24**	Com. Martyr *or* *esp.* 1 Pet. 4. 12–end *also* Matt. 18. 18–22	1 Tim. 2. 1–8 Ps. 28 Luke 7. 1–10	Ps. 123; 124; 125; ***126*** Prov. 25. 1–14 Mark 8. 11–21	Ps. ***127***; 128; 129 2 Sam. 18. 1–18 Acts 10. 34–end
16 Tuesday	**Ninian, Bishop of Galloway, Apostle of the Picts, c. 432** *Edward Bouverie Pusey, Priest, Tractarian, 1882*			
Gw	Com. Missionary *or* *esp.* Acts 13. 46–49 Mark 16. 15–end	1 Tim. 3. 1–13 Ps. 101 Luke 7. 11–17	Ps. ***132***; 133 Prov. 25. 15–end Mark 8. 22–26	Ps. (134); ***135*** 2 Sam. 18.19 – 19.8a Acts 11. 1–18
17 Wednesday	**Hildegard, Abbess of Bingen, Visionary, 1179**			
Gw	Com. Religious *or* *also* 1 Cor. 2. 9–13 Luke 10. 21–24	1 Tim. 3. 14–end Ps. 111. 1–5 Luke 7. 31–35	Ps. 119. 153–end Prov. 26. 12–end Mark 8.27 – 9.1	Ps. 136 2 Sam. 19. 8b–23 Acts 11. 19–end
18 Thursday				
G		1 Tim. 4. 12–end Ps. 111. 6–end Luke 7. 36–end	Ps. ***143***; 146 Prov. 27. 1–22 Mark 9. 2–13	Ps. ***138***; 140; 141 2 Sam. 19. 24–end Acts 12. 1–17
19 Friday	*Theodore of Tarsus, Archbishop of Canterbury, 690*			
G		1 Tim. 6. 2b–12 Ps. 49. 1–9 Luke 8. 1–3	Ps. 142; ***144*** Prov. 30. 1–9, 24–31 Mark 9. 14–29	Ps. 145 2 Sam. 23. 1–7 Acts 12. 18–end
20 Saturday	**John Coleridge Patteson, first Bishop of Melanesia, and his Companions, Martyrs, 1871**			
Gr	Com. Martyr *or* *esp.* 2 Chron. 24. 17–21 *also* Acts 7. 55–end	1 Tim. 6. 13–16 Ps. 100 Luke 8. 4–15	Ps. 147 Prov. 31. 10–end Mark 9. 30–37	Ps. ***148***; 149; 150 2 Sam. ch. 24 Acts 13. 1–12 **ct** *or First EP of Matthew* Ps. 34 Isa. 33. 13–17 Matt. 6. 19–end **R ct**
21 Sunday	**MATTHEW, APOSTLE AND EVANGELIST** (or transferred to 22 September)			
R		Prov. 3. 13–18 Ps. 119. 65–72 2 Cor. 4. 1–6 Matt. 9. 9–13	*MP*: Ps. 49; 117 1 Kings 19. 15–end 2 Tim. 3. 14–end	*EP*: Ps. 119. 33–40, 89–96 Eccles. 5. 4–12 Matt. 19. 16–end
	or, for The Fourteenth Sunday after Trinity (Proper 20):			
G	*Track 1* Jer. 8.18 – 9.1 Ps. 79. 1–9 1 Tim. 2. 1–7 Luke 16. 1–13	*Track 2* Amos 8. 4–7 Ps. 113 1 Tim. 2. 1–7 Luke 16. 1–13	Ps. 130; 131 Isa. 45. 9–22 Rev. 14. 1–5	Ps. [128]; 129 Ezra ch. 1 John 7. 14–36
22 Monday				
G **DEL 25**		Ezra 1. 1–6 Ps. 126 Luke 8. 16–18	Ps. ***1***; 2; 3 Wisd. ch. 1 *or* 1 Chron. 10.1 – 11.9 Mark 9. 38–end	Ps. ***4***; 7 1 Kings 1. 5–31 Acts 13. 13–43

	Calendar and Holy Communion	Morning Prayer	Evening Prayer	NOTES
G		Prov. 25. 1–14 Mark 8. 11–21	2 Sam. 18. 1–18 Acts 10. 34–end	
G		Prov. 25. 15–end Mark 8. 22–26	2 Sam. 18.19 - 19.8a Acts 11. 1–18	
	Lambert, Bishop of Maastricht, Martyr, 709 Ember Day			
Gr	Ember CEG *or* Com. Martyr	Prov. 26. 12–end Mark 8.27 - 9.1	2 Sam. 19. 8b–23 Acts 11. 19–end	
G		Prov. 27. 1–22 Mark 9. 2–13	2 Sam. 19. 24–end Acts 12. 1–17	
	Ember Day			
G	Ember CEG	Prov. 30. 1–9, 24–31 Mark 9. 14–29	2 Sam. 23. 1–7 Acts 12. 18–end	
	Ember Day			
G	Ember CEG	Prov. 31. 10–end Mark 9. 30–37	2 Sam. ch. 24 Acts 13. 1–12 **ct** *or First EP of Matthew* (Ps. 34) Prov. 3. 3–18 Matt. 6. 19–end **R ct**	
	MATTHEW, APOSTLE AND EVANGELIST			
R	Isa. 33. 13–17 Ps. 119. 65–72 2 Cor. 4. 1–6 Matt. 9. 9–13	Ps. 49; 117 1 Kings 19. 15–end 2 Tim. 3. 14–end	Ps. 119. 33–40, 89–96 Eccles. 5. 4–12 Matt. 19. 16–end	
	or, for The Fourteenth Sunday after Trinity (Proper 20):			
G	2 Kings 5. 9–16 Ps. 118. 1–9 Gal. 5. 16–24 Luke 17. 11–19	Ps. 130; 131 Isa. 45. 9–22 Rev. 14. 1–5	Ps. [128]; 129 Ezra ch. 1 John 7. 14–36	
G		Wisd. ch. 1 *or* 1 Chron. 10.1 - 11.9 Mark 9. 38–end	1 Kings 1. 5–31 Acts 13. 13–43	

		Sunday Principal Service Weekday Eucharist	Third Service Morning Prayer	Second Service Evening Prayer
23 Tuesday				
G		Ezra 6. 7–8, 12, 14–20 Ps. 124 Luke 8. 19–21	Ps. ***5***; 6; (8) Wisd. ch. 2 *or* 1 Chron. ch. 13 Mark 10. 1–16	Ps. **9**; 10† 1 Kings 1.32 – 2.4, 10–12 Acts 13.44 – 14.7
24 Wednesday	Ember Day*			
G *or* **R**		Ezra 9. 5–9 *Canticle*: Song of Tobit *or* Ps. 103. 1–6 Luke 9. 1–6	Ps. 119. 1–32 Wisd. 3. 1–9 *or* 1 Chron. 15.1 – 16.3 Mark 10. 17–31	Ps. ***11***; 12; 13 1 Kings ch. 3 Acts 14. 8–end
25 Thursday	**Lancelot Andrewes, Bishop of Winchester, Spiritual Writer, 1626** *Sergei of Radonezh, Russian Monastic Reformer, Teacher, 1392*			
Gw	Com. Bishop *or* *esp.* Isa. 6. 1–8	Hag. 1. 1–8 Ps. 149. 1–5 Luke 9. 7–9	Ps. 14; ***15***; 16 Wisd. 4. 7–end *or* 1 Chron. ch. 17 Mark 10. 32–34	Ps. 18† 1 Kings 4.29 – 5.12 Acts 15. 1–21
26 Friday	Ember Day* *Wilson Carlile, Founder of the Church Army, 1942*			
G *or* **R**		Hag. 1.15b – 2.9 Ps. 43 Luke 9. 18–22	Ps. 17; ***19*** Wisd. 5. 1–16 *or* 1 Chron. 21.1 – 22.1 Mark 10. 35–45	Ps. 22 1 Kings 6. 1, 11–28 Acts 15. 22–35
27 Saturday	**Vincent de Paul, Founder of the Congregation of the Mission (Lazarists), 1660** Ember Day*			
Gw *or* **Rw**	Com. Religious *or* *also* 1 Cor. 1. 25–end Matt. 25. 34–40	Zech. 2. 1–5, 10–11 Ps. 125 *or Canticle*: Jer. 31. 10–13 Luke 9. 43b–45	Ps. 20; 21; ***23*** Wisd. 5.17 – 6.11 *or* 1 Chron. 22. 2–end Mark 10. 46–end	Ps. ***24***; 25 1 Kings 8. 1–30 Acts 15.36 – 16.5 **ct**
28 Sunday	**THE FIFTEENTH SUNDAY AFTER TRINITY (Proper 21)**			
G	*Track 1* Jer. 32. 1–3a, 6–15 Ps. 91. 1–6, 14–end (*or* 91. 11–end) 1 Tim. 6. 6–19 Luke 16. 19–end	*Track 2* Amos. 6. 1a, 4–7 Ps. 146 1 Tim. 6. 6–19 Luke 16. 19–end	Ps. 132 Isa. 48. 12–end Luke 11. 37–end	Ps. 134; 135 (*or* Ps. 135. 1–14) Neh. ch. 2 John 8. 31–38, 48–end *or First EP of Michael and All Angels* Ps. 91 2 Kings 6. 8–17 Matt. 18. 1–6, 10 **W ct**
29 Monday	**MICHAEL AND ALL ANGELS**			
W **DEL 26**		Gen. 28. 10–17 *or* Rev. 12. 7–12 Ps. 103. 19–end Rev. 12. 7–12 *or* Heb. 1. 5–end John 1. 47–end	*MP*: Ps. 34; 150 Tobit 12. 6–end *or* Dan. 12. 1–4 Acts 12. 1–11	*EP*: Ps. 138; 148 Dan. 10. 4–end Rev. ch. 5
30 Tuesday	*Jerome, Translator of the Scriptures, Teacher, 420*			
G		Zech. 8. 20–end Ps. 87 Luke 9. 51–56	Ps. 32; ***36*** Wisd. 7. 1–14 *or* 1 Chron. 28. 11–end Mark 11. 12–26	Ps. 33 1 Kings 8.63 – 9.9 Acts 16. 25–end

*For Ember Day provision, see p. 11.

	Calendar and Holy Communion	Morning Prayer	Evening Prayer
G		Wisd. ch. 2 *or* 1 Chron. ch. 13 Mark 10. 1–16	1 Kings 1.32 – 2.4, 10–12 Acts 13.44 – 14.7
G		Wisd. 3. 1–9 *or* 1 Chron. 15.1 – 16.3 Mark 10. 17–31	1 Kings ch. 3 Acts 14. 8–end
G		Wisd. 4. 7–end *or* 1 Chron. ch. 17 Mark 10. 32–34	1 Kings 4.29 – 5.12 Acts 15. 1–21
	Cyprian, Bishop of Carthage, Martyr, 258		
Gr	Com. Martyr	Wisd. 5. 1–16 *or* 1 Chron. 21.1 – 22.1 Mark 10. 35–45	1 Kings 6. 1, 11–28 Acts 15. 22–35
G		Wisd. 5.17 – 6.11 *or* 1 Chron. 22. 2–end Mark 10. 46–end	1 Kings 8. 1–30 Acts 15.36 – 16.5 **ct**
	THE FIFTEENTH SUNDAY AFTER TRINITY		
G	Josh. 24. 14–25 Ps. 92. 1–6 Gal. 6. 11–end Matt. 6. 24–end	Ps. 132 Isa. 48. 12–end Luke 11. 37–end	Ps. 134; 135 (*or* Ps. 135. 1–14) Neh. ch. 2 John 8. 31–38, 48–end *or First EP of Michael and All Angels* Ps. 91 2 Kings 6. 8–17 John 1. 47–51 **W ct**
	MICHAEL AND ALL ANGELS		
W	Dan. 10. 10–19a Ps. 103. 17–22 Rev. 12. 7–12 Matt. 18. 1–10	(Ps. 34; 150) Tobit 12. 6–end *or* Dan. 12. 1–4 Acts 12. 1–11	(Ps. 138; 148) Gen. 28. 10–17 Rev. ch. 5
	Jerome, Translator of the Scriptures, Teacher, 420		
Gw	Com. Doctor	Wisd. 7. 1–14 *or* 1 Chron. 28. 11–end Mark 11. 12–26	1 Kings 8.63 – 9.9 Acts 16. 25–end

NOTES

		Sunday Principal Service Weekday Eucharist	Third Service Morning Prayer	Second Service Evening Prayer
October 2025				
1 Wednesday	*Remigius, Bishop of Rheims, Apostle of the Franks, 533; Anthony Ashley Cooper, Earl of Shaftesbury, Social Reformer, 1885*			
G		Neh. 2. 1–8 Ps. 137. 1–6 Luke 9. 57–end	Ps. 34 Wisd. 7.15 – 8.4 *or* 1 Chron. 29. 1–9 Mark 11. 27–end	Ps. 119. 33–56 1 Kings 10. 1–25 Acts 17. 1–15
2 Thursday				
G		Neh. 8. 1–12 Ps. 19. 7–11 Luke 10. 1–12	Ps. 37† Wisd. 8. 5–18 *or* 1 Chron. 29. 10–20 Mark 12. 1–12	Ps. 39; **40** 1 Kings 11. 1–13 Acts 17. 16–end
3 Friday	*George Bell, Bishop of Chichester, Ecumenist, Peacemaker, 1958*			
G		Baruch 1. 15–end *or* Deut. 31. 7–13 Ps. 79. 1–9 Luke 10. 13–16	Ps. 31 Wisd. 8.21 – 9.end *or* 1 Chron. 29. 21–end Mark 12. 13–17	Ps. 35 1 Kings 11. 26–end Acts 18. 1–21
4 Saturday	**Francis of Assisi, Friar, Founder of the Friars Minor, 1226**			
Gw	Com. Religious *or* *also* Gal. 6. 14–end Luke 12. 22–34	Baruch 4. 5–12, 27–29 *or* Josh. 22. 1–6 Ps. 69. 33–37 Luke 10. 17–24	Ps. 41; **42**; 43 Wisd. 10.15 – 11.10 *or* 2 Chron. 1. 1–13 Mark 12. 18–27	Ps. 45; **46** 1 Kings 12. 1–24 Acts 18.22 – 19.7 **ct** *or First EP of Dedication Festival* Ps. 24 2 Chron. 7. 11–16 John 4. 19–29 **𝔚 ct**
5 Sunday	**THE SIXTEENTH SUNDAY AFTER TRINITY (Proper 22)**			
G	*Track 1* Lam. 1. 1–6 *Canticle*: Lam. 3. 19–26 *or* Ps. 137 (*or* 137. 1–6) 2 Tim. 1. 1–14 Luke 17. 5–10	*Track 2* Hab. 1. 1–4; 2. 1–4 Ps. 37. 1–9 2 Tim. 1. 1–14 Luke 17. 5–10	Ps. 141 Isa. 49. 13–23 Luke 12. 1–12	Ps. 142 Neh. 5. 1–13 John ch. 9
𝔚	*or, if observed as Dedication Festival*:	1 Chron. 29. 6–19 Ps. 122 Eph. 2. 19–end John 2. 13–22	*MP*: Ps. 48; 150 Hag. 2. 6–9 Heb. 10. 19–25	*EP*: Ps. 132 Jer. 7. 1–11 Luke 19. 1–10
6 Monday	**William Tyndale, Translator of the Scriptures, Reformation Martyr, 1536**			
Gr **DEL 27**	Com. Martyr *or* *also* Prov. 8. 4–11 2 Tim. 3. 12–end	Jonah 1.1 – 2.2, 10 *Canticle*: Jonah 2. 2–4, 7 *or* Ps. 69. 1–6 Luke 10. 25–37	Ps. 44 Wisd. 11.21 – 12.2 *or* 2 Chron. 2. 1–16 Mark 12. 28–34	Ps. **47**; 49 1 Kings 12.25 – 13.10 Acts 19. 8–20

	Calendar and Holy Communion	Morning Prayer	Evening Prayer
	Remigius, Bishop of Rheims, Apostle of the Franks, 533		
Gw	Com. Bishop	Wisd. 7.15 - 8.4 *or* 1 Chron. 29. 1–9 Mark 11. 27–end	1 Kings 10. 1–25 Acts 17. 1–15
G		Wisd. 8. 5–18 *or* 1 Chron. 29. 10–20 Mark 12. 1–12	1 Kings 11. 1–13 Acts 17. 16–end
G		Wisd. 8.21 - 9.end *or* 1 Chron. 29. 21–end Mark 12. 13–17	1 Kings 11. 26–end Acts 18. 1–21
G		Wisd. 10.15 - 11.10 *or* 2 Chron. 1. 1–13 Mark 12. 18–27	1 Kings 12. 1–24 Acts 18.22 - 19.7 **ct** *or First EP of Dedication Festival* Ps. 24 2 Chron. 7. 11–16 John 4. 19–29 **𝔚 ct**
	THE SIXTEENTH SUNDAY AFTER TRINITY		
G	1 Kings 17. 17–end Ps. 102. 12–17 Eph. 3. 13–end Luke 7. 11–17	Ps. 141 Isa. 49. 13–23 Luke 12. 1–12	Ps. 142 Neh. 5. 1–13 John ch. 9
	or, if observed as Dedication Festival:		
𝔚	2 Chron. 7. 11–16 Ps. 122 1 Cor. 3. 9–17 *or* 1 Pet. 2. 1–5 Matt. 21. 12–16 *or* John 10. 22–29	Ps. 48; 150 Hag. 2. 6–9 Heb. 10. 19–25	Ps. 132 Jer. 7. 1–11 Luke 19. 1–10
	Faith of Aquitaine, Martyr, c. 304		
Gr	Com. Virgin Martyr	Wisd. 11.21 - 12.2 *or* 2 Chron. 2. 1–16 Mark 12. 28–34	1 Kings 12.25 - 13.10 Acts 19. 8–20

NOTES

		Sunday Principal Service Weekday Eucharist		Third Service Morning Prayer	Second Service Evening Prayer
7 Tuesday					
G			Jonah ch. 3 Ps. 130 Luke 10. 38–end	Ps. ***48***; 52 Wisd. 12. 12–21 *or* 2 Chron. ch. 3 Mark 12. 35–end	Ps. 50 1 Kings 13. 11–end Acts 19. 21–end
8 Wednesday					
G			Jonah ch. 4 Ps. 86. 1–9 Luke 11. 1–4	Ps. 119. 57–80 Wisd. 13. 1–9 *or* 2 Chron. ch. 5 Mark 13. 1–13	Ps. ***59***; 60; (67) 1 Kings ch. 17 Acts 20. 1–16
9 Thursday	*Denys, Bishop of Paris, and his Companions, Martyrs, c. 250; Robert Grosseteste, Bishop of Lincoln, Philosopher, Scientist, 1253*				
G			Mal. 3.13 – 4.2a Ps. 1 Luke 11. 5–13	Ps. 56; ***57***; (63†) Wisd. 16.15 – 17.1 *or* 2 Chron. 6. 1–21 Mark 13. 14–23	Ps. 61; ***62***; 64 1 Kings 18. 1–20 Acts 20. 17–end
10 Friday	**Paulinus, Bishop of York, Missionary, 644** *Thomas Traherne, Poet, Spiritual Writer, 1674*				
Gw	Com. Missionary *esp.* Matt. 28. 16–end	*or*	Joel 1. 13–15; 2. 1–2 Ps. 9. 1–7 Luke 11. 15–26	Ps. ***51***; 54 Wisd. 18. 6–19 *or* 2 Chron. 6. 22–end Mark 13. 24–31	Ps. 38 1 Kings 18. 21–end Acts 21. 1–16
11 Saturday	*Ethelburga, Abbess of Barking, 675; James the Deacon, Companion of Paulinus, 7th century*				
G			Joel 3. 12–end Ps. 97. 1, 8–end Luke 11. 27–28	Ps. 68 Wisd. ch. 19 *or* 2 Chron. ch. 7 Mark 13. 32–end	Ps. 65; ***66*** 1 Kings ch. 19 Acts 21. 17–36 **ct**
12 Sunday	**THE SEVENTEENTH SUNDAY AFTER TRINITY (Proper 23)**				
G	*Track 1* Jer. 29. 1, 4–7 Ps. 66. 1–11 2 Tim. 2. 8–15 Luke 17. 11–19		*Track 2* 2 Kings 5. 1–3, 7–15c Ps. 111 2 Tim. 2. 8–15 Luke 17. 11–19	Ps. 143 Isa. 50. 4–10 Luke 13. 22–30	Ps. 144 Neh. 6. 1–16 John 15. 12–end
13 Monday	**Edward the Confessor, King of England, 1066**				
Gw **DEL 28**	Com. Saint *also* 2 Sam. 23. 1–5 1 John 4. 13–16	*or*	Rom. 1. 1–7 Ps. 98 Luke 11. 29–32	Ps. 71 1 Macc. 1. 1–19 *or* 2 Chron. 9. 1–12 Mark 14. 1–11	Ps. ***72***; 75 1 Kings ch. 21 Acts 21.37 – 22.21
14 Tuesday					
G			Rom. 1. 16–25 Ps. 19. 1–4 Luke 11. 37–41	Ps. 73 1 Macc. 1. 20–40 *or* 2 Chron. 10.1 – 11.4 Mark 14. 12–25	Ps. 74 1 Kings 22. 1–28 Acts 22.22 – 23.11
15 Wednesday	**Teresa of Avila, Teacher, 1582**				
Gw	Com. Teacher *also* Rom. 8. 22–27	*or*	Rom. 2. 1–11 Ps. 62. 1–8 Luke 11. 42–46	Ps. 77 1 Macc. 1. 41–end *or* 2 Chron. ch. 12 Mark 14. 26–42	Ps. 119. 81–104 1 Kings 22. 29–45 Acts 23. 12–end

	Calendar and Holy Communion	Morning Prayer	Evening Prayer	NOTES
G		Wisd. 12. 12–21 *or* 2 Chron. ch. 3 Mark 12. 35–end	1 Kings 13. 11–end Acts 19. 21–end	
G		Wisd. 13. 1–9 *or* 2 Chron. ch. 5 Mark 13. 1–13	1 Kings ch. 17 Acts 20. 1–16	
	Denys, Bishop of Paris, Martyr, c. 250			
Gr	Com. Martyr	Wisd. 16.15 - 17.1 *or* 2 Chron. 6. 1–21 Mark 13. 14–23	1 Kings 18. 1–20 Acts 20. 17–end	
G		Wisd. 18. 6–19 *or* 2 Chron. 6. 22–end Mark 13. 24–31	1 Kings 18. 21–end Acts 21. 1–16	
G		Wisd. ch. 19 *or* 2 Chron. ch. 7 Mark 13. 32–end	1 Kings ch. 19 Acts 21. 17–36 **ct**	
	THE SEVENTEENTH SUNDAY AFTER TRINITY			
G	Prov. 25. 6–14 Ps. 33. 6–12 Eph. 4. 1–6 Luke 14. 1–11	Ps. 143 Isa. 50. 4–10 Luke 13. 22–30	Ps. 144 Neh. 6. 1–16 John 15. 12–end	
	Edward the Confessor, King of England, 1066			
Gw	Com. Saint	1 Macc. 1. 1–19 *or* 2 Chron. 9. 1–12 Mark 14. 1–11	1 Kings ch. 21 Acts 21.37 - 22.21	
G		1 Macc. 1. 20–40 *or* 2 Chron. 10.1 - 11.4 Mark 14. 12–25	1 Kings 22. 1–28 Acts 22.22 - 23.11	
G		1 Macc. 1. 41–end *or* 2 Chron. ch. 12 Mark 14. 26–42	1 Kings 22. 29–45 Acts 23. 12–end	

		Sunday Principal Service Weekday Eucharist	Third Service Morning Prayer	Second Service Evening Prayer
16 Thursday	*Nicholas Ridley, Bishop of London, and Hugh Latimer, Bishop of Worcester, Reformation Martyrs, 1555*			
G		Rom. 3. 21–30 Ps. 130 Luke 11. 47–end	Ps. 78. 1–39† 1 Macc. 2. 1–28 *or* 2 Chron. 13.1 - 14.1 Mark 14. 43–52	Ps. 78. 40–end† 2 Kings 1. 2–17 Acts 24. 1–23
17 Friday	**Ignatius, Bishop of Antioch, Martyr, c. 107**			
Gr	Com. Martyr *or* *also* Phil. 3. 7–12 John 6. 52–58	Rom. 4. 1–8 Ps. 32 Luke 12. 1–7	Ps. 55 1 Macc. 2. 29–48 *or* 2 Chron. 14. 2–end Mark 14. 53–65	Ps. 69 2 Kings 2. 1–18 Acts 24.24 - 25.12 *or First EP of Luke* Ps. 33 Hos. 6. 1–3 2 Tim. 3. 10–end **R ct**
18 Saturday	**LUKE THE EVANGELIST**			
R		Isa. 35. 3–6 *or* Acts 16. 6–12a Ps. 147. 1–7 2 Tim. 4. 5–17 Luke 10. 1–9	*MP*: Ps. 145; 146 Isa. ch. 55 Luke 1. 1–4	*EP*: Ps. 103 Ecclus. 38. 1–14 *or* Isa. 61. 1–6 Col. 4. 7–end
19 Sunday	**THE EIGHTEENTH SUNDAY AFTER TRINITY (Proper 24)**			
G	*Track 1* Jer. 31. 27–34 Ps. 119. 97–104 2 Tim. 3.14 - 4.5 Luke 18. 1–8	*Track 2* Gen. 32. 22–31 Ps. 121 2 Tim. 3.14 - 4.5 Luke 18. 1–8	Ps. 147 Isa. 54. 1–14 Luke 13. 31–end	Ps. [146]; 149 Neh. 8. 9–end John 16. 1–11
20 Monday				
G **DEL 29**		Rom. 4. 20–end *Canticle*: Benedictus 1–6 Luke 12. 13–21	Ps. ***80***; 82 1 Macc. 3. 1–26 *or* 2 Chron. 17. 1–12 Mark 15. 1–15	Ps. ***85***; 86 2 Kings ch. 5 Acts 26. 1–23
21 Tuesday				
G		Rom. 5. 12, 15, 17–end Ps. 40. 7–12 Luke 12. 35–38	Ps. 87; ***89. 1–18*** 1 Macc. 3. 27–41 *or* 2 Chron. 18. 1–27 Mark 15. 16–32	Ps. 89. 19–end 2 Kings 6. 1–23 Acts 26. 24–end
22 Wednesday				
G		Rom. 6. 12–18 Ps. 124 Luke 12. 39–48	Ps. 119. 105–128 1 Macc. 3. 42–end *or* 2 Chron. 18.28 - 19.end Mark 15. 33–41	Ps. ***91***; 93 2 Kings 9. 1–16 Acts 27. 1–26
23 Thursday				
G		Rom. 6. 19–end Ps. 1 Luke 12. 49–53	Ps. 90; **92** 1 Macc. 4. 1–25 *or* 2 Chron. 20. 1–23 Mark 15. 42–end	Ps. 94 2 Kings 9. 17–end Acts 27. 27–end

	Calendar and Holy Communion	Morning Prayer	Evening Prayer	NOTES
G		1 Macc. 2. 1–28 *or* 2 Chron. 13.1 - 14.1 Mark 14. 43–52	2 Kings 1. 2–17 Acts 24. 1–23	
	Etheldreda, Abbess of Ely, 679			
Gw	Com. Abbess	1 Macc. 2. 29–48 *or* 2 Chron. 14. 2–end Mark 14. 53–65	2 Kings 2. 1–18 Acts 24.24 - 25.12 *or First EP of Luke* (Ps. 33) Hos. 6. 1–3 2 Tim. 3. 10–end **R ct**	
	LUKE THE EVANGELIST			
R	Isa. 35. 3–6 Ps. 147. 1–6 2 Tim. 4. 5–15 Luke 10. 1–9 *or* Luke 7. 36–end	(Ps. 145; 146) Isa. ch. 55 Luke 1. 1–4	(Ps. 103) Ecclus. 38. 1–14 *or* Isa. 61. 1–6 Col. 4. 7–end	
	THE EIGHTEENTH SUNDAY AFTER TRINITY			
G	Deut. 6. 4–9 Ps. 122 1 Cor. 1. 4–8 Matt. 22. 34–end	Ps. 147 Isa. 54. 1–14 Luke 13. 31–end	Ps. [146]; 149 Neh. 8. 9–end John 16. 1–11	
G		1 Macc. 3. 1–26 *or* 2 Chron. 17. 1–12 Mark 15. 1–15	2 Kings ch. 5 Acts 26. 1–23	
G		1 Macc. 3. 27–41 *or* 2 Chron. 18. 1–27 Mark 15. 16–32	2 Kings 6. 1–23 Acts 26. 24–end	
G		1 Macc. 3. 42–end *or* 2 Chron. 18.28 - 19.end Mark 15. 33–41	2 Kings 9. 1–16 Acts 27. 1–26	
G		1 Macc. 4. 1–25 *or* 2 Chron. 20. 1–23 Mark 15. 42–end	2 Kings 9. 17–end Acts 27. 27–end	

		Sunday Principal Service Weekday Eucharist	Third Service Morning Prayer	Second Service Evening Prayer
24 Friday				
G		Rom. 7. 18–end Ps. 119. 33–40 Luke 12. 54–end	Ps. ***88***; (95) 1 Macc. 4. 26–35 *or* 2 Chron. 22.10 – 23.end Mark 16. 1–8	Ps. 102 2 Kings 12. 1–19 Acts 28. 1–16
25 Saturday	*Crispin and Crispinian, Martyrs at Rome, c. 287*			
G		Rom. 8. 1–11 Ps. 24. 1–6 Luke 13. 1–9	Ps. 96; ***97***; 100 1 Macc. 4. 36–end *or* 2 Chron. 24. 1–22 Mark 16. 9–end	Ps. 104 2 Kings 17. 1–23 Acts 28. 17–end **ct**
26 Sunday	**THE LAST SUNDAY AFTER TRINITY***			
G	*Track 1* Joel 2. 23–end Ps. 65 (*or* 65. 1–7) 2 Tim. 4. 6–8, 16–18 Luke 18. 9–14	*Track 2* Ecclus. 35. 12–17 *or* Jer. 14. 7–10, 19–end Ps. 84. 1–7 2 Tim. 4. 6–8, 16–18 Luke 18. 9–14	Ps. 119. 105–128 Isa. 59. 9–20 Luke 14. 1–14	Ps. 119. 1–16 Eccles. chs 11 & 12 2 Tim. 2. 1–7 *Gospel*: Matt. 22. 34–end
	or, if being observed as Bible Sunday:			
G		Isa. 45. 22–end Ps. 119. 129–136 Rom. 15. 1–6 Luke 4. 16–24	Ps. 119. 105–128 1 Kings 22. 1–17 Rom. 15. 4–13 *or* Luke 14. 1–14	Ps. 119. 1–16 Jer. 36. 9–end Rom. 10. 5–17 *Gospel*: Matt. 22. 34–40
27 Monday				
G **DEL 30**		Rom. 8. 12–17 Ps. 68. 1–6, 19 Luke 13. 10–17	Ps. ***98***; 99; 101 1 Macc. 6. 1–17 *or* 2 Chron. 26. 1–21 John 13. 1–11	Ps. ***105***† (*or* 103) 2 Kings 17. 24–end Phil. 1. 1–11 *or First EP of Simon and Jude* Ps. 124; 125; 126 Deut. 32. 1–4 John 14. 15–26 **R ct**
28 Tuesday	**SIMON AND JUDE, APOSTLES**			
R		Isa. 28. 14–16 Ps. 119. 89–96 Eph. 2. 19–end John 15. 17–end	*MP*: Ps. 116; 117 Wisd. 5. 1–16 *or* Isa. 45. 18–end Luke 6. 12–16	*EP*: Ps. 119. 1–16 1 Macc. 2. 42–66 *or* Jer. 3. 11–18 Jude 1–4, 17–end
29 Wednesday	**James Hannington, Bishop of Eastern Equatorial Africa, Martyr in Uganda, 1885**			
Gr	Com. Martyr *or* *esp.* Matt. 10. 28–39	Rom. 8. 26–30 Ps. 13 Luke 13. 22–30	Ps. 110; ***111***; 112 1 Macc. 7. 1–20 *or* 2 Chron. 29. 1–19 John 13. 21–30	Ps. 119. 129–152 2 Kings 18. 13–end Phil. 2. 1–13
30 Thursday				
G		Rom. 8. 31–end Ps. 109. 20–26, 29–30 Luke 13. 31–end	Ps. 113; ***115*** 1 Macc. 7. 21–end *or* 2 Chron. 29. 20–end John 13. 31–end	Ps. 114; ***116***; 117 2 Kings 19. 1–19 Phil. 2. 14–end

*If the Dedication Festival is kept on this Sunday, use the provision given on 4 and 5 October.

	Calendar and Holy Communion	Morning Prayer	Evening Prayer	NOTES
G		1 Macc. 4. 26–35 *or* 2 Chron. 22.10 – 23.end Mark 16. 1–8	2 Kings 12. 1–19 Acts 28. 1–16	
	Crispin, Martyr at Rome, c. 287			
Gr	Com. Martyr	1 Macc. 4. 36–end *or* 2 Chron. 24. 1–22 Mark 16. 9–end	2 Kings 17. 1–23 Acts 28. 17–end **ct**	
	THE NINETEENTH SUNDAY AFTER TRINITY			
G	Gen. 18. 23–32 Ps. 141. 1–9 Eph. 4. 17–end Matt. 9. 1–8	Ps. 119. 105–128 Isa. 59. 9–20 Luke 14. 12–24	Ps. 119. 1–16 Eccles. chs 11 & 12 2 Tim. 2. 1–7	
G		1 Macc. 6. 1–17 *or* 2 Chron. 26. 1–21 John 13. 1–11	2 Kings 17. 24–end Phil. 1. 1–11 *or First EP of Simon and Jude* (Ps. 124; 125; 126) Deut. 32. 1–4 John 14. 15–26 **R ct**	
	SIMON AND JUDE, APOSTLES			
R	Isa. 28. 9–16 Ps. 116. 11–end Jude 1–8 *or* Rev. 21. 9–14 John 15. 17–end	(Ps. 119. 89–96) Wisd. 5. 1–16 *or* Isa. 45. 18–end Luke 6. 12–16	(Ps. 119. 1–16) 1 Macc. 2. 42–66 *or* Jer. 3. 11–18 Eph. 2. 19–end	
G		1 Macc. 7. 1–20 *or* 2 Chron. 29. 1–19 John 13. 21–30	2 Kings 18. 13–end Phil. 2. 1–13	
G		1 Macc. 7. 21–end *or* 2 Chron. 29. 20–end John 13. 31–end	2 Kings 19. 1–19 Phil. 2. 14–end	

		Sunday Principal Service Weekday Eucharist	Third Service Morning Prayer	Second Service Evening Prayer
31 Friday	*Martin Luther, Reformer, 1546*			
G		Rom. 9. 1-5 Ps. 147. 13-end Luke 14. 1-6	Ps. 139 1 Macc. 9. 1-22 *or* 2 Chron. ch. 30 John 14. 1-14	*First EP of All Saints* Ps. 1; 5 Ecclus. 44. 1-15 *or* Isa. 40. 27-end Rev. 19. 6-10 **𝔚 ct** *or, if All Saints is observed on 2 November*: Ps. ***130***; 131; 137 2 Kings 19. 20-36 Phil. 3.1 - 4.1 **ct**

November 2025

		Sunday Principal Service Weekday Eucharist	Third Service Morning Prayer	Second Service Evening Prayer
1 Saturday	**ALL SAINTS' DAY**			
𝔚		Dan. 7. 1-3, 15-18 Ps. 149 Eph. 1. 11-end Luke 6. 20-31	*MP*: Ps. 15; 84; 149 Isa. ch. 35 Luke 9. 18-27	*EP*: Ps. 148; 150 Isa. 65. 17-end Heb. 11.32 - 12.2
	or, if the readings above are used on Sunday 2 November:			
𝔚		Isa. 56. 3-8 *or* 2 Esdras 2. 42-end Ps. 33. 1-5 Heb. 12. 18-24 Matt. 5. 1-12	*MP*: 111; 112; 117 Wisd. 5. 1-16 *or* Jer. 31. 31-34 2 Cor. 4. 5-12	*EP*: Ps. 145 Isa. 66. 20-23 Col. 1. 9-14
	or, if kept as a feria:			
G		Rom. 11. 1-2, 11-12, 25-29 Ps. 94. 14-19 Luke 14. 1, 7-11	Ps. 120; ***121***; 122 1 Macc. 13. 41-end; 14. 4-15 *or* 2 Chron. 32. 1-22 John 14. 15-end	Ps. 118 2 Kings ch. 20 Phil. 4. 2-end **ct**
2 Sunday	**THE FOURTH SUNDAY BEFORE ADVENT**			
R *or* **G**		Isa. 1. 10-18 Ps. 32. 1-8 2 Thess. ch. 1 Luke 19. 1-10	Ps. 87 Job ch. 26 Col. 1. 9-14	Ps. 145 (*or* 145. 1-9) Lam. 3. 22-33 John 11. [1-31] 32-44
𝔚	*or ALL SAINTS' SUNDAY (see readings for 1 November throughout the day)*			
3 Monday	**Richard Hooker, Priest, Anglican Apologist, Teacher, 1600** *Martin of Porres, Friar, 1639*			
Rw *or* **Gw** **DEL 31**		Rom. 11. 29-end Ps. 69. 31-37 Luke 14. 12-14	Ps. **2**; 146 *alt.* Ps. 123; 124; 125; ***126*** Isa. 1. 1-20 Matt. 1. 18-end	Ps. **92**; 96; 97 *alt.* Ps. ***127***; 128; 129 Dan. ch. 1 Rev. ch. 1
4 Tuesday				
R *or* **G**		Rom. 12. 5-16 Ps. 131 Luke 14. 15-24	Ps. ***5***; 147. 1-12 *alt.* Ps. ***132***; 133 Isa. 1. 21-end Matt. 2. 1-15	Ps. 98; 99; ***100*** *alt.* Ps. (134); ***135*** Dan. 2. 1-24 Rev. 2. 1-11

	Calendar and Holy Communion	Morning Prayer	Evening Prayer	NOTES
G		1 Macc. 9. 1–22 *or* 2 Chron. ch. 30 John 14. 1–14	*First EP of All Saints* Ps. 1; 5 Ecclus. 44. 1–15 *or* Isa. 40. 27–end Rev. 19. 6–10 **W ct**	
	ALL SAINTS' DAY			
W	Isa. 66. 20–23 Ps. 33. 1–5 Rev. 7. 2–4 [5–8] 9–12 Matt. 5. 1–12	Ps. 15; 84; 149 Isa. ch. 35 Luke 9. 18–27	Ps. 148; 150 Isa. 65. 17–end Heb. 11.32 – 12.2	
	THE TWENTIETH SUNDAY AFTER TRINITY			
G	Prov. 9. 1–6 Ps. 145. 15–end Eph. 5. 15–21 Matt. 22. 1–14	Ps. 87 Job ch. 26 Luke 19. 1–10	Ps. 145 (*or* 145. 1–9) Lam. 3. 22–33 John 11. [1–31] 32–44	
G		Isa. 1. 1–20 Matt. 1. 18–end	Dan. ch. 1 Rev. ch. 1	
G		Isa. 1. 21–end Matt. 2. 1–15	Dan. 2. 1–24 Rev. 2. 1–11	

		Sunday Principal Service Weekday Eucharist	Third Service Morning Prayer	Second Service Evening Prayer
5 Wednesday				
R *or* **G**		Rom. 13. 8–10 Ps. 112 Luke 14. 25–33	Ps. ***9***; 147. 13–end *alt.* Ps. 119. 153–end Isa. 2. 1–11 Matt. 2. 16–end	Ps. 111; ***112***; 116 *alt.* Ps. 136 Dan. 2. 25–end Rev. 2. 12–end
6 Thursday	*Leonard, Hermit, 6th century; William Temple, Archbishop of Canterbury, Teacher, 1944*			
R *or* **G**		Rom. 14. 7–12 Ps. 27. 14–end Luke 15. 1–10	Ps. 11; ***15***; 148 *alt.* Ps. ***143***; 146 Isa. 2. 12–end Matt. ch. 3	Ps. 118 *alt.* Ps. ***138***; 140; 141 Dan. 3. 1–18 Rev. 3. 1–13
7 Friday	**Willibrord of York, Bishop, Apostle of Frisia, 739**			
Rw *or* **Gw**	Com. Missionary *or* *esp.* Isa. 52. 7–10 Matt. 28. 16–end	Rom. 15. 14–21 Ps. 98 Luke 16. 1–8	Ps. ***16***; 149 *alt.* Ps. 142; ***144*** Isa. 3. 1–15 Matt. 4. 1–11	Ps. 137; 138; ***143*** *alt.* Ps. 145 Dan. 3. 19–end Rev. 3. 14–end
8 Saturday	**The Saints and Martyrs of England**			
Rw *or* **Gw**	Isa. 61. 4–9 *or* *or* Ecclus. 44. 1–15 Ps. 15 Rev. 19. 5–10 John 17. 18–23	Rom. 16. 3–9, 16, 22–end Ps. 145. 1–7 Luke 16. 9–15	Ps. ***18. 31–end***; 150 *alt.* Ps. 147 Isa. 4.2 – 5.7 Matt. 4. 12–22	Ps. 145 *alt.* Ps. ***148***; 149; 150 Dan. 4. 1–18 Rev. ch. 4 **ct**
9 Sunday	**THE THIRD SUNDAY BEFORE ADVENT** (Remembrance Sunday)			
R *or* **G**		Job 19. 23–27a Ps. 17. 1–9 (*or* 17. 1–8) 2 Thess. 2. 1–5, 13–end Luke 20. 27–38	Ps. 20; 90 Isa. 2. 1–5 James 3. 13–end	Ps. 40 1 Kings 3. 1–15 Rom. 8. 31–end *Gospel*: Matt. 22. 15–22
10 Monday	**Leo the Great, Bishop of Rome, Teacher, 461**			
Rw *or* **Gw** **DEL 32**	Com. Teacher *or* *also* 1 Pet. 5. 1–11	Wisd. 1. 1–7 *or* Titus 1. 1–9 Ps. 139. 1–9 *or* Ps. 24. 1–6 Luke 17. 1–6	Ps. 19; ***20*** *alt.* Ps. ***1***; 2; 3 Isa. 5. 8–24 Matt. 4.23 – 5.12	Ps. 34 *alt.* Ps. ***4***; 7 Dan. 4. 19–end Rev. ch. 5
11 Tuesday	**Martin, Bishop of Tours, c. 397**			
Rw *or* **Gw**	Com. Bishop *or* *also* 1 Thess. 5. 1–11 Matt. 25. 34–40	Wisd. 2.23 – 3.9 *or* Titus 2. 1–8, 11–14 Ps. 34. 1–6 *or* Ps. 37. 3–5, 30–32 Luke 17. 7–10	Ps. ***21***; 24 *alt.* Ps. ***5***; 6; (8) Isa. 5. 25–end Matt. 5. 13–20	Ps. 36; ***40*** *alt.* Ps. ***9***; 10† Dan. 5. 1–12 Rev. ch. 6
12 Wednesday				
R *or* **G**		Wisd. 6. 1–11 *or* Titus 3. 1–7 Ps. 82 *or* Ps. 23 Luke 17. 11–19	Ps. ***23***; 25 *alt.* Ps. 119. 1–32 Isa. ch. 6 Matt. 5. 21–37	Ps. 37 *alt.* Ps. ***11***; 12; 13 Dan. 5. 13–end Rev. 7. 1–4, 9–end

	Calendar and Holy Communion	Morning Prayer	Evening Prayer	NOTES
G		Isa. 2. 1–11 Matt. 2. 16–end	Dan. 2. 25–end Rev. 2. 12–end	
	Leonard, Hermit, 6th century			
Gw	Com. Abbot	Isa. 2. 12–end Matt. ch. 3	Dan. 3. 1–18 Rev. 3. 1–13	
G		Isa. 3. 1–15 Matt. 4. 1–11	Dan. 3. 19–end Rev. 3. 14–end	
G		Isa. 4.2 – 5.7 Matt. 4. 12–22	Dan. 4. 1–18 Rev. ch. 4 **ct**	
	THE TWENTY-FIRST SUNDAY AFTER TRINITY			
G	Gen. 32. 24–29 Ps. 90. 1–12 Eph. 6. 10–20 John 4. 46b–end	Ps. 20; 90 Isa. 2. 1–5 James 3. 13–end	Ps. 40 1 Kings 3. 1–15 Luke 20. 27–38	
G		Isa. 5. 8–24 Matt. 4.23 – 5.12	Dan. 4. 19–end Rev. ch. 5	
	Martin, Bishop of Tours, c. 397			
Gw	Com. Bishop	Isa. 5. 25–end Matt. 5. 13–20	Dan. 5. 1–12 Rev. ch. 6	
G		Isa. ch. 6 Matt. 5. 21–37	Dan. 5. 13–end Rev. 7. 1–4, 9–end	

		Sunday Principal Service Weekday Eucharist	Third Service Morning Prayer	Second Service Evening Prayer
13 Thursday	**Charles Simeon, Priest, Evangelical Divine, 1836**			
Rw *or* **Gw**	Com. Pastor *or* *esp.* Mal. 2. 5–7 *also* Col. 1. 3–8 Luke 8	Wisd. 7.22 – 8.1 *or* Philemon 7–20 Ps. 119. 89–96 *or* Ps. 146. 4–end Luke 17. 20–25	Ps. ***26***; 27 *alt.* Ps. 14; ***15***; 16 Isa. 7. 1–17 Matt. 5. 38–end	Ps. 42; ***43*** *alt.* Ps. 18† Dan. ch. 6 Rev. ch. 8
14 Friday	*Samuel Seabury, first Anglican Bishop in North America, 1796*			
R *or* **G**		Wisd. 13. 1–9 *or* 2 John 4–9 Ps. 19. 1–4 *or* Ps. 119. 1–8 Luke 17. 26–end	Ps. 28; ***32*** *alt.* Ps. 17; ***19*** Isa. 8. 1–15 Matt. 6. 1–18	Ps. 31 *alt.* Ps. 22 Dan. 7. 1–14 Rev. 9. 1–12
15 Saturday				
R *or* **G**		Wisd. 18. 14–16; 19. 6–9 *or* 3 John 5–8 Ps. 105. 1–5, 35–42 *or* Ps. 112 Luke 18. 1–8	Ps. 33 *alt.* Ps. 20; 21; ***23*** Isa. 8.16 – 9.7 Matt. 6. 19–end	Ps. 84; ***86*** *alt.* Ps. ***24***; 25 Dan. 7. 15–end Rev. 9. 13–end **ct**
16 Sunday	**THE SECOND SUNDAY BEFORE ADVENT**			
R *or* **G**		Mal. 4. 1–2a Ps. 98 2 Thess. 3. 6–13 Luke 21. 5–19	Ps. 132 1 Sam. 16. 1–13 Matt. 13. 44–52	Ps. [93]; 97 Dan. ch. 6 Matt. 13. 1–9, 18–23
17 Monday	**Hugh, Bishop of Lincoln, 1200**			
Rw *or* **Gw** **DEL 33**	Com. Bishop *or* *also* 1 Tim. 6. 11–16	1 Macc. 1. 10–15, 41–43, 54–57, 62–64 *or* Rev. 1. 1–4; 2. 1–5 Ps. 79. 1–5 *or* Ps. 1 Luke 18. 35–end	Ps. 46; ***47*** *alt.* Ps. 27; ***30*** Isa. 9.8 – 10.4 Matt. 7. 1–12	Ps. 70; ***71*** *alt.* Ps. 26; ***28***; 29 Dan. 8. 1–14 Rev. ch. 10
18 Tuesday	**Elizabeth of Hungary, Princess of Thuringia, Philanthropist, 1231**			
Rw *or* **Gw**	Com. Saint *or* *esp.* Matt. 25. 31–end *also* Prov. 31. 10–end	2 Macc. 6. 18–end *or* Rev. 3. 1–6, 14–31 Ps. 11 *or* Ps. 15 Luke 19. 1–10	Ps. 48; ***52*** *alt.* Ps. 32; ***36*** Isa. 10. 5–19 Matt. 7. 13–end	Ps. ***67***; 72 *alt.* Ps. 33 Dan. 8. 15–end Rev. 11. 1–14
19 Wednesday	**Hilda, Abbess of Whitby, 680** *Mechtild, Béguine of Magdeburg, Mystic, 1280*			
Rw *or* **Gw**	Com. Religious *or* *esp.* Isa. 61.10 – 62.5	2 Macc. 7. 1, 20–31 *or* Rev. ch. 4 Ps. 116. 10–end *or* Ps. 150 Luke 19. 11–28	Ps. ***56***; 57 *alt.* Ps. 34 Isa. 10. 20–32 Matt. 8. 1–13	Ps. 73 *alt.* Ps. 119. 33–56 Dan. 9. 1–19 Rev. 11. 15–end
20 Thursday	**Edmund, King of the East Angles, Martyr, 870** *Priscilla Lydia Sellon, a Restorer of the Religious Life in the Church of England, 1876*			
R *or* **Gr**	Com. Martyr *or* *also* Prov. 20. 28; 21. 1–4, 7	1 Macc. 2. 15–29 *or* Rev. 5. 1–10 Ps. 129 *or* Ps. 149. 1–5 Luke 19. 41–44	Ps. 61; ***62*** *alt.* Ps. 37† Isa. 10.33 – 11.9 Matt. 8. 14–22	Ps. 74; ***76*** *alt.* Ps. 39; ***40*** Dan. 9. 20–end Rev. ch. 12

	Calendar and Holy Communion	Morning Prayer	Evening Prayer	NOTES
	Britius, Bishop of Tours, 444			
Gw	Com. Bishop	Isa. 7. 1–17 Matt. 5. 38–end	Dan. ch. 6 Rev. ch. 8	
G		Isa. 8. 1–15 Matt. 6. 1–18	Dan. 7. 1–14 Rev. 9. 1–12	
	Machutus, Bishop, Apostle of Brittany, c. 564			
Gw	Com. Bishop	Isa. 8.16 - 9.7 Matt. 6. 19–end	Dan. 7. 15–end Rev. 9. 13–end **ct**	
	THE TWENTY-SECOND SUNDAY AFTER TRINITY			
G	Gen. 45. 1–7, 15 Ps. 133 Phil. 1. 3–11 Matt. 18. 21–end	Ps. 132 1 Sam. 16. 1–13 Matt. 13. 44–52	Ps. [93]; 97 Dan. ch. 6 Matt. 13. 1–9, 18–23	
	Hugh, Bishop of Lincoln, 1200			
Gw	Com. Bishop	Isa. 9.8 - 10.4 Matt. 7. 1–12	Dan. 8. 1–14 Rev. ch. 10	
G		Isa. 10. 5–19 Matt. 7. 13–end	Dan. 8. 15–end Rev. 11. 1–14	
G		Isa. 10. 20–32 Matt. 8. 1–13	Dan. 9. 1–19 Rev. 11. 15–end	
	Edmund, King of the East Angles, Martyr, 870			
Gr	Com. Martyr	Isa. 10.33 - 11.9 Matt. 8. 14–22	Dan. 9. 20–end Rev. ch. 12	

		Sunday Principal Service Weekday Eucharist	Third Service Morning Prayer	Second Service Evening Prayer
21 Friday				
R *or* **G**		1 Macc. 4. 36–37, 52–59 *or* Rev. 10. 8–11 Ps. 122 *or* Ps. 119. 65–72 Luke 19. 45–48	Ps. ***63***; 65 *alt.* Ps. 31 Isa. 11.10 - 12.end Matt. 8. 23–end	Ps. 77 *alt.* Ps. 35 Dan. 10.1 - 11.1 Rev. 13. 1–10
22 Saturday	*Cecilia, Martyr at Rome,* c. *230*			
R *or* **G**		1 Macc. 6. 1–13 *or* Rev. 11. 4–12 Ps. 124 *or* Ps. 144. 1–9 Luke 20. 27–40	Ps. 78. 1–39 *alt.* Ps. 41; ***42***; 43 Isa. 13. 1–13 Matt. 9. 1–17	Ps. 78. 40–end *alt.* Ps. 45; ***46*** Dan. ch. 12 Rev. 13. 11–end **ct** *or First EP of Christ the King* Ps. 99; 100 Isa. 10.33 - 11.9 1 Tim. 6. 11–16 **R** *or* **W ct**
23 Sunday	**CHRIST THE KING** The Sunday Next Before Advent			
R *or* **W**		Jer. 23. 1–6 Ps. 46 Col. 1. 11–20 Luke 23. 33–43	*MP*: Ps. 29; 110 Zech. 6. 9–end Rev. 11. 15–18	*EP*: Ps. 72 (*or* 72. 1–7) 1 Sam. 8. 4–20 John 18. 33–37
24 Monday				
R *or* **G** **DEL 34**		Dan. 1. 1–6, 8–20 *Canticle*: Bless the Lord Luke 21. 1–4	Ps. 92; ***96*** *alt.* Ps. 44 Isa. 14. 3–20 Matt. 9. 18–34	Ps. ***80***; 81 *alt.* Ps. ***47***; 49 Isa. 40. 1–11 Rev. 14. 1–13
25 Tuesday	*Catherine of Alexandria, Martyr, 4th century; Isaac Watts, Hymn Writer, 1748*			
R *or* **G**		Dan. 2. 31–45 *Canticle*: Benedicite 1–3 Luke 21. 5–11	Ps. ***97***; 98; 100 *alt.* Ps. ***48***; 52 Isa. ch. 17 Matt. 9.35 - 10.15	Ps. 99; ***101*** *alt.* Ps. 50 Isa. 40. 12–26 Rev. 14.14 - 15.end
26 Wednesday				
R *or* **G**		Dan. 5. 1–6, 13–14, 16–17, 23–28 *Canticle*: Benedicite 4–5 Luke 21. 12–19	Ps. 110; 111; ***112*** *alt.* Ps. 119. 57–80 Isa. ch. 19 Matt. 10. 16–33	Ps. 121; ***122***; 123; 124 *alt.* Ps. ***59***; 60; (67) Isa. 40.27 - 41.7 Rev. 16. 1–11
27 Thursday				
R *or* **G**		Dan. 6. 12–end *Canticle*: Benedicite 6–8a Luke 21. 20–28	Ps. ***125***; 126; 127; 128 *alt.* Ps. 56; ***57***; (63†) Isa. 21. 1–12 Matt. 10.34 - 11.1	Ps. 131; 132; ***133*** *alt.* Ps. 61; ***62***; 64 Isa. 41. 8–20 Rev. 16. 12–end
28 Friday				
R *or* **G**		Dan. 7. 2–14 *Canticle*: Benedicite 8b–10a Luke 21. 29–33	Ps. 139 *alt.* Ps. ***51***; 54 Isa. 22. 1–14 Matt. 11. 2–19	Ps. ***146***; 147 *alt.* Ps. 38 Isa. 41.21 - 42.9 Rev. ch. 17

	Calendar and Holy Communion	Morning Prayer	Evening Prayer	NOTES
G		Isa. 11.10 - 12.end Matt. 8. 23-end	Dan. 10.1 - 11.1 Rev. 13. 1-10	
	Cecilia, Martyr at Rome, c. 230			
Gr	Com. Virgin Martyr	Isa. 13. 1-13 Matt. 9. 1-17	Dan. ch. 12 Rev. 13. 11-end **ct**	
	THE SUNDAY NEXT BEFORE ADVENT To celebrate Christ the King, see *Common Worship* provision.			
G	Jer. 23. 5-8 Ps. 85. 8-end Col. 1. 13-20 John 6. 5-14	Ps. 29; 110 Zech. 6. 9-end Rev. 11. 15-18	Ps. 72 (*or* 72. 1-7) 1 Sam. 8. 4-20 John 18. 33-37	
G		Isa. 14. 3-20 Matt. 9. 18-34	Isa. 40. 1-11 Rev. 14. 1-13	
	Catherine of Alexandria, Martyr, 4th century			
Gr	Com. Virgin Martyr	Isa. ch. 17 Matt. 9.35 - 10.15	Isa. 40. 12-26 Rev. 14.14 - 15.end	
G		Isa. ch. 19 Matt. 10. 16-33	Isa. 40.27 - 41.7 Rev. 16. 1-11	
G		Isa. 21. 1-12 Matt. 10.34 - 11.1	Isa. 41. 8-20 Rev. 16. 12-end	
G		Isa. 22. 1-14 Matt. 11. 2-19	Isa. 41.21 - 42.9 Rev. ch. 17	

		Sunday Principal Service Weekday Eucharist	Third Service Morning Prayer	Second Service Evening Prayer
29 Saturday				
R *or* **G**		Dan. 7. 15–27 *Canticle*: Benedicite 10b–end Luke 21. 34–36	Ps. 145 *alt.* Ps. 68 Isa. ch. 24 Matt. 11. 20–end	Ps. 148; 149; ***150*** *alt.* Ps. 65; ***66*** Isa. 42. 10–17 Rev. ch. 18 **P ct**
	Day of Intercession and Thanksgiving for the Missionary Work of the Church	Isa. 49. 1–6; Isa. 52. 7–10; Mic. 4. 1–5 Acts 17. 12–end; 2 Cor. 5. 14 - 6.2; Eph. 2. 13–end Ps. 2; 46; 47 Matt. 5. 13–16; Matt. 28. 16–end; John 17. 20–end		
30 Sunday	**THE FIRST SUNDAY OF ADVENT** (Andrew transferred to 1 December) *Common Worship* Year A begins			
P		Isa. 2. 1–5 Ps. 122 Rom. 13. 11–end Matt. 24. 36–44	Ps. 44 Mic. 4. 1–7 1 Thess. 5. 1–11	Ps. 9 (*or* 9. 1–8) Isa. 52. 1–12 Matt. 24. 15–28 *or First EP of Andrew the Apostle* Ps. 48 Isa. 49. 1–9a 1 Cor. 4. 9–16 **R ct**

December 2025

1 Monday	**ANDREW THE APOSTLE**			
R		Isa. 52. 7–10 Ps. 19. 1–6 Rom. 10. 12–18 Matt. 4. 18–22	*MP*: Ps. 47; 147. 1–12 Ezek. 47. 1–12 *or* Ecclus. 14. 20–end John 12. 20–32	*EP*: Ps. 87; 96 Zech. 8. 20–end John 1. 35–42
2 Tuesday	Daily Eucharistic Lectionary Year 2 begins			
P		Isa. 11. 1–10 Ps. 72. 1–4, 18–19 Luke 10. 21–24	Ps. ***80***; 82 *alt.* Ps. ***5***; 6; (8) Isa. 26. 1–13 Matt. 12. 22–37	Ps. ***74***; 75 *alt.* Ps. ***9***; 10† Isa. 43. 1–13 Rev. ch. 20
3 Wednesday	*Francis Xavier, Missionary, Apostle of the Indies, 1552*			
P		Isa. 25. 6–10a Ps. 23 Matt. 15. 29–37	Ps. 5; ***7*** *alt.* Ps. 119. 1–32 Isa. 28. 1–13 Matt. 12. 38–end	Ps. 76; ***77*** *alt.* Ps. ***11***; 12; 13 Isa. 43. 14–end Rev. 21. 1–8
4 Thursday	*John of Damascus, Monk, Teacher, c. 749; Nicholas Ferrar, Deacon, Founder of the Little Gidding Community, 1637*			
P		Isa. 26. 1–6 Ps. 118. 18–27a Matt. 7. 21, 24–27	Ps. ***42***; 43 *alt.* Ps. 14; ***15***; 16 Isa. 28. 14–end Matt. 13. 1–23	Ps. ***40***; 46 *alt.* Ps. 18† Isa. 44. 1–8 Rev. 21. 9–21
5 Friday				
P		Isa. 29. 17–end Ps. 27. 1–4, 16–17 Matt. 9. 27–31	Ps. ***25***; 26 *alt.* Ps. 17; ***19*** Isa. 29. 1–14 Matt. 13. 24–43	Ps. 16; ***17*** *alt.* Ps. 22 Isa. 44. 9–23 Rev. 21.22 - 22.5

	Calendar and Holy Communion	Morning Prayer	Evening Prayer	NOTES
G		Isa. ch. 24 Matt. 11. 20–end	Isa. 42. 10–17 Rev. ch. 18 **P ct**	
	To celebrate the Day of Intercession and Thanksgiving for the Missionary Work of the Church, see *Common Worship* provision.			
	THE FIRST SUNDAY OF ADVENT (Andrew transferred to 1 December) Advent 1 Collect until Christmas Eve			
P	Mic. 4. 1–4, 6–7 Ps. 25. 1–9 Rom. 13. 8–14 Matt. 21. 1–13	Ps. 44 Isa. 2. 1–5 1 Thess. 5. 1–11	Ps. 9 (*or* 9. 1–8) Isa. 52. 1–12 Matt. 24. 15–28 *or First EP of Andrew the Apostle* Ps. 48 Isa. 49. 1–9a 1 Cor. 4. 9–16 **R ct**	
	ANDREW THE APOSTLE			
R	Zech. 8. 20–end Ps. 92. 1–5 Rom. 10. 9–end Matt. 4. 18–22	(Ps. 47; 147. 1–12) Ezek. 47. 1–12 *or* Ecclus. 14. 20–end John 12. 20–32	(Ps. 87; 96) Isa. 52. 7–10 John 1. 35–42	
P		Isa. 26. 1–13 Matt. 12. 22–37	Isa. 43. 1–13 Rev. ch. 20	
P		Isa. 28. 1–13 Matt. 12. 38–end	Isa. 43. 14–end Rev. 21. 1–8	
P		Isa. 28. 14–end Matt. 13. 1–23	Isa. 44. 1–8 Rev. 21. 9–21	
P		Isa. 29. 1–14 Matt. 13. 24–43	Isa. 44. 9–23 Rev. 21.22 - 22.5	

			Sunday Principal Service Weekday Eucharist	Third Service Morning Prayer	Second Service Evening Prayer
6 Saturday		**Nicholas, Bishop of Myra, *c.* 326**			
	Pw	Com. Bishop *or* *also* Isa. 61. 1–3 1 Tim. 6. 6–11 Mark 10. 13–16	Isa. 30. 19–21, 23–26 Ps. 146. 4–9 Matt. 9.35 - 10.1, 6–8	Ps. ***9***; 10 *alt.* Ps. 20; 21; ***23*** Isa. 29. 15–end Matt. 13. 44–end	Ps. ***27***; 28 *alt.* Ps. ***24***; 25 Isa. 44.24 - 45.13 Rev. 22. 6–end **ct**
7 Sunday		**THE SECOND SUNDAY OF ADVENT**			
	P		Isa. 11. 1–10 Ps. 72. 1–7, 18–19 (*or* 72. 1–7) Rom. 15. 4–13 Matt. 3. 1–12	Ps. 80 Amos ch. 7 Luke 1. 5–20	Ps. 11; [28] 1 Kings 18. 17–39 John 1. 19–28
8 Monday		**The Conception of the Blessed Virgin Mary**			
	Pw	Com. BVM *or*	Isa. ch. 35 Ps. 85. 7–end Luke 5. 17–26	Ps. 44 *alt.* Ps. 27; ***30*** Isa. 30. 1–18 Matt. 14. 1–12	Ps. ***144***; 146 *alt.* Ps. 26; ***28***; 29 Isa. 45. 14–end 1 Thess. ch. 1
9 Tuesday					
	P		Isa. 40. 1–11 Ps. 96. 1, 10–end Matt. 18. 12–14	Ps. ***56***; 57 *alt.* Ps. 32; ***36*** Isa. 30. 19–end Matt. 14. 13–end	Ps. ***11***; 12; 13 *alt.* Ps. 33 Isa. ch. 46 1 Thess. 2. 1–12
10 Wednesday		Ember Day*			
	P		Isa. 40. 25–end Ps. 103. 8–13 Matt. 11. 28–end	Ps. ***62***; 63 *alt.* Ps. 34 Isa. ch. 31 Matt. 15. 1–20	Ps. ***10***; 14 *alt.* Ps. 119. 33–56 Isa. ch. 47 1 Thess. 2. 13–end
11 Thursday					
	P		Isa. 41. 13–20 Ps. 145. 1, 8–13 Matt. 11. 11–15	Ps. 53; ***54***; 60 *alt.* Ps. 37† Isa. ch. 32 Matt. 15. 21–28	Ps. 73 *alt.* Ps. 39; ***40*** Isa. 48. 1–11 1 Thess. ch. 3
12 Friday		Ember Day*			
	P		Isa. 48. 17–19 Ps. 1 Matt. 11. 16–19	Ps. 85; ***86*** *alt.* Ps. 31 Isa. 33. 1–22 Matt. 15. 29–end	Ps. 82; ***90*** *alt.* Ps. 35 Isa. 48. 12–end 1 Thess. 4. 1–12
13 Saturday		**Lucy, Martyr at Syracuse, 304** Ember Day* *Samuel Johnson, Moralist, 1784*			
	Pr	Com. Martyr *or* *also* Wisd. 3. 1–7 2 Cor. 4. 6–15	Ecclus. 48. 1–4, 9–11 *or* 2 Kings 2. 9–12 Ps. 80. 1–4, 18–19 Matt. 17. 10–13	Ps. 145 *alt.* Ps. 41; ***42***; 43 Isa. ch. 35 Matt. 16. 1–12	Ps. 93; ***94*** *alt.* Ps. 45; ***46*** Isa. 49. 1–13 1 Thess. 4. 13–end **ct**

*For Ember Day provision, see p. 11.

	Calendar and Holy Communion	Morning Prayer	Evening Prayer	NOTES
	Nicholas, Bishop of Myra, c. 326			
Pw	Com. Bishop	Isa. 29. 15–end Matt. 13. 44–end	Isa. 44.24 – 45.13 Rev. 22. 6–end	
			ct	
	THE SECOND SUNDAY IN ADVENT			
P	2 Kings 22. 8–10; 23. 1–3 Ps. 50. 1–6 Rom. 15. 4–13 Luke 21. 25–33	Ps. 80 Amos ch. 7 Luke 1. 5–20	Ps. 11; [28] 1 Kings 18. 17–39 Matt. 3. 1–12	
	The Conception of the Blessed Virgin Mary			
Pw		Isa. 30. 1–18 Matt. 14. 1–12	Isa. 45. 14–end 1 Thess. ch. 1	
P		Isa. 30. 19–end Matt. 14. 13–end	Isa. ch. 46 1 Thess. 2. 1–12	
P		Isa. ch. 31 Matt. 15. 1–20	Isa. ch. 47 1 Thess. 2. 13–end	
P		Isa. ch. 32 Matt. 15. 21–28	Isa. 48. 1–11 1 Thess. ch. 3	
P		Isa. 33. 1–22 Matt. 15. 29–end	Isa. 48. 12–end 1 Thess. 4. 1–12	
	Lucy, Martyr at Syracuse, 304 Com. Virgin Martyr			
Pr		Isa. ch. 35 Matt. 16. 1–12	Isa. 49. 1–13 1 Thess. 4. 13–end	
			ct	

		Sunday Principal Service Weekday Eucharist	Third Service Morning Prayer	Second Service Evening Prayer
14 Sunday	**THE THIRD SUNDAY OF ADVENT**			
P		Isa. 35. 1–10 Ps. 146. 4–10 *or Canticle*: Magnificat James 5. 7–10 Matt. 11. 2–11	Ps. 68. 1–19 Zeph. 3. 14–end Phil. 4. 4–7	Ps. 12; [14] Isa. 5. 8–end Acts 13. 13–41 *Gospel*: John 5. 31–40
15 Monday				
P		Num. 24. 2–7, 15–17 Ps. 25. 3–8 Matt. 21. 23–27	Ps. 40 *alt*. Ps. 44 Isa. 38. 1–8, 21–22 Matt. 16. 13–end	Ps. 25; ***26*** *alt*. Ps. ***47***; 49 Isa. 49. 14–25 1 Thess. 5. 1–11
16 Tuesday				
P		Zeph. 3. 1–2, 9–13 Ps. 34. 1–6, 21–22 Matt. 21. 28–32	Ps. ***70***; 74 *alt*. Ps. ***48***; 52 Isa. 38. 9–20 Matt. 17. 1–13	Ps. ***50***; 54 *alt*. Ps. 50 Isa. ch. 50 1 Thess. 5. 12–end
17 Wednesday	O Sapientia *Eglantyne Jebb, Social Reformer, Founder of 'Save the Children', 1928*			
P		Gen. 49. 2, 8–10 Ps. 72. 1–5, 18–19 Matt. 1. 1–17	Ps. ***75***; 96 *alt*. Ps. 119. 57–80 Isa. ch. 39 Matt. 17. 14–21	Ps. 25; ***82*** *alt*. Ps. ***59***; 60; (67) Isa. 51. 1–8 2 Thess. ch. 1
18 Thursday				
P		Jer. 23. 5–8 Ps. 72. 1–2, 12–13, 18–end Matt. 1. 18–24	Ps. ***76***; 97 *alt*. Ps. 56; ***57***; (63†) Zeph. 1.1 – 2.3 Matt. 17. 22–end	Ps. 44 *alt*. Ps. 61; ***62***; 64 Isa. 51. 9–16 2 Thess. ch. 2
19 Friday				
P		Judg. 13. 2–7, 24–end Ps. 71. 3–8 Luke 1. 5–25	Ps. 144; ***146*** Zeph. 3. 1–13 Matt. 18. 1–20	Ps. 10; ***57*** Isa. 51. 17–end 2 Thess. ch. 3
20 Saturday				
P		Isa. 7. 10–14 Ps. 24. 1–6 Luke 1. 26–38	Ps. ***46***; 95 Zeph. 3. 14–end Matt. 18. 21–end	Ps. ***4***; 9 Isa. 52. 1–12 Jude **ct**
21 Sunday	**THE FOURTH SUNDAY OF ADVENT**			
P		Isa. 7. 10–16 Ps. 80. 1–8, 18–20 (*or* 80. 1–8) Rom. 1. 1–7 Matt. 1. 18–end	Ps. 144 Mic. 5. 2–5a Luke 1. 26–38	Ps. 113; [126] 1 Sam. 1. 1–20 Rev. 22. 6–end *Gospel*: Luke 1. 39–45

	Calendar and Holy Communion	Morning Prayer	Evening Prayer	NOTES
	THE THIRD SUNDAY IN ADVENT			
P	Isa. ch. 35 Ps. 80. 1–7 1 Cor. 4. 1–5 Matt. 11. 2–10	Ps. 68. 1–19 Zeph. 3. 14–end James 5. 7–10	Ps. 12; [14] Isa. 5. 8–end Acts 13. 13–41	
P		Isa. 38. 1–8, 21–22 Matt. 16. 13–end	Isa. 49. 14–25 1 Thess. 5. 1–11	
	O Sapientia			
P		Isa. 38. 9–20 Matt. 17. 1–13	Isa. ch. 50 1 Thess. 5. 12–end	
	Ember Day			
P	Ember CEG	Isa. ch. 39 Matt. 17. 14–21	Isa. 51. 1–8 2 Thess. ch. 1	
P		Zeph. 1.1 – 2.3 Matt. 17. 22–end	Isa. 51. 9–16 2 Thess. ch. 2	
	Ember Day			
P	Ember CEG	Zeph. 3. 1–13 Matt. 18. 1–20	Isa. 51. 17–end 2 Thess. ch. 3	
	Ember Day			
P	Ember CEG	Zeph. 3. 14–end Matt. 18. 21–end	Isa. 52. 1–12 Jude **ct**	
	THE FOURTH SUNDAY OF ADVENT (Thomas transferred to 22 December)			
P	Isa. 40. 1–9 Ps. 145. 17–end Phil. 4. 4–7 John 1. 19–28	Ps. 144 Mic. 5. 2–5a Luke 1. 26–38	Ps. 113; [126] 1 Sam. 1. 1–20 Rev. 22. 6–end *or First EP of Thomas* Ps. 27 Isa. ch. 35 Heb. 10.35 – 11.1 **R ct**	

		Sunday Principal Service Weekday Eucharist	Third Service Morning Prayer	Second Service Evening Prayer
22 Monday*				
P		1 Sam. 1. 24-end Ps. 113 Luke 1. 46-56	Ps. ***124***; 125; 126; 127 Mal. 1. 1, 6-end Matt. 19. 1-12	Ps. 24; ***48*** Isa. 52.13 - 53.end 1 Pet. 1. 1-15
23 Tuesday				
P		Mal. 3. 1-4; 4. 5-end Ps. 25. 3-9 Luke 1. 57-66	Ps. 128; 129; ***130***; 131 Mal. 2. 1-16 Matt. 19. 13-15	Ps. 89. 1-37 Isa. ch. 54 2 Pet. 1.16 - 2.3
24 Wednesday	**CHRISTMAS EVE**			
P		*Morning Eucharist* 2 Sam. 7. 1-5, 8-11, 16 Ps. 89. 2, 19-27 Acts 13. 16-26 Luke 1. 67-79	Ps. ***45***; 113 Mal. 2.17 - 3.12 Matt. 19. 16-end	Ps. 85 Zech. ch. 2 Rev. 1. 1-8
25 Thursday	**CHRISTMAS DAY**			
𝔚	*Any of the following sets of readings may be used on the evening of Christmas Eve and on Christmas Day. Set III should be used at some service during the celebration.*	*I* Isa. 9. 2-7 Ps. 96 Titus 2. 11-14 Luke 2. 1-14 [15-20] *II* Isa. 62. 6-end Ps. 97 Titus 3. 4-7 Luke 2. [1-7] 8-20 *III* Isa. 52. 7-10 Ps. 98 Heb. 1. 1-4 [5-12] John 1. 1-14	*MP*: Ps. ***110***; 117 Isa. 62. 1-5 Matt. 1. 18-end	*EP*: Ps. 8 Isa. 65. 17-25 Phil. 2. 5-11 *or* Luke 2. 1-20 *if it has not been used at the principal service of the day*
26 Friday	**STEPHEN, DEACON, FIRST MARTYR**			
R		2 Chron. 24. 20-22 *or* Acts 7. 51-end Ps. 119. 161-168 Acts 7. 51-end *or* Gal. 2. 16b-20 Matt. 10. 17-22	*MP*: Ps. ***13***; 31. 1-8; 150 Jer. 26. 12-15 Acts ch. 6	*EP*: Ps. 57; ***86*** Gen. 4. 1-10 Matt. 23. 34-end
27 Saturday	**JOHN, APOSTLE AND EVANGELIST**			
W		Exod. 33. 7-11a Ps. 117 1 John ch. 1 John 21. 19b-end	*MP*: Ps. ***21***; 147. 13-end Exod. 33. 12-end 1 John 2. 1-11	*EP*: Ps. 97 Isa. 6. 1-8 1 John 5. 1-12

*Thomas the Apostle may be celebrated on 22 December this year instead of 3 July.

	Calendar and Holy Communion	Morning Prayer	Evening Prayer	NOTES
	THOMAS THE APOSTLE (transferred from 21 December)			
R	Job 42. 1–6 Ps. 139. 1–11 Eph. 2. 19–end John 20. 24–end	(Ps. 92; 146) 2 Sam. 15. 17–21 *or* Ecclus. ch. 2 John 11. 1–16	(Ps. 139) Hab. 2. 1–4 1 Pet. 1. 3–12	
P		Mal. 2. 1–16 Matt. 19. 13–15	Isa. ch. 54 2 Pet. 1.16 – 2.3	
	CHRISTMAS EVE			
P	Collect (1) Christmas Eve (2) Advent 1 Mic. 5. 2–5a Ps. 24 Titus 3. 3–7 Luke 2. 1–14	Mal. 2.17 – 3.12 Matt. 19. 16–end	Zech. ch. 2 Rev. 1. 1–8	
	CHRISTMAS DAY			
W	Isa. 9. 2–7 Ps. 98 Heb. 1. 1–12 John 1. 1–14	Ps. 110; 117 Isa. 62. 1–5 Matt. 1. 18–end	Ps. 8 Isa. 65. 17–25 Phil. 2. 5–11 *or* Luke 2. 1–20	
	STEPHEN, DEACON, FIRST MARTYR			
R	Collect (1) Stephen (2) Christmas 2 Chron. 24. 20–22 Ps. 119. 161–168 Acts 7. 55–end Matt. 23. 34–end	(Ps. 13; 31. 1–8; 150) Jer. 26. 12–15 Acts ch. 6	(Ps. 57; 86) Gen. 4. 1–10 Matt. 10. 17–22	
	JOHN, APOSTLE AND EVANGELIST			
W	Collect (1) John (2) Christmas Exod. 33. 18–end Ps. 92. 11–end 1 John ch. 1 John 21. 19b–end	(Ps. 21; 147. 13–end) Exod. 33. 7–11a 1 John 2. 1–11	(Ps. 97) Isa. 6. 1–8 1 John 5. 1–12	

		Sunday Principal Service Weekday Eucharist	Third Service Morning Prayer	Second Service Evening Prayer
28 Sunday	**THE HOLY INNOCENTS** (or transferred to 29 December)			
R		Jer. 31. 15–17 Ps. 124 1 Cor. 1. 26–29 Matt. 2. 13–18	*MP*: Ps. ***36***; 146 Baruch 4. 21–27 *or* Gen. 37. 13–20 Matt. 18. 1–10	*EP*: Ps. 123; ***128*** Isa. 49. 14–25 Mark 10. 13–16
	or, for The First Sunday of Christmas:			
W		Isa. 63. 7–9 Ps. 148 (*or* 148. 7–end) Heb. 2. 10–end Matt. 2. 13–end	Ps. 105. 1–11 Isa. 35. 1–6 Gal. 3. 23–end	Ps. 132 Isa. 49. 7–13 Phil. 2. 1–11 *Gospel*: Luke 2. 41–52
29 Monday	**Thomas Becket, Archbishop of Canterbury, Martyr, 1170***			
Wr	Com. Martyr *or* *esp.* Matt. 10. 28–33 *also* Ecclus. 51. 1–8	1 John 2. 3–11 Ps. 96. 1–4 Luke 2. 22–35	Ps. ***19***; 20 Jonah ch. 1 Col. 1. 1–14	Ps. 131; ***132*** Isa. 57. 15–end John 1. 1–18
30 Tuesday				
W		1 John 2. 12–17 Ps. 96. 7–10 Luke 2. 36–40	Ps. 111; 112; ***113*** Jonah ch. 2 Col. 1. 15–23	Ps. ***65***; 84 Isa. 59. 1–15a John 1. 19–28
31 Wednesday	*John Wyclif, Reformer, 1384*			
W		1 John 2. 18–21 Ps. 96. 1, 11–end John 1. 1–18	Ps. 102 Jonah chs 3 & 4 Col. 1.24 – 2.7	Ps. ***90***; 148 Isa. 59. 15b–end John 1. 29–34 *or First EP of The Naming of Jesus* Ps. 148 Jer. 23. 1–6 Col. 2. 8–15 **ct**

*Thomas Becket may be celebrated on 7 July instead of 29 December.

	Calendar and Holy Communion	Morning Prayer	Evening Prayer
	THE HOLY INNOCENTS		
R	Collect (1) Innocents (2) Christmas Jer. 31. 10–17 Ps. 123 Rev. 14. 1–5 Matt. 2. 13–18	Ps. 36; 146 Baruch 4. 21–27 *or* Gen. 37. 13–20 Matt. 18. 1–10	Ps. 124; 128 Isa. 49. 14–25 Mark 10. 13–16
	or, for The Sunday after Christmas Day:		
W	Isa. 62. 10–12 Ps. 45. 1–7 Gal. 4. 1–7 Matt. 1. 18–end	Ps. 105. 1–11 Isa. 35. 1–6 Gal. 3. 23–end	Ps. 132 Isa. 49. 7–13 Phil. 2. 1–11
W		Jonah ch. 1 Col. 1. 1–14	Isa. 57. 15–end John 1. 1–18
W		Jonah ch. 2 Col. 1. 15–23	Isa. 59. 1–15a John 1. 19–28
	Silvester, Bishop of Rome, 335		
W	Com. Bishop	Jonah chs 3 & 4 Col. 1.24 - 2.7	Isa. 59. 15b–end John 1. 29–34 *or First EP of The Circumcision of Christ* (Ps. 148) Jer. 23. 1–6 Col. 2. 8–15 **ct**

NOTES

The *Common Worship* Additional Weekday Lectionary

The Additional Weekday Lectionary provides two readings on a one-year cycle for each day (except for Sundays, Principal Feasts and Holy Days, Festivals and Holy Week). They 'stand alone' and are intended particularly for use in those churches and cathedrals that attract occasional rather than regular congregations. The Additional Weekday Lectionary has been designed to complement rather than replace the existing Weekday Lectionary. Thus a church with a regular congregation in the morning and a congregation made up mainly of visitors in the evening would continue to use the Weekday Lectionary in the morning but might choose to use this Additional Weekday Lectionary for Evening Prayer.

Psalms are not provided, since the Weekday Lectionary already offers a variety of approaches with regard to psalmody. This Lectionary is not intended for use at the Eucharist; the Daily Eucharistic Lectionary is already authorized for that purpose.

On Sundays, Principal Feasts, other Principal Holy Days, Festivals, and in Holy Week, where no readings are provided in this table, the lectionary provision in the main part of this volume should be used.

December 2024

Date		Old Testament	New Testament
1	S	THE FIRST SUNDAY OF ADVENT	
2	M	Mal. 3. 1–6	Matt. 3. 1–6
3	Tu	Zeph. 3. 14–end	1 Thess. 4. 13–end
4	W	Isa. 65.17 – 66.2	Matt. 24. 1–14
5	Th	Mic. 5. 2–5a	John 3. 16–21
6	F	Isa. 66. 18–end	Luke 13. 22–30
7	Sa	Mic. 7. 8–15	Rom. 15.30 – 16.7, 25–end
8	S	THE SECOND SUNDAY OF ADVENT	
9	M	Jer. 7. 1–11	Phil. 4. 4–9
10	Tu	Dan. 7. 9–14	Matt. 24. 15–28
11	W	Amos 9. 11–end	Rom. 13. 8–14
12	Th	Jer. 23. 5–8	Mark 11. 1–11
13	F	Jer. 33. 14–22	Luke 21. 25–36
14	Sa	Zech. 14. 4–11	Rev. 22. 1–7
15	S	THE THIRD SUNDAY OF ADVENT	
16	M	Isa. 40. 1–11	Matt. 3. 1–12
17	Tu	Ecclus. 24. 1–9 *or* Prov. 6. 22–31	1 Cor. 2. 1–13
18	W	Exod. 3. 1–6	Acts 7. 20–36
19	Th	Isa. 11. 1–9	Rom. 15. 7–13
20	F	Isa. 22. 21–23	Rev. 3. 7–13
21	Sa	Num. 24. 15b–19	Rev. 22. 10–21
22	S	THE FOURTH SUNDAY OF ADVENT	
23	M	Isa. 7. 10–15	Matt. 1. 18–23
24	Tu	*At Evening Prayer the readings for Christmas Eve are used. At other services the following readings are used:* Isa. 29. 13–18	1 John 4. 7–16
25	W	**CHRISTMAS DAY**	
26	Th	STEPHEN	
27	F	JOHN THE EVANGELIST	
28	Sa	THE HOLY INNOCENTS	
29	S	THE FIRST SUNDAY OF CHRISTMAS	
30	M	Isa. 9. 2–7	John 8. 12–20
31	Tu	Eccles. 3. 1–13	Rev. 21. 1–8

January 2025

Date		Old Testament	New Testament
1	W	**NAMING AND CIRCUMCISION OF JESUS**	
2	Th	Isa. 66. 6–14	Matt. 12. 46–50
3	F	Deut. 6. 4–15	John 10. 31–end
4	Sa	Isa. 63. 7–16 *Where, for pastoral reasons, The Epiphany is celebrated on Sunday 5 January, the readings for the Eve of Epiphany are used at Evening Prayer.*	Gal. 3.23 – 4.7
5	S	THE SECOND SUNDAY OF CHRISTMAS (*or The Epiphany*) *Where The Epiphany is celebrated on Monday 6 January, the readings for the Eve of Epiphany are used at Evening Prayer.*	
6	M	**THE EPIPHANY** *Where, for pastoral reasons, The Epiphany is celebrated on 5 January, the following readings are used:* Isa. ch. 12	2 Cor. 2. 12–end
7	Tu	Gen. 25. 19–end	Eph. 1. 1–6
8	W	Joel 2. 28–end	Eph. 1. 7–14
9	Th	Prov. 8. 12–21	Eph. 1. 15–end
10	F	Gen. 19. 15–29	Eph. 2. 1–10
11	Sa	*At Evening Prayer the readings for the Eve of the Baptism of Christ are used. At other services the following readings are used:* Gen. 17. 1–14	Eph. 2. 11–end
12	S	THE BAPTISM OF CHRIST (The First Sunday of Epiphany)	
13	M	Isa. 41. 14–20	John 1. 29–34
14	Tu	Exod. 17. 1–7	Acts 8. 26–end
15	W	Exod. 15. 1–19	Col. 2. 8–15
16	Th	Zech. 6. 9–15	1 Pet. 2. 4–10
17	F	Isa. 51. 7–16	Gal. 6. 14–18
18	Sa	Lev. 16. 11–22	Heb. 10. 19–25
19	S	THE SECOND SUNDAY OF EPIPHANY	
20	M	1 Kings 17. 8–16	Mark 8. 1–10
21	Tu	1 Kings 19. 1–9a	Mark 1. 9–15
22	W	1 Kings 19. 9b–18	Mark 9. 2–13
23	Th	Lev. 11. 1–8, 13–19, 41–45	Acts 10. 9–16
24	F	Isa. 49. 8–13	Acts 10. 34–43
25	Sa	THE CONVERSION OF PAUL	
26	S	THE THIRD SUNDAY OF EPIPHANY	
27	M	Ezek. 37. 15–end	John 17. 1–19
28	Tu	Ezek. 20. 39–44	John 17. 20–end
29	W	Neh. 2. 1–10	Rom. 12. 1–8
30	Th	Deut. 26. 16–end	Rom. 14. 1–9
31	F	Lev. 19. 9–28	Rom. 15. 1–7

February 2025

Date		Old Testament	New Testament
1	Sa	Jer. 33. 1–11	1 Pet. 5. 5b–end
2	S	**THE PRESENTATION**	
3	M	Isa. 42. 10–21	Luke 1. 5–25
4	Tu	1 Sam. 4. 12–end	Luke 1. 57–80
5	W	Baruch 5 *or* Hag. 1. 1–11	Mark 1. 1–11
6	Th	Isa. ch. 35	Matt. 11. 2–19
7	F	2 Sam. 11. 1–17	Matt. 14. 1–12
8	Sa	Isa. 43. 15–21	Acts 19. 1–10
9	S	THE FOURTH SUNDAY BEFORE LENT	
10	M	Gen. 1. 26–end	Mark 10. 1–16
11	Tu	Ruth 1. 1–18	1 John 3. 14–end
12	W	1 Sam. 1. 19b–end	Luke 2. 41–end
13	Th	Gen. 47. 1–12	Eph. 3. 14–end
14	F	2 Sam. 1. 17–end	Rom. 8. 28–end
15	Sa	Song of Sol. 2. 8–end	1 Cor. ch. 13
16	S	THE THIRD SUNDAY BEFORE LENT	
17	M	Exod. 23. 1–13	James 2. 1–13
18	Tu	Deut. 10. 12–end	Heb. 13. 1–16
19	W	Isa. 58. 6–end	Matt. 25. 31–end
20	Th	Isa. 42. 1–9	Luke 4. 14–21
21	F	Amos 5. 6–15	Eph. 4. 25–end
22	Sa	Amos 5. 18–24	John 2. 13–22
23	S	THE SECOND SUNDAY BEFORE LENT	
24	M	Isa. 61. 1–9	Mark 6. 1–13
25	Tu	Isa. 52. 1–10	Rom. 10. 5–21
26	W	Isa. 52.13 – 53.6	Rom. 15. 14–21
27	Th	Isa. 53. 4–12	2 Cor. 4. 1–10

28 F Zech. 8. 16–end Matt. 10. 1–15

March 2025

1 Sa Jer. 1. 4–10 Matt. 10. 16–22
2 S THE SUNDAY NEXT BEFORE LENT
3 M 2 Kings 2. 13–22 3 John
4 Tu Judges 14. 5–17 Rev. 10. 4–11
5 W **ASH WEDNESDAY**
6 Th Gen. 2. 7–end Heb. 2. 5–end
7 F Gen. 4. 1–12 Heb. 4. 12–end
8 Sa 2 Kings 22. 11–end Heb. 5. 1–10
9 S THE FIRST SUNDAY OF LENT
10 M Gen. 6. 11–end; 7. 11–16 Luke 4. 14–21
11 Tu Deut. 31. 7–13 1 John 3. 1–10
12 W Gen. 11. 1–9 Matt. 24. 15–28
13 Th Gen. 13. 1–13 1 Pet. 2. 13–end
14 F Gen. 21. 1–8 Luke 9. 18–27
15 Sa Gen. 32. 22–32 2 Pet. 1. 10–end
16 S THE SECOND SUNDAY OF LENT
17 M 1 Chron. 21. 1–17 1 John 2. 1–8
18 Tu Zech. ch. 3 2 Pet. 2. 1–10a
19 W JOSEPH OF NAZARETH
20 Th 2 Chron. 29. 1–11 Mark 11. 15–19
21 F Exod. 19. 1–9a 1 Pet. 1. 1–9
22 Sa Exod. 19. 9b–19 Acts 7. 44–50
23 S THE THIRD SUNDAY OF LENT
24 M Josh. 4. 1–13 Luke 9. 1–11
25 Tu **THE ANNUNCIATION**
26 W Gen. 9. 8–17 1 Pet. 3. 18–end
27 Th Dan. 12. 5–end Mark 13. 21–end
28 F Num. 20. 1–13 1 Cor. 10. 23–end
29 Sa Isa. 43. 14–end Heb. 3. 1–15
30 S THE FOURTH SUNDAY OF LENT **(Mothering Sunday)**
31 M 2 Kings 24.18 – 25.7 1 Cor. 15. 20–34

April 2025

1 Tu Jer. 13. 12–19 Acts 13. 26–35
2 W Jer. 13. 20–27 1 Pet. 1.17 – 2.3
3 Th Jer. 22. 11–19 Luke 11. 37–52
4 F Jer. 17. 1–14 Luke 6. 17–26
5 Sa Ezra ch. 1 2 Cor. 1. 12–19
6 S THE FIFTH SUNDAY OF LENT **(Passiontide begins)**
7 M Joel 2. 12–17 2 John
8 Tu Isa. 58. 1–14 Mark 10. 32–45
9 W Joel 36. 1–12 John 14. 1–14
10 Th Jer. 9. 17–22 Luke 13. 31–35
11 F Lam. 5. 1–3, 19–22 John 12. 20–26
12 Sa Job 17. 6–end John 12. 27–36
13 S PALM SUNDAY
HOLY WEEK
20 S **EASTER DAY**
21 M Isa. 54. 1–14 Rom. 1. 1–7
22 Tu Isa. 51. 1–11 John 5. 19–29
23 W Isa. 26. 1–19 John 20. 1–10
24 Th Isa. 43. 14–21 Rev. 1. 4–end
25 F Isa. 42. 10–17 1 Thess. 5. 1–11
26 Sa Job 14. 1–14 John 21. 1–14
27 S THE SECOND SUNDAY OF EASTER
28 M GEORGE
29 Tu MARK
30 W Hos. 5.15 – 6.6 1 Cor. 15. 1–11

May 2025

1 Th PHILIP AND JAMES
2 F Gen. 6. 9–end 1 Pet. 3. 8–end
3 Sa 1 Sam. 2. 1–8 Matt. 28. 8–15
4 S THE THIRD SUNDAY OF EASTER
5 M Exod. 24. 1–11 Rev. ch. 5
6 Tu Lev. 19. 9–18, 32–end Matt. 5. 38–end
7 W Gen. 3. 8–21 1 Cor. 15. 12–28
8 Th Isa. 33. 13–22 Mark 6. 47–end
9 F Neh. 9. 6–17 Rom. 5. 12–end
10 Sa Isa. 61.10 – 62.5 Luke 24. 1–12
11 S THE FOURTH SUNDAY OF EASTER
12 M Jer. 31. 10–17 Rev. 7. 9–end
13 Tu Job 31. 13–23 Matt. 7. 1–12
14 W MATTHIAS
Where Matthias is celebrated on Monday 24 February:
Gen. 2. 4b–9 1 Cor. 15. 35–49
15 Th Prov. 28. 3–end Mark 10. 17–31
16 F Eccles. 12. 1–8 Rom. 6. 1–11
17 Sa 1 Chron. 29. 10–13 Luke 24. 13–35
18 S THE FIFTH SUNDAY OF EASTER
19 M Gen. 15. 1–18 Rom. 4. 13–end
20 Tu Deut. 8. 1–10 Matt. 6. 19–end
21 W Hos. 13. 4–14 1 Cor. 15. 50–end
22 Th Exod. 3. 1–15 Mark 12. 18–27
23 F Ezek. 36. 33–end Rom. 8. 1–11
24 Sa Isa. 38. 9–20 Luke 24. 33–end
25 S THE SIXTH SUNDAY OF EASTER
26 M Prov. 4. 1–13 Phil. 2. 1–11
27 Tu Isa. 32. 12–end Rom. 5. 1–11
28 W *At Evening Prayer the readings for the Eve of Ascension Day are used. At other services the following readings are used:*
Isa. 43. 1–13 Titus 2.11 – 3.8
29 Th **ASCENSION DAY**
30 F Exod. 35.30 – 36.1 Gal. 5. 13–end
31 Sa THE VISITATION
Where The Visitation is celebrated on 2 July:
Num. 11. 16–17, 24–29 1 Cor. ch. 2

June 2025

1 S THE SEVENTH SUNDAY OF EASTER (Sunday after Ascension Day)
2 M Num. 27. 15–end 1 Cor. ch. 3
3 Tu 1 Sam. 10. 1–10 1 Cor. 12. 1–13
4 W 1 Kings 19. 1–18 Matt. 3. 13–end
5 Th Ezek. 11. 14–20 Matt. 9.35 – 10.20
6 F Ezek. 36. 22–28 Matt. 12. 22–32
7 Sa *At Evening Prayer the readings for the Eve of Pentecost are used. At other services the following readings are used:*
Mic. 3. 1–8 Eph. 6. 10–20
8 S **PENTECOST** (Whit Sunday)
9 M Gen. 12. 1–9 Rom. 4. 13–end
10 Tu Gen. 13. 1–12 Rom. 12. 9–end
11 W BARNABAS
12 Th Gen. 22. 1–18 Heb. 11. 8–19
13 F Isa. 51. 1–8 John 8. 48–end
14 Sa *At Evening Prayer the readings for the Eve of Trinity Sunday are used. At other services the following readings are used:*
Ecclus. 44. 19–23 James 2. 14–26
or Josh. 2. 1–15
15 S **TRINITY SUNDAY**
16 M Exod. 2. 1–10 Heb. 11. 23–31
17 Tu Exod. 2. 11–end Acts 7. 17–29
18 W Exod. 3. 1–12 Acts 7. 30–38
19 Th *Day of Thanksgiving for the Institution of the Holy Communion (Corpus Christi), or, where Corpus Christi is celebrated as a Lesser Festival:*
Exod. 6. 1–13 John 9. 24–38
20 F Exod. 34. 1–10 Mark 7. 1–13
21 Sa Exod. 34. 27–end 2 Cor. 3. 7–end
22 S THE FIRST SUNDAY AFTER TRINITY
23 M Gen. 37. 1–11 Rom. 12. 9–21
24 Tu THE BIRTH OF JOHN THE BAPTIST
25 W Gen. 42. 17–end Matt. 18. 1–14
26 Th Gen. 45. 1–15 Acts 7. 9–16
27 F Gen. 47. 1–12 1 Thess. 5. 12–end
28 Sa Gen. 50. 4–21 Luke 15. 11–end
29 S PETER AND PAUL (THE SECOND SUNDAY AFTER TRINITY)

30 M *Where Peter and Paul are celebrated on Sunday 29 June*:
Isa. ch. 32 | James 3. 13–end

July 2025

1 Tu Prov. 3. 1–18 | Matt. 5. 1–12
2 W Judg. 6. 1–16 | Matt. 5. 13–24
3 Th **THOMAS**
Where Thomas is celebrated on 21 December:
Jer. 6. 9–15 | 1 Tim. 2. 1–6
4 F 1 Sam. 16. 14–end | John 14. 15–end
5 Sa Isa. 6. 1–9 | Rev. 19. 9–end
6 S **THE THIRD SUNDAY AFTER TRINITY**
7 M Exod. 13. 13b–end | Luke 15. 1–10
8 Tu Prov. 1. 20–end | James 5. 13–end
9 W Isa. 5. 8–24 | James 1. 17–25
10 Th Isa. 57. 14–end | John 13. 1–17
11 F Jer. 15. 15–end | Luke 16. 19–31
12 Sa Isa. 25. 1–9 | Acts 2. 22–33
13 S **THE FOURTH SUNDAY AFTER TRINITY**
14 M Exod. 20. 1–17 | Matt. 6. 1–15
15 Tu Prov. 6. 6–19 | Luke 4. 1–14
16 W Isa. 24. 1–15 | 1 Cor. 6. 1–11
17 Th Job ch. 7 | Matt. 7. 21–29
18 F Jer. 20. 7–end | Matt. 27. 27–44
19 Sa Job ch. 28 | Heb. 11.32 – 12.2
20 S **THE FIFTH SUNDAY AFTER TRINITY**
21 M Exod. 32. 1–14 | Col. 3. 1–11
22 Tu **MARY MAGDALENE**
23 W Isa. 26. 1–9 | Rom. 8. 12–27
24 Th Jer. 8.18 – 9.6 | John 13. 21–35
25 F **JAMES**
26 Sa Hos. 11. 1–11 | Matt. 28. 1–7
27 S **THE SIXTH SUNDAY AFTER TRINITY**
28 M Exod. 40. 1–16 | Luke 14. 15–24
29 Tu Prov. 11. 1–12 | Mark 12. 38–44
30 W Isa. 33. 2–10 | Phil. 1. 1–11
31 Th Job ch. 38 | Luke 18. 1–14

August 2025

1 F Job 42. 1–6 | John 3. 1–15
2 Sa Eccles. 9. 1–11 | Heb. 1. 1–9
3 S **THE SEVENTH SUNDAY AFTER TRINITY**
4 M Num. 23. 1–12 | 1 Cor. 1. 10–17
5 Tu Prov. 12. 1–12 | Gal. 3. 1–14
6 W **THE TRANSFIGURATION**
7 Th Hos. ch. 14 | John 15. 1–17
8 F 2 Sam. 18. 18–end | Matt. 27. 57–66
9 Sa Isa. 55. 1–7 | Mark 6. 1–8
10 S **THE EIGHTH SUNDAY AFTER TRINITY**
11 M Joel 3. 16–21 | Mark 4. 21–34
12 Tu Prov. 12. 13–end | John 1. 43–51
13 W Isa. 55. 8–end | 2 Tim. 2. 8–19
14 Th Isa. 38. 1–8 | Mark 5. 21–43
15 F **THE BLESSED VIRGIN MARY**
When the Blessed Virgin Mary is celebrated on 8 September:
Jer. 14. 1–9 | Luke 8. 4–15
16 Sa Eccles. 5. 10–19 | 1 Tim. 6. 6–16
17 S **THE NINTH SUNDAY AFTER TRINITY**
18 M Josh. 1. 1–9 | 1 Cor. 9. 19–end
19 Tu Prov. 15. 1–11 | Gal. 2. 15–end
20 W Isa. 49. 1–7 | 1 John 1
21 Th Prov. 27. 1–12 | John 15. 12–27
22 F Isa. 59. 8–end | Mark 15. 6–20
23 Sa Zech. 7.8 – 8.8 | Luke 20. 27–40
24 S **BARTHOLOMEW (THE TENTH SUNDAY AFTER TRINITY)**
25 M *Where Bartholomew is celebrated on Sunday 24 August*:
Judg. 13. 1–23 | Luke 10. 38–42
or Bartholomew
26 Tu Prov. 15. 15–end | Matt. 15. 21–28
27 W Isa. 45. 1–7 | Eph. 4. 1–16
28 Th Jer. 16. 1–5 | Luke 12. 35–48
29 F Jer. 18. 1–11 | Heb. 1. 1–9
30 Sa Jer. 26. 1–19 | Eph. 3. 1–13
31 S **THE ELEVENTH SUNDAY AFTER TRINITY**

September 2025

1 M Ruth 2. 1–13 | Luke 10. 25–37
2 Tu Prov. 16. 1–11 | Phil. 3. 4b–end
3 W Deut. 11. 1–21 | 2 Cor. 9. 6–end
4 Th Ecclus. ch. 2 | John 16. 1–15
or Eccles. 2. 12–25
5 F Obadiah 1–10 | John 19. 1–16
6 Sa 2 Kings 2. 11–14 | Luke 24. 36–end
7 S **THE TWELFTH SUNDAY AFTER TRINITY**
8 M 1 Sam. 17. 32–50 | Matt. 8. 14–22
9 Tu Prov. 17. 1–15 | Luke 7. 1–17
10 W Jer. 5. 20–end | 2 Pet. 3. 8–end
11 Th Dan. 2. 1–23 | Luke 10. 1–20
12 F Dan. 3. 1–28 | Rev. ch. 15
13 Sa Dan. ch. 6 | Phil. 2. 14–24
14 S **HOLY CROSS DAY (THE THIRTEENTH SUNDAY AFTER TRINITY)**
15 M *When Holy Cross Day is celebrated on Sunday 14 September*:
2 Sam. 7. 4–17 | 2 Cor. 5. 1–10
or Holy Cross Day
16 Tu Prov. 18. 10–21 | Rom. 14. 10–end
17 W Judg. 4. 1–10 | Rom. 1. 8–17
18 Th Isa. 49. 14–end | John 16. 16–24
19 F Job 9. 1–24 | Mark 15. 21–32
20 Sa Exod. 19. 1–9 | John 20. 11–18
21 S **MATTHEW (THE FOURTEENTH SUNDAY AFTER TRINITY)**
22 M *When Matthew is celebrated on Sunday 21 September*:
Hagg. ch. 1 | Mark 7. 9–23
or Matthew
23 Tu Prov. 21. 1–18 | Mark 6. 30–44
24 W Hos. 11. 1–11 | 1 John 4. 9–end
25 Th Lam. 3. 34–48 | Rom. 7. 14–end
26 F 2 Kings 19. 4–18 | 1 Thess. ch. 3
27 Sa Ecclus. 4. 1–28 | 2 Tim. 3. 10–end
or Deut. 29. 2–15
28 S **THE FIFTEENTH SUNDAY AFTER TRINITY**
29 M **MICHAEL AND ALL ANGELS**
30 Tu Prov. 8. 1–11 | Luke 6. 39–end

October 2025

1 W Prov. 2. 1–15 | Col. 1. 9–20
2 Th Baruch 3. 14–end | John 1. 1–18
or Gen. 1. 1–13
3 F Ecclus. 1. 1–20 | 1 Cor. 1. 18–end
or Deut. 7. 7–16
4 Sa Wisd. 9. 1–12 | Luke 2. 41–end
or Jer. 1. 4–10
5 S **THE SIXTEENTH SUNDAY AFTER TRINITY**
6 M Gen. 21. 1–13 | Luke 1. 26–38
7 Tu Ruth 4. 7–17 | Luke 2. 25–38
8 W 2 Kings 4. 1–7 | John 2. 1–11
9 Th 2 Kings 4. 25b–37 | Mark 3. 19b–35
10 F Judith 8. 9–17, 28–36 | John 19. 25b–30
or Ruth 1. 1–18
11 Sa Exod. 15. 19–27 | Acts 1. 6–14
12 S **THE SEVENTEENTH SUNDAY AFTER TRINITY**
13 M Exod. 19. 16–end | Heb. 12. 18–end
14 Tu 1 Chron. 16. 1–13 | Rev. 11. 15–end
15 W 1 Chron. 29. 10–19 | Col. 3. 12–17
16 Th Neh. 8. 1–12 | 1 Cor. 14. 1–12
17 F Isa. 1. 10–17 | Mark 12. 28–34
18 Sa **LUKE**
19 S **THE EIGHTEENTH SUNDAY AFTER TRINITY**
20 M 2 Sam. 22. 4–7, 17–20 | Heb. 7.26 – 8.6

21	Tu	Prov. 22. 17–end	2 Cor. 12. 1–10
22	W	Hos. ch. 14	James 2. 14–26
23	Th	Isa. 24. 1–15	John 16. 25–33
24	F	Jer. 14. 1–9	Luke 23. 44–56
25	Sa	Zech. 8. 14–end	John 20. 19–end
26	S	**THE LAST SUNDAY AFTER TRINITY**	
27	M	Isa. 42. 14–21	Luke 1. 5–25
28	Tu	**SIMON AND JUDE**	
29	W	Baruch ch. 5 *or* Hag. 1. 1–11	Mark 1. 1–11
30	Th	Isa. ch. 35	Matt. 11. 2–19
31	F	*At Evening Prayer the readings for the Eve of All Saints are used. At other services the following readings are used:* 2 Sam. 11. 1–17	Matt. 14. 1–12

November 2025

1	Sa	**ALL SAINTS' DAY** *or, where All Saints' Day is celebrated on Sunday 2 November only:* Isa. 43. 15–21	Acts 19. 1–10
2	S	**THE FOURTH SUNDAY BEFORE ADVENT**	
3	M	Esther 3. 1–11; 4. 7–17	Matt. 18. 1–10
4	Tu	Ezek. 18. 21–end	Matt. 18. 12–20
5	W	Prov. 3. 27–end	Matt. 18. 21–end
6	Th	Exod. 23. 1–9	Matt. 19. 1–15
7	F	Prov. 3. 13–18	Matt. 19. 16–end
8	Sa	Deut. 28. 1–6	Matt. 20. 1–16
9	S	**THE THIRD SUNDAY BEFORE ADVENT**	
10	M	Isa. 40. 21–end	Rom. 11. 25–end
11	Tu	Ezek. 34. 20–end	John 10. 1–18
12	W	Lev. 26. 3–13	Titus 2. 1–10
13	Th	Hos. 6. 1–6	Matt. 9. 9–13
14	F	Mal. ch. 4	John 4. 5–26
15	Sa	Mic. 6. 6–8	Col. 3. 12–17
16	S	**THE SECOND SUNDAY BEFORE ADVENT**	
17	M	Mic. 7. 1–7	Matt. 10. 24–39
18	Tu	Hab. 3. 1–19a	1 Cor. 4. 9–16
19	W	Zech. 8. 1–13	Mark 13. 3–8
20	Th	Zech. 10. 6–end	1 Pet. 5. 1–11
21	F	Mic. 4. 1–5	Luke 9. 28–36
22	Sa	*At Evening Prayer the readings for the Eve of Christ the King are used. At other services the following readings are used:* Exod. 16. 1–21	John 6. 3–15
23	S	**CHRIST THE KING** (The Sunday next before Advent)	
24	M	Jer. 30. 1–3, 10–17	Rom. 12. 9–21
25	Tu	Jer. 30. 18–24	John 10. 22–30
26	W	Jer. 31. 1–9	Matt. 15. 21–31
27	Th	Jer. 31. 10–17	Matt. 16. 13–end
28	F	Jer. 31. 31–37	Heb. 10. 11–18
29	Sa	Isa. 51.17 – 52.2	Eph. 5. 1–20
30	S	**THE FIRST SUNDAY OF ADVENT**	

December 2025

1	M	**ANDREW** (transferred from 30 November)	
2	Tu	Zeph. 3. 14–end	1 Thess. 4. 13–end
3	W	Isa. 65.17 – 66.2	Matt. 24. 1–14
4	Th	Mic. 5. 2–5a	John 3. 16–21
5	F	Isa. 66. 18–end	Luke 13. 22–30
6	Sa	Mic. 7. 8–15	Rom. 15.30 – 16.7, 25–end
7	S	**THE SECOND SUNDAY OF ADVENT**	
8	M	Jer. 7. 1–11	Phil. 4. 4–9
9	Tu	Dan. 7. 9–14	Matt. 24. 15–28
10	W	Amos 9. 11–end	Rom. 13. 8–14
11	Th	Jer. 23. 5–8	Mark 11. 1–11
12	F	Jer. 33. 14–22	Luke 21. 25–36
13	Sa	Zech. 14. 4–11	Rev. 22. 1–7
14	S	**THE THIRD SUNDAY OF ADVENT**	
15	M	Isa. 40. 1–11	Matt. 3. 1–12
16	Tu	Lam. 3. 22–33	1 Cor. 1. 1–9
17	W	Ecclus. 24. 1–9 *or* Prov. 6. 22–31	1 Cor. 2. 1–13
18	Th	Exod. 3. 1–6	Acts 7. 20–36
19	F	Isa. 11. 1–9	Rom. 15. 7–13
20	Sa	Isa. 22. 21–23	Rev. 3. 7–13
21	S	**THE FOURTH SUNDAY OF ADVENT**	
22	M	Jer. 30. 7–11a	Acts 4. 1–12
23	Tu	Isa. 7. 10–15	Matt. 1. 18–23
24	W	*At Evening Prayer the readings for Christmas Eve are used. At other services the following readings are used:* Isa. 29. 13–18	1 John 4. 7–16
25	Th	**CHRISTMAS DAY**	
26	F	**STEPHEN**	
27	Sa	**JOHN THE EVANGELIST**	
28	S	**THE HOLY INNOCENTS (THE FIRST SUNDAY OF CHRISTMAS)**	
29	M	*Where The Holy Innocents is celebrated on Sunday 28 December:* Mic. 1. 1–4; 2. 12–13 *or The Holy Innocents*	Luke 2. 1–7
30	Tu	Isa. 9. 2–7	John 8. 12–20
31	W	Eccles. 3. 1–13	Rev. 21. 1–8

CALENDAR 2025

JANUARY

Su	..	X^2	B	E^2	E^3	..
M	..	E	13	20	27	..
Tu	..	7	14	21	28	..
W	1	8	15	22	29	..
Th	2	9	16	23	30	..
F	3	10	17	24	31	..
Sa	4	11	18	25	..	..

FEBRUARY

Su	..	Pr	L^{-4}	L^{-3}	L^{-2}	..
M	..	3	10	17	24	..
Tu	..	4	11	18	25	..
W	..	5	12	19	26	..
Th	..	6	13	20	27	..
F	..	7	14	21	28	..
Sa	1	8	15	22	..	..

MARCH

Su	..	L^{-1}	L^1	L^2	L^3	L^4
M	..	3	10	17	24	31
Tu	..	4	11	18	An	..
W	..	A	12	19	26	..
Th	..	6	13	20	27	..
F	..	7	14	21	28	..
Sa	1	8	15	22	29	..

APRIL

Su	..	L^5	P	E	E^2	..
M	..	7	14	21	28	..
Tu	1	8	15	22	29	..
W	2	9	16	23	30	..
Th	3	10	M	24	..	..
F	4	11	F	25	..	..
Sa	5	12	19	26	..	..

MAY

Su	..	E^3	E^4	E^5	E^6	..
M	..	5	12	19	26	..
Tu	..	6	13	20	27	..
W	..	7	14	21	28	..
Th	1	8	15	22	A	..
F	2	9	16	23	30	..
Sa	3	10	17	24	31	..

JUNE

Su	E^7	W	T	T^1	T^2	..
M	2	9	16	23	30	..
Tu	3	10	17	24	..	..
W	4	11	18	25	..	..
Th	5	12	19	26	..	..
F	6	13	20	27	..	..
Sa	7	14	21	28	..	..

JULY

Su	..	T^3	T^4	T^5	T^6	..
M	..	7	14	21	28	..
Tu	1	8	15	22	29	..
W	2	9	16	23	30	..
Th	3	10	17	24	31	..
F	4	11	18	25	..	..
Sa	5	12	19	26	..	..

AUGUST

Su	..	T^7	T^8	T^9	T^{10}	T^{11}
M	..	4	11	18	25	..
Tu	..	5	12	19	26	..
W	..	6	13	20	27	..
Th	..	7	14	21	28	..
F	1	8	15	22	29	..
Sa	2	9	16	23	30	..

SEPTEMBER

Su	..	T^{12}	T^{13}	T^{14}	T^{15}	..
M	1	8	15	22	29	..
Tu	2	9	16	23	30	..
W	3	10	17	24	..	..
Th	4	11	18	25	..	..
F	5	12	19	26	..	..
Sa	6	13	20	27	..	..

OCTOBER

Su	..	T^{16}	T^{17}	T^{18}	T^L	..
M	..	6	13	20	27	..
Tu	..	7	14	21	28	..
W	1	8	15	22	29	..
Th	2	9	16	23	30	..
F	3	10	17	24	31	..
Sa	4	11	18	25	..	..

NOVEMBER

Su	..	A^{-4}	A^{-3}	A^{-2}	A^{-1}	A
M	..	3	10	17	24	..
Tu	..	4	11	18	25	..
W	..	5	12	19	26	..
Th	..	6	13	20	27	..
F	..	7	14	21	28	..
Sa	AS	8	15	22	29	..

DECEMBER

Su	..	A^2	A^3	A^4	X^1	..
M	1	8	15	22	29	..
Tu	2	9	16	23	30	..
W	3	10	17	24	31	..
Th	4	11	18	X	..	..
F	5	12	19	26	..	..
Sa	6	13	20	27	..	..

A = Ash Wednesday, Ascension, Advent
A^- = Before Advent
A^{-4} = also All Saints, 2025 (if transferred)
A^{-1} = Christ the King
An = Annunciation
AS = All Saints (also Fourth Sunday before Advent, 2026)
B = Baptism
E = Epiphany, Easter
(E^3 = also Conversion of Paul, 2026)
E^4 = also Presentation, 2026 (if transferred)
G = Good Friday
L = Lent

CALENDAR 2026

JANUARY

Su	..	X^2	B	E^2	E^3	..
M	..	5	12	19	26	..
Tu	..	E	13	20	27	..
W	..	7	14	21	28	..
Th	1	8	15	22	29	..
F	2	9	16	23	30	..
Sa	3	10	17	24	31	..

FEBRUARY

Su	E^4	L^{-2}	L^{-1}	L^1	..	..
M	Pr	9	16	23	..	..
Tu	3	10	17	24	..	..
W	4	11	A	25	..	..
Th	5	12	19	26	..	..
F	6	13	20	27	..	..
Sa	7	14	21	28	..	..

MARCH

Su	L^2	L^3	L^4	L^5	P	..
M	2	9	16	23	30	..
Tu	3	10	17	24	31	..
W	4	11	18	An	..	..
Th	5	12	19	26	..	..
F	6	13	20	27	..	..
Sa	7	14	21	28	..	..

APRIL

Su	..	E	E^2	E^3	E^4	..
M	..	6	13	20	27	..
Tu	..	7	14	21	28	..
W	1	8	15	22	29	..
Th	M	9	16	23	30	..
F	G	10	17	24	..	..
Sa	4	11	18	25	..	..

MAY

Su	..	E^5	E^6	E^7	W	T
M	..	4	11	18	25	..
Tu	..	5	12	19	26	..
W	..	6	13	20	27	..
Th	..	7	A	21	28	..
F	1	8	15	22	29	..
Sa	2	9	16	23	30	..

JUNE

Su	..	T^1	T^2	T^3	T^4	..
M	1	8	15	22	29	..
Tu	2	9	16	23	30	..
W	3	10	17	24	..	..
Th	4	11	18	25	..	..
F	5	12	19	26	..	..
Sa	6	13	20	27	..	..

JULY

Su	..	T^5	T^6	T^7	T^8	..
M	..	6	13	20	27	..
Tu	..	7	14	21	28	..
W	1	8	15	22	29	..
Th	2	9	16	23	30	..
F	3	10	17	24	31	..
Sa	4	11	18	25	..	..

AUGUST

Su	..	T^9	T^{10}	T^{11}	T^{12}	T^{13}
M	..	3	10	17	24	31
Tu	..	4	11	18	25	..
W	..	5	12	19	26	..
Th	..	6	13	20	27	..
F	..	7	14	21	28	..
Sa	1	8	15	22	29	..

SEPTEMBER

Su	..	T^{14}	T^{15}	T^{16}	T^{17}	..
M	..	7	14	21	28	..
Tu	1	8	15	22	29	..
W	2	9	16	23	30	..
Th	3	10	17	24	..	..
F	4	11	18	25	..	..
Sa	5	12	19	26	..	..

OCTOBER

Su	..	T^{18}	T^{19}	T^{20}	T^L	..
M	..	5	12	19	26	..
Tu	..	6	13	20	27	..
W	..	7	14	21	28	..
Th	1	8	15	22	29	..
F	2	9	16	23	30	..
Sa	3	10	17	24	31	..

NOVEMBER

Su	AS	A^{-3}	A^{-2}	A^{-1}	A	..
M	2	9	16	23	30	..
Tu	3	10	17	24	..	..
W	4	11	18	25	..	..
Th	5	12	19	26	..	..
F	6	13	20	27	..	..
Sa	7	14	21	28	..	..

DECEMBER

Su	..	A^2	A^3	A^4	X^1	..
M	..	7	14	21	28	..
Tu	1	8	15	22	29	..
W	2	9	16	23	30	..
Th	3	10	17	24	31	..
F	4	11	18	X	..	..
Sa	5	12	19	26	..	..

L^- = Before Lent
M = Maundy Thursday
P = Palm Sunday
Pr = Presentation
T = Trinity
(T^2 = also Peter and Paul, 2025)
(T^{13} = also Holy Cross Day, 2025)
(T^{14} = also Matthew, 2025)
(T^{20} = also Luke, 2026)
T^L = Last Sunday after Trinity
W = Pentecost (Whit Sunday)
X = Christmas
(X^1 = also John, 2026)
X^2 = also Epiphany, 2026 (if transferred)